COORDINATION
WITHOUT
HIERARCHY

COORDINATION WITHOUT HIERARCHY

INFORMAL STRUCTURES IN MULTIORGANIZATIONAL SYSTEMS

Donald Chisholm

UNIVERSITY OF CALIFORNIA PRESS

Berkeley   Los Angeles   Oxford

University of California Press
Berkeley and Los Angeles, California

University of California Press, Ltd.
Oxford, England
© 1989 by
The Regents of the University of California
First Paperback Printing 1992

LIBRARY OF CONGRESS
Library of Congress Cataloging-in-Publication Data

Chisholm, Donald William.
Coordination without Hierarchy: informal structures in multiorganizational
  systems / Donald Chisholm.
    p.   cm.
    Bibliography: p.
    Includes index.
    ISBN 0-520-08037-8
    1. Organizational behavior.   I. Title.
HD58.7.C487 1989
388.4'068—dc19   88-4214
                                                           CIP

Printed in the United States of America

1   2   3   4   5   6   7   8   9

Contents

List of Tables, Figures, and Maps

Tables

Figures

Maps

Preface

It is remarkable that political science and public administration seem only recently to be discovering (or rediscovering) what sociologists have known all along: informal aspects of organization are not only powerful determinants of behavior within and among organizations but possess characteristics rendering them effective as instruments for such tasks as coordination. The trend among some public choice theorists toward assumptions of multiple encounters of interdependent actors and the evolution of powerful behavioral norms, along with increasingly sophisticated discussions of organizations as political coalitions, are but two encouraging examples of this (re)discovery. Why has the pathbreaking work of the Hawthorne studies, or the subsequent work of Fenno and others on legislatures, waited so long to be integrated into research on problems of collective action and the design of formal organizations? Perhaps the delay is a phenomenon most readily explained as the result of different paradigmatic approaches to slightly dissimilar problems: the sociological approach, along with that of cognitive psychology, versus the microeconomic approach.[1]

The approach taken in this study is intentionally pragmatic and opportunistic, moving from a specific practical problem in the real world of politics and public administration—the coordination of the public transit system of the San Francisco Bay Area—to a direct and practical solution and a foundation for a generalizable theory of coordination by informal mechanisms. In so doing it borrows liberally from contemporary and earlier efforts in other domains. In this conjunction of finding solutions to the practical problem with developing general scientific propositions, I would like to think that I am continuing in the tradition of Charles E. Merriam and the other progenitors of modern political science.

My approach is characterized by observation of how decision makers actually behave, rather than reliance on a closed deductive analytical system replete with a full complement of assumptions about human behavior. In this regard, I take seriously Wesley Mitchell's critical comments about the economists of his time:

> Their habit has been to set up simplified conditions in their imaginations, and draw conclusions about what would happen in an unreal world—conclusions that cannot be refuted by an appeal to actual experience.[2]

I am less interested in finding out what an already well developed deductive theory might have to say about some problem to which it has not yet been applied than in developing a relatively powerful theory that explains that problem. Nor did I feel it appropriate to study the relevant organizations and their activities from a distance; I employed direct personal (what Fenno calls interactive) observation to bring me closer to the data.[3]

I have borrowed freely from whatever theories seemed most useful for understanding the problem. My debt is greatest to sociology and social psychology, but I also owe something to theories of public choice. In the tradition of Herbert Simon, I take generally conservative, even pessimistic, positions on the extent of individual human capacities for rationality; the availability of information to decision makers; and human capacity to design and administer effective, large-scale, formal organizations in the face of complex problems.[4]

In the research reported here, I used an intensive analysis of activities in the public transit systems of the San Francisco Bay Area and Washington, D.C., to generate a series of broader theoretical statements about problems of coordination and their resolution in multiorganizational systems more generally. The theory was only partially developed when the research commenced, and theory building became intimately intertwined with data collection. I followed Darwin's dictum: "Science consists in grouping facts so that general laws or conclusions may be drawn from them."[5] In this sense, this essay does not adhere closely to the standard presentation of results found in most scientific papers. My account reflects the actual development of the theory, that is, the argument more closely follows the "logic-in-use" than the "reconstructed logic of presentation."[6] In this breach I hope I will be indulged by those interested in the material and forgiven by those less patient.

My conclusions and recommendations may be regarded by some as extreme and radical—at a minimum they will be considered counterintuitive—given traditional approaches to the problem of coordination and current prevailing wisdom in the public administration. My hope, however, is that at least some of them will be recognized as practical, pragmatic proposals concerning the often intransigent problem of coordination.

Although books are mostly solitary endeavors, one usually has more collaborators than one realizes. This essay is no exception. In its lengthy gestation I incurred considerable debts to many people for many reasons.

I wish first to thank the men and women of the public transit systems of the San Francisco Bay Area and the Washington Metropolitan Area for their gracious participation in this study. They often made time for my questions in the midst of pressing job demands. Without their active assistance, this study would have been impossible.

Thomas Cordi, James Desveaux, and David Richman each contributed their support and criticism as the project began to take shape. Charles Ostrom and Jack Knott provided needed encouragement and advice during a later, very difficult period of writing. Nelson Polsby and Melvin Webber each contributed their sage counsel during the project's early stages, while throughout Jack Citrin performed the difficult dual roles of friend and critic. Steve Erie contributed valuable advice about writing as I began the inevitable revisions.

The Berkeley academic community provided a unique and stimulating environment for research and discussion. I wish particularly to thank the Institute of Governmental Studies of the University of California, Berkeley, for providing during much of the writing such a splendid place to be. Initial research support was provided by the Urban Mass Transportation Administration and Berkeley's Institute of Urban and Regional Development. The National Policy Studies Program at Berkeley provided funds that enabled me to conduct the Washington portion of the research. The Joseph P. Harris Fund made possible several months of uninterrupted writing, while funding from the Institute of Transportation Studies at Berkeley permitted me to write for a year without other obligations.

However, it is Martin Landau to whom I owe my deepest personal and intellectual debts. He provoked me to think hard and without regard to academic orthodoxy. In the absence of his criticism, tempered by his patience and kind support throughout the early stages when there was only a slight promise of completion and little visible progress and during the later stages of outside criticism and internal self-doubt, this tale would not now be seeing the light of day.

1

Multiorganizational Systems

In ancient times alchemists believed implicitly
in a philosopher's stone which would provide
the key to the universe and, in effect, solve all
of the problems of mankind. The quest for coordination is in many respects the twentieth
century equivalent of the medieval search for
the philosopher's stone. If only we can find the
right formula for coordination, we can recon-
cile the irreconcilable, harmonize competing
and wholly divergent interests, overcome irra-
tionalities in our government structures, and
make hard policy choices to which no one will
dissent.

—Harold Seidman, *Politics,
Position, and Power*

I begin with a problem. Not long ago the (then) general
manager of the San Francisco Public Utilities Commission, referring
to the public transit system of the Bay Area, declared that "decision-
making should be centralized, the different properties can't get together on the simplest things."[1] Commenting on the same transit
system, transportation engineer David Jones observed that project-by-
project development has produced an extensive but ill-coordinated
network of services and facilities, that the area's transit networks display significant gaps where controversies have stalled development

and where competing interests of independent jurisdictions frustrate coordination and connectivity, and that the rivalry of these jurisdictions has resulted in a diffusion of transportation responsibilities to the point where the Bay Area "is an extreme case of jurisdictional fragmentation." [2]

In a similar vein, a recent *San Francisco Chronicle* article commented on the great gap between the promise of Bay Area transit and the reality:

> The idea was brilliant: The Bay Area would build the best transit network in America, a system good enough to compete with the private automobile.
>
> Twenty years and more than $3 billion later, public transit is big business—and it is in big trouble.
>
> Instead of the best network in America, the region has 17 separate transit baronies that war with each other over passengers and waste money on a huge scale.[3]

Put bluntly, the system is uncoordinated and in disarray. The result is inefficient use of resources, lost opportunities, and useless conflict. The cause is faulty organization.

As this was being written, California State Senator Quentin Kopp, a former San Francisco Supervisor, was drafting legislation to force the Bay Area's seventeen transit systems to merge into three or four superagencies, in an effort to eliminate costly duplication and competition. All of the East Bay systems would be consolidated into one organization; Santa Clara and San Mateo would merge with the San Francisco system; a North Bay transport agency would also be created; and the Bay Area Rapid Transit District would remain an independent entity.[4]

Elsewhere, the California State Assembly was holding hearings on proposals to reorganize and consolidate public transportation for Los Angeles County. Southern California Rapid Transit District (SCRTD) currently operates the major bus system for the county and is building a subway line in downtown Los Angeles, while the Los Angeles County Transportation Commission (LACTC) is building a trolley line from Long Beach to downtown; twelve smaller cities operate bus systems of their own.

The problem is described by the chief administrative officer for Los Angeles County:

The absence of a specific hierarchy or reporting relationship between SCRTD and the LACTC, the similar composition of each agency's governing board and the responsibility of SCRTD for Metro Rail planning and construction and LACTC for light-rail project planning and construction create the impression they are parallel, independent entities. . . . These give the appearance of a lack of accountability to the public and to other officials.[5]

The statement by State Assemblyman Richard Katz, chairman of the Assembly Transportation Committee, and sponsor of the consolidation bill, is a classic justification for reorganizations of this sort:

Having two competing Los Angeles transportation bodies has resulted in a lack of coordinated planning, duplication of efforts, overlapping jurisdiction, and a lack of accountability.[6]

The Transportation Committee passed the bill by a 22-to-0 vote to send it to the assembly floor where it passed with little debate and with a 65-to-0 vote.[7]

Referring to urban politics more generally, Douglas Yates makes a claim with which Henry Bruere would have been more than sympathetic: "Policy making takes place in a political and administrative system that is fragmented to the point of chaos."[8] Too often the policies that result are incomplete, contradictory, and ineffective. Problems surpass the ability of any one agency or governmental entity to solve. "Municipal officials in cities like San Clemente, Kingburg, Galt, Delano, and Watsonville say poverty, crime, and community blight are problems that spill over into their communities from developments just beyond their jurisdictions."[9]

In this view, the components of the organizational system impinge on each other in significant ways that preclude treating them as independent units. They are composed of interdependent parts that must be coordinated on a comprehensive basis. The need for coordination is a function of the interdependence of the parts of an organizational system: existing formal coordinative arrangements are unable to manage interdependencies effectively. In the face of this inadequacy, coordination fails to occur, and irrational, chaotic public policy results. The problem is in no way limited to public transportation or local government; it occurs at all levels of government, in virtually all policy areas, and in all countries and cultures. San Francisco Bay

Area and Los Angeles public transit merely exemplify the problem in its more extreme forms.

In response to the perceived need to do *something* concrete to improve the organization of the San Francisco Bay Area public transit system, the Urban Mass Transportation Administration (UMTA) commissioned the study *Redundancy in Public Transit*.[10] In this study, of which I was a coauthor, we introduced that transit system in the following way:

> It may be the most generously endowed with public transport services of any metropolitan area anywhere. It has cable cars, trolley cars, subway cars, both modern-light and modern-heavy rail. It has traditional local buses, luxury express buses, and specialized subscription buses. Besides all this, there are governmentally sponsored car and van pools; there are taxis and a rare but viable jitney service; there are high-speed ferries, an old-fashioned suburban railroad and soon even a local helicopter. That smorgasbord is offered by some thirty-five organizations, not counting the numerous taxi, jitney and specialized van and bus operators. All but four of those outfits are now governmental agencies, most of them operating autonomously, almost as though they were private firms openly competing with each other in an unregulated market.[11]

The roles of these organizational actors vary widely, as do their organizational structures, scopes of authority, and sources of funding. Some have only a single transit mode, others are multimodal. Some are strictly operators. Others regulate and coordinate. Some are part of municipal or county governments; some exist independently as special-purpose districts. Some rely on property taxes, others on sales taxes and bridge tolls, while all of them depend on state and federal assistance for operating and capital funds. When viewed as a whole, they appear to be a collection of distinct entities that overlap in jurisdictions and duplicate services, with little overall shape or form. "Bay Area transit appears to be a far cry from the integrated transit system sought by Jones: it is 'chaotic and irrational.'"[12] It makes the Los Angeles system, with only a few major actors, look well ordered and highly efficient.

The assertion that the Bay Area transit is an egregious example of a fragmented organizational system, however, is self-contradictory. "Fragmented" suggests a fracture of something that was once whole, while "system" implies an interrelatedness of parts such that each can only be comprehended in terms of the others. Fortunately, we can readily make sense of this apparent paradox. Those, such as Jones, who describe Bay Area transit as a "fragmented system" refer to fragmentation of the *formal* organizational arrangements—to the fact of many different independent operating entities in a single geographic area. On the other hand, "system" implies that the agencies are functionally related: the alteration of one aspect will affect the others to a significant degree. Evidently, there is a disjuncture between the organizational character and the functional properties of the system.

But it is a great leap from finding a degree of interdependence among the components of an organizational system to the conclusion that such a system, if it has no formal unified authority, is uncoordinated. That is, however, precisely the leap made by those who see multiorganization as evidence of a serious weakness: because each organization pursues its own goals, such a system permits the coexistence of incompatible goals, encourages the avoidance of responsibility, and involves costly duplication and overlap. The technical expression of this state is "multiorganizational suboptimality." Lack of coordination is its principal characteristic.[13] Although not often made explicit, the source of comparison for this criticism of the multiorganizational system is a model of organization characterized by a high degree of internal order and interconnection of parts, high levels of efficiency, and an absence of redundancy. When examined against the backdrop of this model, any multiorganizational system inevitably proves problematic and inadequate.[14]

Ironically, this concept of multiorganizational suboptimality is applied almost exclusively to the public sector. What is recommended as the prescription for this malady is nothing less than complete monopoly, involving central control and vertical integration. Thus put, the key to problems of coordination is hierarchical organization.[15]

Yet in the private sector, tendencies toward consolidation and merger are not only considered an anathema on an ideological basis, but are judged in restraint of trade and in violation of law; they have been in particular disfavor during the past decade. We need look no further than the efforts of the Carter and Reagan administrations to deregulate and promote competition in a range of private markets, a process that included the dismantling of AT&T. Withal, the canons of classic economic theory that resound the virtues of the coordinat-

ing and regulating properties of the market system are rarely applied
to the realm of public organizations. Those who view natural market
forces as operating as a profound coordinating mechanism abandon
this view when it comes to the public administration, arguing that,
because public organizations specialize in necessary services that
cannot be sold for dollars at a per unit rate, market rules do not apply.[16] Therefore, the public arena requires regulation and control in
the form of a single center of authority and responsibility.

Reorganization and Coordination

Even if the distinction between public and private organizations as regards types of products and services and the nature of prof-
its and grants is accepted, it is not a necessary conclusion that only
hierarchical schemes can ensure effective performance. The assumed
virtues and economies of vertical integration schemes and of efforts
to streamline multiorganizational sectors by eliminating duplication
and overlap are exaggerated. In fact, they have more to do with bureaucratic politics than with effective performance.[17] Even where
such reorganizations are genuinely intended to improve performance,
the record indicates the failures; in some cases they have caused considerable damage and brought few benefits.

Large-scale efforts to reorganize and reform public agencies at all
levels are by no means new. Since the dawn of the twentieth century
there have been seemingly endless waves of consolidation and integration of public organization for the sake of efficiency and effectiveness, beginning with the Keep Commission (1904–09) on through
the President's Reorganization Project (1977–80); the most famous
and influential was Roosevelt's Committee on Administrative Management (1933–37), chaired by Louis Brownlow.[18] Throughout, the
reorganizers have been hunting for *the* system that, in the words of
the 1949 reorganization statute, would reduce expenditures and promote economy, better execution of the laws, and the expeditious administration of the public business.[19] All the proposed programs,
however, involved tremendous financial cost, not to mention disruption caused by reorganization.

"Hunting" stands out in sharp relief from "learning." The record
does not indicate steady and continuous adaptations in organizational

structures as responses to experience or careful experimentation. Instead we find the propensity for organizations to "oscillate from one form to another" even in the face of "generally stable environmental conditions." [20] Persistence in the face of apparent failure and indifference to careful evaluation of the consequences of action are, of course, often observed in human behavior—particularly in domains of strong beliefs and ambiguous experience.[21] Our administrative history is rife with radical reorganizations that shuffle and combine agencies, redistribute authority, and incorporate comprehensive coordinating arrangements ranging from direct consolidation to management-control systems such as Planning, Programming, Budgeting (PPB) and Program Evaluation Review Technique (PERT) and now strategic planning.

In public transit, formal reconstructions of organizational arrangements on occasion have included tariff associations, transit communities, and transit federations;[22] but, as elsewhere, mergers and consolidations have been proposed most frequently, and they continue to dominate other approaches to problems of coordination. Witness, for example, the creation of the Metropolitan Transportation Authority in New York, which in 1967 took jurisdiction over the subways, the commuter rail services, the city's bus lines, and the Triboro Bridge and Tunnel Authority. The underlying assumption (rarely put to the empirical test) common to these reorganizations is that problems of coordination can be solved and difficulties removed by structural reform.

However, despite our history of organizational reform, some problems are unrelated to structural defects and will likely remain irrespective of the organizational design. Genuine differences in interest among groups, asymmetrical distributions of costs and benefits in issues of coordination, and thorny technical problems are not susceptible to resolution through structural reform. Or, as Harold Seidman has noted,

> Where conflicts result from clashes in statutory missions or differences in legislative mandates, they cannot be reconciled through the magic of coordination. Too often organic disease is diagnosed as a simple case of inadequate coordination.[23]

Certainly, not all government reorganizations have been directed toward formal integration and consolidation. From time to time there

decentralization

have been countermoves toward decentralization. Usually, however, these countermoves have been of short duration and less than monumental consequence, in part because pressures for integration and consolidation have resulted from enduring orthodox administrative philosophy, whereas moves toward decentralization have come as a result of practical necessity. Observe, for example, the U.S. Civil Service Commission:

> Decentralization of authority was one of the effects of World War II on administrative development. The change, for the most part, was made not because of any change in the philosophy of the men who led the (Civil Service) Commission, but was rather the result of necessity.[24]

In this case, decentralization resulted from the need for "speed of operations" and the greatly expanded activities of the war effort. As soon as the war ended, the president ordered the commission to return to its prewar rules.[25] However, where decentralization has been defended on more general grounds, the justifications have been sensible: it increases innovation, encourages public participation, strengthens local governing capacities, and places responsibility for decision making at the level where spillover effects are at a minimum.[26]

Inevitably, however, the cry of fragmentation is heard once again, the trend toward decentralization is reversed, and another drive toward integration and consolidation is begun. A once-decomposable set of components is now considered a complex, tightly interdependent system where decisions affecting one component affect all, directly or indirectly. In such a situation it becomes imperative to eliminate fragmentary and disjointed approaches and to seek an agenda of "purposive and coordinative action."[27] Land use planning provides a prime example:

> Planners have been introducing a greater degree of flexibility into land use decisions through the use of flexible zoning techniques as a means of improving the traditional system of land use regulation. But this has been a cause for concern and planners are also calling for the preparation of rules to limit discretion.[28]

Reorganizations in the direction of consolidation and merger, which concentrate authority at the top, have not provided the advances in coordination or significant improvements in performance expected from them. The same academics and policy makers who wring their hands at the presence of the multiorganizational system also bewail the inherent inflexibility, slowness to change, and inability to contend with anomaly that characterize large bureaucratic organizations.[29] Such large bureaucracies are rigid and do not learn easily or quickly. Nor are they especially powerful coordinating agents. Do we forget that many of our bureaucracies were created to coordinate the smaller agencies that now compose them? Though intended to produce an integrated set of policies, consistent and well coordinated, these large bureaucracies remain little more than holding companies for elements that remain largely independent. Huge agencies such as the departments of Health and Human Services, Education, and Transportation have yet to display the positive attributes of vertical integration while continuing to exhibit all the deficiencies of large bureaucracies. The old problems of coordination have not been solved, and new problems have been created. Under the Carter administration the organization of a Department of Energy merely transformed into discrete subunits several previously independent agencies. Like the other superagencies, it is nothing more than a holding company.[30]

Decomposability and Organizational Structure

Irrespective of the general coordinative capacities of large bureaucratic forms of organization, in particular situations overcentralization can occur. Referring to the relationship of a brain to its environment, Ashby queried: "Is it not good that a brain should have its parts in rich functional connection?"[31] Answering his own question, he replied:

> No—not in general; only when the environment itself is richly connected. When the environment's parts are not richly connected (when it is highly reducible, in other words), adaptation will go on faster if the brain is also highly reducible, i.e., if its connectivity is small. Thus the degree of organization can be too high as well as too low.[32]

Thus, an analogy is posited between the brain and organizations; we will expect the formal structure for a given organizational system to be more effective if the extent of its connectivity matches the level of connectivity (interdependence) in that system. Higher levels of interdependence may require higher levels of connectivity in the formal structure. But one cannot simply assume high levels of interdependence for a system. The extent of interdependence is an empirical question that can be resolved only by careful examination of the particular domain.

If one must make any assumptions at all about interdependence, one might do well to assume lower levels rather than higher, because, as Simon has observed:

> Hierarchic systems are . . . often nearly decomposable. Hence only aggregative properties of their parts enter into the descriptions of the interactions of these parts. A generalization of the notion of near decomposability might be called the "empty world hypothesis"—most things are only weakly connected with most other things; for a tolerable description of reality only a tiny fraction of all possible interactions needs be taken into account.[33]

Simon thus contradicts the conventional tendency to impute on an a priori basis high levels of interdependence to the parts of a system by arguing that even most complex systems are nearly decomposable: "Intracomponent linkages are generally stronger than intercomponent linkages."[34]

Central coordinating schemes do work effectively under conditions where the task environment is known and unchanging, where it can be treated as a closed system. In such a situation, coordination can be programmed, but the tendency has been (and continues to be) to apply such coordinating schemes to situations marked instead by variability and conflict. More than twenty-five years ago, Burton Klein noted that military research and development was "suffering from too much direction and control." He found it remarkable that "many people who otherwise deplore a high degree of centralized planning regard it as a panacea when it comes to the conduct of R. and D."[35] The rigid character of standardized procedures inherent in formal centralized structures precludes adaptive responses to surprise, and the organizational system suffers accordingly. This crucial point is still not well understood: in a discussion of fostering innovation in urban transportation systems, Martin Wachs, for example, urges that "fragmentation of decision-making, finance, and administrative control must be reduced as an obstacle to innovation."[36]

Formal routines tend to take on a life of their own, commonly undergoing a conversion from purely instrumental devices to intrinsically valuable entities, leading to "displacement of goals." Goal orientation is lost and adherence to rules becomes the prime motivation for behavior.[37]

Additionally, formal systems often create a gap between the formal authority to make decisions and the capacity to make them, owing to a failure to recognize the necessity for a great deal of technical information for effective coordination. Ad hoc coordinating committees staffed by personnel with the requisite professional skills appear far more effective than permanent central coordinating committees run by professional coordinators.[38] Assuming that coordination can occur through formal mechanisms only, or that in some cases it can occur through them at all, is a mistake. I return to Harold Seidman: "Formal coordinating processes are time consuming and the results are generally inconclusive. True coordination is sometimes obtained only by going outside the formal processes." [39]

Informal Organization and Loosely Coupled Systems

Although the contention that higher levels of interdependence in a system demand more coordination is empirically strong, the argument that only formal schemes of a centralized character can provide that coordination remains weak. Because that position has been held so tenaciously, other highly effective devices for coordination have been ignored, and their latent utility wasted.

One of the principal mechanisms for coordinating transit activities in the San Francisco Bay Area fails to appear on any organization chart or in newspaper accounts of transit events. It has no board of directors, no employees of its own, and it cannot raise taxes. In fact, this mechanism has no legal standing. Some classical theorists of public administration might consider it extralegal, if not illegal.[40] Yet the importance and influence of this mechanism is pervasive and persistent. This shadowy, elusive mechanism is a system of informal channels, behavioral norms, and agreements.

These informal organizational features develop on the basis of need. They derive from the everyday processes of mutual adjustment that are exhibited by all large-scale systems, public and private.[41] Informal channels of communication, informal bargains and agreements, and norms of reciprocity all contribute directly and indirectly to processes of coordination. They also form the foundation for formal schemes of coordination, especially by promoting consensus in situations initially characterized by conflict and dissension.

In this sense, Jones's criticism of Bay Area transit for producing "consensus instead of policy" is misplaced.[42] In an informal organization, as opposed to the situation in a formal hierarchy, roles and definitions of tasks are set not by any single authority but by the components themselves. Roles are continuously redefined on the basis of experience, and specific tasks are determined by negotiation. The parties to the bargain are determined not by an organization chart but by the character of the issues at hand.[43]

Informal systems of coordination have many virtues. They tend to be flexible and adaptive. The disruptive effects of innovation in a formal hierarchy, because of its tightly coupled interdependencies, are avoided in the more loosely coupled, flat, informal system of coordination. Such informal systems are problem oriented and pragmatic. They are self-organizing in the sense that they respond to the effects of experience rather than to the a priori demands of organizational designers.[44] Against the canons of classical management theory, they appear to be uncoordinated; but, to use Seidman's words, this is a false impression. Because they are flat, they cannot and do not coordinate by hierarchy. But they are marked by extensive lateral coordination, which occurs at virtually every level of activity—producing an overall system that is quite resistant to serious disruption.[45]

Nonetheless, academics and policy makers regularly ignore or underestimate the potential of informal mechanisms for coordinating different organizations operating in the same domain. In part, this attitude is accounted for by the attractiveness of formal, centralized approaches to coordination and the certainty they promise. But why the unattractiveness of informal organization? Why discount, ignore, or decry such mechanisms when they already exist and when they can provide effective coordination?

Suppose an ostensibly "fragmented" group of organizations shows a surprising capacity for coordination in the absence of any kind of formal consolidation or centralization. Would the automatic response to such "fragmentation" still be a demand for formal centralization and hierarchy? Several factors intrude to prevent a negative answer to this query. As I have already noted, there appears to be a process of transmutation whereby coordination and centralization have become virtually synonymous. Where a need for coordination is perceived, the reflexive response is centralization.

But to coordinate means to place or arrange things in proper position relative to each other and to the system of which they form parts—to bring into proper combined order as parts of a whole.[46] It means, in essence, to bring about some kind of order, not to provide a hierarchical, unified structure. Coordination may consist of a number of things of equal rank or of a number of actions or processes properly combined. But although things may be ordered without reference to hierarchy, the connection between coordination and centralization, if not immutable, is made all too frequently. Look no further than arguments in favor of comprehensive transportation planning:

> This acceptance [of comprehensive planning] has come about through federal pressures and incentives and through recognition at the local level that certain pressing problems of physical and economic development and of environmental deterioration do, in fact, transcend municipal corporate lines and require for sound resolution the cooperative efforts of all the levels, units, and agencies of government concerned.[47]

Or arguments for centralized coordinating agencies:

> If the [Los Angeles County Transportation] Commission chooses to select a strong centralized approach, it would . . . give Los Angeles County every opportunity to provide, for the first time, a coordinated and integrated transit service.[48]

While I do not quarrel with the contention that interdependence requires coordination, I strongly dispute the reflexive assumption that coordination is inexorably tied to centralized arrangements such as comprehensive plans and consolidated agencies.

In part this is a problem of language, which stems from the use of such terms as "fragmented" to characterize multiorganizational systems. The subjective connotation of the term can easily lead to judgments that are not only incorrect but preclude seeing the real issues. Although "fragmented" may be presented as a neutral descriptive term, its normative associations are negative. "Fragmented" implies breakage, disconnection, incompleteness, and disjointedness, terms that presuppose that an entity once whole has since been broken up.[49] To seek "integration" is the "natural" solution. "It brings together the broken pieces, the disconnected and disjointed parts, and renders them entire—one symmetrical and harmonious whole."[50] Thus, "fragmented" organizational arrangements are something to be fixed.

But suppose one were to characterize a multiorganizational system such as Bay Area public transit using different language, language that carries with it different connotations? Suppose one described the transit system as a loosely coupled organizational domain, with flat instead of hierarchical structure, with horizontal instead of vertical linkages tying the components of the system together. Without the pejorative connotations of "fragmented," the reflexive assumption that the organizational system is in need of remedy is absent. To be sure, if the system did suffer breakdowns of one sort or another, we would see them, but it would not be a necessary conclusion that a solution involved formal integration and consolidation.[51]

The bias against multiorganizational systems stems not only from the transmutation of coordination and centralization, but also from a misapprehension of the character of informal organization, as to both the nature of its origins and its potential for coordination. Although informal organization is by no means unknown to students of public organization, its positive role in solving problems of coordination is far from universally apprehended either by academics or policy makers. Nor, more generally, is the nature of informal organization well understood.

Theoretical Perspectives on Organization

The view one adopts on the character and utility of informal mechanisms depends on larger perspectives on the nature of organization.[52] Students of organization, such as Weber, Taylor, and Fayol, who emphasize rationally designed formal structures and tend to consider the organization as separable from its environment (a "closed system") are apt simply to ignore entirely the existence of informal aspects of organization. If the researcher adopts the view, as Roethlisberger and Dickson did, that organizations can be considered apart from their environments, yet allow for organic processes, formal structures will be considered the creations of rational design processes of the managers, and informal features, the aggregation of the personal interests of the organization members. Or one may embrace the perspective, as did Barnard, that though essentially closed systems, organizations are the result of both rational decisions and spontaneous and basically unplanned processes that serve an array of goals, including communication within the organizations. In this case, one may admit to the utility of informal organization but may still fail to recognize the planned, intentional character of many informal mechanisms, especially as they pertain to coordination.[53]

Compounding cloudy perceptions of (and misapprehensions about) the utility of informal organization for the problem of coordination are other failings common to social science research. Empirical work on informal organization has remained largely descriptive in character. Generalizations from this body of research have been narrow in focus, or more concerned with other issues.[54] Conversely, research containing more general and theoretical statements about informal organization has not been well grounded empirically. At the worst, these statements have been offered as virtual proverbs whose empirical warrant is unquestioned.[55]

Our best understanding of informal organization has resulted from the work of sociologists such as Rcbert Merton, Alvin Gouldner, and Philip Selznick.[56] However, even Merton's oft-quoted work on the political machine is only part of a chapter on manifest and latent functions; it is not, overtly at least, about informal organization. In Gouldner's study of the gypsum factory, important information emerges about informal organization, but only in the context of an attempt to understand the growth or contraction of processes of bureaucratization.

Problems resulting from the disjuncture between empirical research and theoretical claims are magnified by difficulties of definition. Insufficient attention has been devoted to providing an accepted, useful definition of the element that gives clear and fixed meaning to the term informal organization. The supposition has been, apparently, that common usage is sufficiently precise—"informal" somehow denotes all aspects of organizations that are not formal:

> There is a noteworthy ambiguity in the natural-system model concerning the meaning of "informal organization." In other words, al-

though it is clear that the natural-system model directs attention beyond and away from the formally constituted organizational system, there remains a question concerning what it is that the model directs attention towards. The notion of informal organization is a residual or cafeteria concept of diverse and sprawling contents.[57]

However, we *have* descriptions of informal organization. It is spontaneous in character and omnipresent within formal organizations. It is composed of group behavior and personal relationships. Occasionally it performs functions for the formal organization in which it develops. More often it serves personal or group ends that are either tangential to the ends of the formal organization or are in conflict with them:

> There will develop an informal structure within the organization which will reflect the spontaneous efforts of individuals and subgroups to control the conditions of their existence. There will also develop informal lines of communication and control to and from other organizations in the environment.[58]

Ambiguity does not exhaust the definitional problems attendant to informal organization. The term has not enjoyed a neutral cast. Because of its general theoretical perspective, the pioneering work of Roethlisberger and Dickson loaded the term with pejorative connotations. By focusing on practices that violated the assumption that the worker's role is a strict devotion to duty, they directed their attention to how the informal organization of the workers interfered with the goals of the formal organization:

> It has been shown that the members of the bank wiring room possessed an intricate social organization in terms of which much of their contact was determined. Restriction of output was the chief outer manifestation of this complex of human relations. . . . There is no doubt that *the most pronounced overall characteristic of the interhuman activities described was their peculiarly protective or resistive quality.*[59]

In fact, concern for the formal design of organizations, combined with a virtual blindness to informal mechanisms on the one hand and an overt hostility to informal mechanisms on the other, is evidence of a theory that constitutes not a descriptive or explanatory analysis of an empirical phenomenon, but a set of prescriptive rules that identify which organizational features are good and which are bad. This bears more than a vague similarity to the Moral Newtonianism of the nineteenth century:

> When scientific models are transferred from their domains of literal meaning, they frequently give rise to sets of moral principles which determine the goals to be sought. The powerful theory of mechanics became, in the secondary domain, Moral Newtonianism, while the theory of evolution became Social Darwinism.[60]

March and Olson go so far as to link the prescriptive orientation of "administrative orthodoxy" to religious and moral movements, a conclusion that should make us question the "rational" character of such orthodoxy.[61]

Thus, one finds on the one hand an overconfidence in the capacity of formal centralized organization to provide the coordination required by multiorganizational systems and, on the other, a misconception and underevaluation of informal, flat organization for the provision of the same. There are multiple causes for this orientation, but its single most important result is an overemphasis on formal reorganization that does not solve the problems it is intended to solve but creates new problems, while alternative means of coordination are ignored.

The argument made in this essay is a straightforward one. In situations where the components of an organizational system are functionally interdependent, the resulting uncertainty creates pressures for coordination. The parts cannot behave without affecting each other; they cannot be understood without reference to each other and to the whole. Historically, the modal response to such pressures for coordination has been to consolidate and integrate formally the separate organizations of the system into a unitary whole, typified by a hierarchical structure of authority and vertical lines of communication.

However, where formal organizational arrangements are absent, insufficient, or inappropriate for providing the requisite coordination (and I argue that they frequently are), informal adaptations develop to satisfy that need. The informal organization thus realized may be quite stable and effective, more so perhaps than formal hierarchical arrangements. Furthermore, because informal organization permits the continued existence of formally autonomous organizations in the face of mutual interdependence, it can achieve other values, such as reliability, flexibility, and representativeness, that would otherwise be precluded or substantially diminished under formal consolidation.

The public transit system of the San Francisco Bay Area clearly evidences both a complex set of functional interdependencies and a set of formally autonomous public agencies. Duplication and overlap of jurisdictions and services as well as competition characterize Bay Area transit. The transit system of the Washington, D.C., metropolitan area also possesses many of these characteristics, yet has a substantially different set of organizational arrangements: the Bay Area transit has a decentralized system of multiple independent organizations whereas Washington possesses a much more consolidated, unitary, hierarchical system. Some comparisons of the two systems permit an understanding of the informal organization and its utility for coordination.

The research reported here differs in a number of ways from previous research involving informal organization. It focuses not on the general properties of informal organization, but on informal mechanisms as they relate directly and indirectly to problems of coordination in a multiorganizational domain. Interest in informal organization stems from its capacity to resolve problems of coordination and its potential as an alternative to the orthodox views of public administration on coordination. I am not concerned with whatever personal or group functions informal features may perform, except as they relate to problems of coordination. Furthermore, whereas most research on informal mechanisms has centered on those found within individual organizations (for example, the formal structure provides a context or environment within which informal features develop), the research reported here examines a stable informal organization that exists in an interagency context apart from any single formal organization.

The research reported here also differs significantly from contemporary studies in its treatment of the problem of coordination. Where recent formal modeling and game theory approaches have largely cast coordination as a problem of finding solutions that maximize the self-interest of the parties involved, employing microeconomic techniques of analysis and often making assumptions about perfect knowledge and the rational calculation of costs and benefits in the absence of behavioral norms,[62] this study emphasizes the development and maintenance of mechanisms through which coordination may take place and the norms that bound the behavior of the actors involved. In this sense, it complements rather than competes with formal modeling and game theory approaches to coordination.

Although the empirical portion of this study is grounded in a case study, my specific intent is to develop general propositions that transcend those cases and that will help both theorists *and* practitioners rethink their ideas about possible and appropriate devices for solving coordination problems at all levels of government and across a wide range of policy areas. At the same time, I would like to think that there are some specific lessons here that are applicable to public transit.

2

Formal Failures and Informal Compensations

See how beautiful a Tammany city government runs, with a so-called boss directin' the whole shootin' match! The machinery moves so noiseless that you wouldn't think there was any.

—George Washington Plunkitt,
a Sachem of Tammany Hall

Virtually everywhere one turns in the domain of organizations, one finds evidence of informal organization.[1] One *expects* to find the formal features of organization. Formal organizations are designed more or less intentionally to perform certain tasks in order to achieve certain goals in the context of particular assumptions about the relevant operating conditions. Public organizations are consciously chosen instruments intended to achieve legally mandated goals.

Informal organization has no such legal rationale for existence, however. It is not considered part of the design of organizations, yet it is a pervasive factor in the life of organizations. Moreover, these durable informal organizations frequently transcend mere extra-legality to illegality; and despite strenuous attempts to stamp them out they continue to thrive. Where might one start the search to explain this phenomenon? If formal designs may be so drawn as to be perfectly suited to achieving their stated goals, any development of informal organization must be treated as an unwarranted intrusion that, at a minimum, is potentially damaging to the achievement of those goals. Furthermore, if it is also assumed that salaries or wages and position within the organization suffice to secure employee loyalty and productivity, without considering survival needs and needs for affiliation and social interaction in the workplace, any informal features that develop will be perceived as problematic. They are phenomena to be suppressed rather than useful devices to be understood and carefully exploited: "The laborer's role is expected to be a strict devotion to technical duty . . . mediated by a competitive orientation toward reward and advancement." [2]

The famous Hawthorne studies by Roethlisberger and Dickson include an early empirical analysis of informal organization. Among other things, they sought to explain the existence of an intricate social organization that determined much employee behavior in the bank wiring room:

> In certain departments at the Hawthorne plant there existed informal employee organizations resulting in problems such as "restriction of output, faulty supervision or mismanagement." The significant problem appeared to be that of specifying the factors which gave rise to such informal organization. [3]

From the first, their attention focused on informalities because they created "problems" for the formal organization. Roethlisberger and Dickson found that the men had "elaborated, spontaneously and quite unconsciously, an intricate social organization around their collective beliefs and sentiments." [4] They concluded that the social organization developed to protect the group in the bank wiring room from internal indiscretions, largely having to do with production levels, and it also served to protect the bank wiring room from outside interference, particularly with respect to change:

> It can be seen that one of the chief sources of constraint in a working group can be a logic which does not take into account the workers' sentiments. Any activity not strictly in accordance with such a logic (and sometimes this means most sorts of social activity) may be judged "wrong." As a result, such activity can only be indulged in

openly within the protection of the informal group, which, in turn, may become organized in opposition to the effective purpose of the total organization.[5]

One concludes from the Roethlisberger and Dickson account that the managers neglected to take into account workers' needs that might run counter to the logic of efficiency and pecuniary reward, thereby virtually ensuring that the workers would attempt to protect themselves from these problems. They did so by creating an informal organization. One begins to get a notion of why informal organization is so persistent.

Merton also found a similar persistence to informal organization. However, in his discussion of political machines, which provide a striking example of informal organization, he came to different conclusions about its origins. Machines persisted over time, despite efforts to eradicate them. In the words of George Washington Plunkitt:

> One year it goes down in defeat and the prediction is made that it will never again raise its head. The district leader, undaunted by defeat, collects his scattered forces, organizes them as only Tammany knows how to organize, and in a little while the organization is as strong as ever.[6]

Political machines tend to run counter to mores, at least as they are publicly expostulated. But "political machines have had the phoenix-like quality of arising strong and unspoiled from their ashes. . . . this structure has exhibited a notable vitality in many areas of political life."[7]

How does Merton explain this persistence? Should it be attributed to the innate corrupting influence of positions of power and the opportunity for "honest graft"? Could it be the intrinsic propensity of people to act illicitly if given half a chance? Merton suggests a more surprising yet ultimately more powerful explanation having less to do with personal motivations than with failures of formal organization.

In particular, the political machine compensated for structural problems (especially the dispersion of power) in municipal government that made coordination for the purposes of positive action difficult if not impossible. Furthermore, political machines met the needs of "diverse subgroups in the larger community which (were) not adequately satisfied by legally devised and culturally approved substructures."[8] Municipal reformers came to associate decentralized city governments with the strength of political machines. Not until fractionalized municipal government was "fixed" through the short ballot and unification of powers in a single governing body did the political machines begin to wither and disappear. While Roethlisberger and Dickson recognized that the informal organization protected individuals and subgroups against the intrusion of the formal organization, Merton directly connected the existence of the informal organization (the political machine) to failures of the official political structure to achieve its intended goals.

Without requiring the adoption of latent functional analysis as a causal explanation, Merton's approach leads us to think about informal organization as a compensatory device for failures of formal structures: they have consequences that make them very valuable. What sorts of consequences might these be? Wilbert Moore recognized that formal designs are essentially incomplete, that they specify vertical lines of authority far more thoroughly than horizontal lines of communication. More important, Moore perceived the inevitability of informal patterns of interaction among workers, documenting various features of what he called "cliques" within organizations, observing that cliques within organizations may well be related to "off-the-job attitudes and modes of association."

Moore observed that groups (or cliques) initiate new members into the accepted norms of behavior for the organization. They also develop and maintain technical languages specific to the routines of the organization (what Arrow has called the organization's "code"). Additionally, groups provide recreational play that serves as an outlet for boredom and dissatisfaction, while maintaining group norms through standard customs of behavior toward individuals.[9]

Seeking to understand the restriction of output observed by Roethlisberger and Dickson, Moore suggested that informalities substitute group ends for individual competitive ends. Because individual competition can be divisive, certain informal mechanisms that promote group cohesiveness develop, though they might be antithetical to the ends both of individuals and of the organization as a whole.[10]

Moore correctly concluded that informal patterns serve to protect *group* ends, through the control of output (neither too little nor too much), a norm prohibiting "squealing," and a norm emphasizing good personal relations and minimizing social distance. Moore noted that a vital organizational end was indirectly served by the informal group activities—the maintenance of a foundation for coordination—albeit indirectly. An exclusive concern for competitive performance is "not only destructive of group morale, but may actually subvert the general ends of the cooperative system by destroying the basis for joint activity." [11]

The Informal Organization: Planned or Spontaneous?

Among early researchers who delved into the mysteries of informal organization, the subtlest discussion of the relationship between the formal and informal comes from Chester Barnard. According to Barnard, informal organization provides effective communication within the organization, which improves the ability of the formal organization to be an effective system for cooperation (or coordination). Furthermore, informal organization maintains "cohesiveness in formal organization through regulating the willingness to serve and the stability of objective authority." [12] Informal mechanisms also provide for the "maintenance of the feeling of personal integrity, of self-respect, of independent choice," among the members of the organization. Although often deemed destructive to formal organization, this aspect of informalities is "to be regarded as a means of maintaining the personality of the individual against certain effects of formal organizations which tend to disintegrate the personality," [13] and indirectly assists in maintaining the viability of the organization through improved morale.

More recently, Victor Thompson has sought to understand the character of what he calls the "natural system" of organization as distinguished from the "artificial system." [14] These terms equate with "informal" organization and "formal" organization, respectively, as they are used in this study. In a discussion of the problem of instrumentality (the nature of the functions performed), Thompson argues that "it is often mistakenly assumed that natural systems are concerned with maintenance functions and artificial systems with instrumental-adaptive functions. However, both systems perform both kinds of functions." [15]

For Thompson, the key functional distinction between the two systems hinges on the referent of their consequences: "internal for the natural system, external for the artificial system." [16] "The most important, or central, characteristic of the natural system is neither its residual nor its spontaneous character, but its internal reference. *It is not a tool* of anyone or anything but itself." [17]

Referring to the men of the bank wiring room, Roethlisberger and Dickson wrote: "there was nothing in the behavior of this group that even faintly resembled conscious, planned opposition to management." [18] Thompson takes a more qualified view of the planned nature of informalities: the modal characteristic of the natural system is spontaneity (which is a connotation of the very word he uses to denote the phenomenon), but planning is possible within the natural system. Thompson contends, however, that planning does not go beyond individual or group protection: "conscious planning takes place within the natural system, as when a group gets together to plan a defense against a threatening procedure or superior." [19] Thompson agrees with Merton that the development of informalities may be related to failures of the formal structure—not simply that informalities achieve important ends but that some of the ends they achieve are related to distinct failures of the formal.

Despite Barnard's subtle understanding of informal organization, particularly for the formal organization as a unit, his analysis only implicitly suggests that informalities compensated for formal failures. Nor does Barnard believe that the consequences of informal mechanisms for the formal were anything but incidental. Referring to informalities, he argues that "though common or joint purposes are excluded by definition, common or joint results of important character nevertheless come from such organization." [20] Perhaps, for Barnard, informal organization comprised the processes of society "which are unconscious as contrasted with those of formal organization which are conscious." [21]

Thompson's discussion of natural systems makes several valuable contributions toward understanding informal organization. Although informal organization is primarily spontaneous in character, it may sometimes be planned intentionally; nonetheless, intentional uses of informal organization have a strictly internal referent. This position stands in clear contrast to Barnard's. The conscious motivation for informal organization, if one exists (and it need not), may be quite distinct from and even antithetical to some of its consequences. Informal channels may be developed to meet individual or group ends and simultaneously have consequences that compensate for formal structure failures. Precisely the opposite may also be true, however. For an illustration of this point, contrast Devons's observations on the British Ministry of Aircraft Production with Sapolsky's description of the Polaris system development. Both were concerned with the collection of sensitive information about production schedules from subunits or subcontractors by a central coordinating body for a program. Of Polaris, Sapolsky wrote:

> When the technical officers wanted accurate data on development slippages in Plant X they would call a former Navy buddy in quality control, visit with the redhead who was the design group's secretary, or wire the cooperative salesmanager of Plant X's subcontractor. . . . The PERT system, though supposedly designed to overcome one set of biases, was, in their opinion, riddled with other unintended and uncompensated biases.[22]

Concerning the Ministry of Aircraft Production (MAP) in Great Britain during World War II, Ely Devons wrote:

> In order to get the information they needed the planning directorate used two main lines of attack. First, they engaged in the most subtle forms of spying they could contrive. The most effective was to find some person in the production directorate who had a grievance, worm one's way into his confidence, and get him to "spill the beans" on what was really happening in his directorate. . . . The other main line of attack was to discover officials either at MAP, the firms or the Air Ministry who realized the importance of coordination and were not oversensitive about the prestige of their own directorate, cultivate their acquaintance or friendship where this was possible, and use them as the main instruments of coordination, especially in an emergency when quick decisions were necessary.[23]

Both Devons and Sapolsky describe the use of informal channels to compensate for coordination failures of the formal mechanism. Each shows a perspective quite dissimilar to the picture drawn by Roethlisberger and Dickson. They point out that informal mechanisms were directly used for the task of coordination. The two observations diverge in the way they depict the development and use of informal channels. Sapolsky gives the impression that informal channels existed only because of previous personal relationships and fortuitous circumstance. Existing channels were exploited for the purpose of coordination without having been developed intentionally for that purpose. Conversely, Devons shows clearly the deliberate, conscious development of informal relationships, not for personal survival needs or group protection, but with the specific intent to exploit them for purposes of coordination. The consequences are the same in both cases, but for Devons the intended purpose of the informal channels is an organizational end (although they may also incidentally meet group or personal needs). In the former case, informalities serve the formal organization only incidentally. They remain directed toward individual or group needs. We would expect the channels in Devons's example ultimately to prove more dependable and durable because they were developed and maintained especially for coordination.

Thus, the picture drawn by Devons is at odds with those drawn by Thompson, Barnard, Moore, and Roethlisberger and Dickson with respect to the reasons why informalities develop. If we keep this distinction in mind, the two-way Table 1 can help us to understand the problem.

Cell A contains those aspects of informal organization intended to achieve ends for the individual or group, with consequences only for the individual or group. Cell C contains informal features intended for individual or group ends but having consequences for the formal organization as well. In Cell B are those informalities intended to serve the organization's goals but which also have positive consequences for the group or individual. Finally, Cell D contains informal devices intended to serve the ends of formal organization and which in fact have consequences for those ends.

If we associate the authors discussed previously with the cells of Table 1 according to their perspectives on the intentions and consequences of informal organization, the following arrangement results. Roethlisberger and Dickson, who do not believe that informal organization serves other than group or individual ends, fall into Cell A. Any consequences for the formal organization are deemed negative. On the other hand, Moore belongs in Cell C. For Moore, the informal is developed because of benefits it can provide for the group, but it also performs incidental functions for the larger organization. Thompson, Barnard, and Sapolsky also belong in Cell C, along with

Table 1   Consequences of Informal Organization

	Intended Ends	
	Group or Individual	Formal Organization
Actual consequences for		
Group or individual	A	B
Formal organization	C	D

Merton. Only Devons would be found in Cell D, where informalities are intended to serve the ends of the larger organization and perhaps also in Cell B where informal mechanisms have incidental positive consequences for the individual or group.

The conclusion drawn from existing analyses (those discussed are a representative sample) is that by and large informalities are believed to result from personal or group needs. Disagreement exists over whether informalities are strictly spontaneous or whether, as Thompson suggests, they are at times consciously developed. For the most part, commentators believe that ends of the larger organization are met only adventitiously by informal mechanisms. Such consequences are not a principal intention of informalities. Only Devons has ventured to hazard otherwise.

Failures in the Process of Coordination

"Coordination describes both a process—the act of coordinating—and a goal." [24] If coordination is considered as an end state, the result of some process, it is defined as a "harmonious combination of agents or functions toward the production of a result." [25] Such a definition of coordination does not assist us to understand how coordination is achieved. On the other hand, the definition of the verb form, to coordinate, is somewhat different: "to place or arrange (things) in proper position relatively to each other and to the system of which they form parts; to bring into proper combined order as parts of a whole." [26]

To comprehend formal failures, coordination must be understood as a process as well as a desired end state. This approach permits decomposing the process of coordination into its several components. In this way we can attain a more complete understanding of formal failure and pinpoint the exact nature of the compensatory role of informal mechanisms.

According to Simon, three main elements compose any formal process of coordination: a plan of action must be developed; the plan of action must be communicated to the parties who will carry it out; and the plan as developed and communicated must be accepted by those parties.[27] To these three steps, a fourth may be added: pertinent information must be acquired through research and intelligence. Before a plan of action can be developed information about goals and cause-effect relationships must be obtained. These four steps may be more accurately considered essential components of coordination, rather than steps to be followed in precise order. Certainly, for example, acceptance of a plan is generated throughout the entire process of developing it, not solely after it has been developed.

Sapolsky and Devons illustrate some failures of formal organization regarding these components, particularly regarding the acquisition of necessary information. Where else among these components of coordination should we expect to find formal failures? Coordination is an activity that is understood to occur only after sufficient community of interest develops among the relevant parties, forming a foundation for later efforts. This process is not necessarily understood by everyone. Seidman notes that when efforts at coordination in the federal government fail, the fault is placed in the formula, not in deeper, underlying causes. Formal efforts at coordination are often destined to fail because they are expected to do the impossible:

> Too often organic disease is diagnosed as a case of inadequate coordination. . . . Without . . . a community of interests and compatible objectives, problems cannot be resolved by coordination.[28]

The failure to develop a community of interest, or as Barnard refers to it, "community of purpose," precludes effective coordination. Formal mechanisms are notoriously ineffective at developing such community. Informal devices are often more effective for this purpose.

Acceptance of a plan by relevant parties is also something that cannot be achieved by formal design. Formal inducement/reward and

Table 2   Components of Coordination and Types of Failure

Component	Permanent Failure	Episodic Failure
Development of plan of action	No provision for building coalitions No provision for building community of interest	—
Communication of plan of action	Mismatched channels Incomplete channels	Slow channels
Acceptance of plan of action	No provision for building coalitions	Inability to expand zone of acceptance
Collection of essential information	Mismatched channels Inability to collect sensitive information Formal structure incomplete	Slow channels Mismatched channels

coercive mechanisms often prove inadequate to the task of gaining acceptance, even though all means of expanding the "zone of acceptance" have been exhausted.[29] Most of the burden here falls to the informal structures of organization, principally because they are founded on personal trust, reciprocity, and persuasion.

Formal failures in the process of coordination are summarized in Table 2, which combines the components of coordination with permanent and episodic failures.

Coordination may be (and often is) intentionally achieved by informal organization in ways that have generally gone unnoticed. As a way of understanding the problem of coordination, consider the broader role of informal mechanisms as they relate to the failures of formal organization. Although informalities often result from personal motivations of individual organization members, the formal organization also frequently fails to provide sufficient means for the achievement of its own goals. Informal mechanisms can compensate for these failures, although their role is grossly underrated. There are endemic, pervasive failures of formal organization as instrument, which may result in part from the inevitable impossibility of specifying all standards, rules of behavior, and relationships for any given organization. "Even if it were desirable, the formal structure could not be specified in such detail as to obviate the need for an informal supplement." [30] Or, as Simon, Smithburg, and Thompson contend:

> There are wide differences in the degrees to which various organizations attempt to plan formally the behavior of their employees. In some organizations the plan is very sketchy. It consists of little more than a few verbal or written instructions that assign tasks to employees, and perhaps specify the principal lines of legitimate authority. . . . In other organizations the plan is very elaborate. . . . The incompleteness of the formal plan provides a vacuum which, like other vacuums, proves abhorrent to nature. The members of an organization gradually develop patterns of behavior and relationships with each other." [31]

Aside from problems of incompleteness, there are other endemic failures of formal organization that no amount of tinkering or revision can eliminate. For the most part the formal organization is hopelessly incapable of meeting individual or group needs. In some cases it even works against them, as when formal organization creates problems for individuals concerning self-respect and personal integrity.

Consider the possibility that there are some ends of the organization as a unit that the formal organizational structure is poorly adapted to perform. Simultaneously, there may be ends of the organization as a unit that informal mechanisms are singularly well suited to perform. If fortune is beneficent, those ends that formal structures cannot perform well and those that informalities are peculiarly fitted to perform will be roughly equivalent. Devons provides some insight on this point. Again, referring to the problem of coordinating British aircraft production during World War II, and specifically the problem of acquiring accurate information on production estimates, he wrote:

> To the newcomer to the problem of coordination it seemed easy to ensure that the planning directorate were given the necessary advance information. It merely needed an instruction to the production directors that they should provide the central directorate with the earliest warning of any sign that the programmes for which they were responsible would not be fulfilled. In fact *such coordination by instruction never worked.* . . . Such an instruction invariably aroused the suspicion in the production directorates that the planning directorate were trying to interfere in matters which did not concern them. [32]

Certain information is essential to the task of effective coordination, but the formal system often lacks the ability to obtain this information. For example, formal channels tend to be public channels, which in bureaucracies are almost always documented on paper, often making information transmitted through them subject to unwanted scrutiny. The information most needed for coordination is often potentially damaging to the party who is supposed to supply it. Confessions of failure are hardly likely, especially when some sort of punishment may result. This is one of the major problems of coordinating the production of goods and services in centrally planned economies, such as that of the Soviet Union. The pioneering studies of Berliner have shown that, were it not for an elaborate system of illegal but widely tolerated informal structures, the Soviet economy would crumble almost straightaway.[33]

Strict reliance on formal channels compounds the problem: reliable information will not be supplied, and the failure will not be uncovered until it is too late to compensate for it. Informal channels, by their typically clandestine nature and foundation on reciprocity and mutual trust, provide appropriate means for surmounting problems associated with formal channels of communication. In this case the informal structures neatly compensate for the failings of the formal. Inasmuch as coordination is largely based on accurate, reliable information, acquiring that information is indispensable. Referring to the informal, Devons wrote: "It was by such channels that the most efficient coordination was achieved and yet it would have been quite impossible to bring such a system into being by administrative (e.g., formal) arrangements."[34]

Informalities may also be developed because of "episodic" failures of formal organization that interfere with the performance of important ends. The formal structure may work most of the time, but tend to break down at certain times, under certain conditions. Such failures may result from the slowness of formal channels in the face of urgent situations. Informal channels, which tend to cut through layers of authority and provide direct contact between relevant parties, are often effective remedies. When such formal failures occur, the power of informal mechanisms to compensate for them may be so great that employees frequently resort to channels of communication that are not only extralegal but even illegal: "When employees find that it is too complicated to do things 'through channels,' new and often explicitly forbidden channels are employed to supplement and bypass the formal ones."[35] An illustration from the staff of the commander in chief of the U.S. Fleet (COMINCH) during World War II makes the point:

The COMINCH organization had to adapt to the expanding demands of a burgeoning navy fighting a global war. [Admiral Ernest J.] King wanted a small staff for reasons of efficiency; any request for increased numbers required ample justification and King's grudging approval. The staff nevertheless grew to over six hundred officers and enlisted personnel. It concurrently became less efficient. "I found out early in the game," recalled staff officer Robert B. Pirie, "that, working on a big staff like that, to try to get action taken on dispatches or papers that I was trying to move in a hurry . . . would just take days, literally to go around and get initials from half a dozen people between my level and Admiral King. So I finally just took the things up and got him to release them direct. . . . Admiral King was very good about that." [36]

Figure 1 shows differences in the directness of informal versus formal channels of communication between two organizations, 1 and 2. Situation A shows the operation of formal channels between the two organizations. In order for interorganizational communication to occur, the communication must pass through several layers of each organization. The picture is obviously simplified, because formal communication between organizations may go on between formally designated liaisons located at middle levels of each organization. However, the general point remains the same. Situation B illustrates the shorter, more direct character of informal channels between the same two organizations. Formal communication between X and V, is a more laborious and circuitous process (and therefore more time consuming) than informal communication. In the informal case the people needing to talk to one another simply do so directly.

Informal features are also developed to compensate for failures resulting from formal maladaptation to specific circumstances. Such failures may result from forcing a formal design into a situation when the design is inappropriate. A frequent occurrence of this type is the imposition of a programmed structure (such as a management-control system) onto a situation featuring substantial value disagreement. In such a case, unless informal patterns of bargaining and accommodation are developed and used, the organization will be incapacitated. [37]

All organizations are designed to deal with a particular set of problems possessing certain attendant characteristics. If organizations are well designed, most of the problems they face will have those characteristics. Invariably, however, the organization will come face to face with anomalous problems for which it was not de-

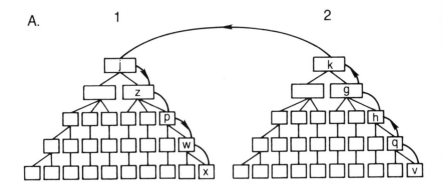

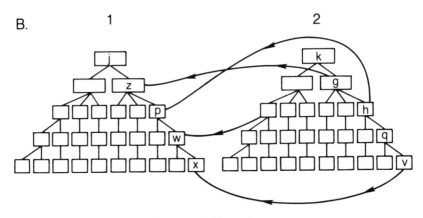

Figure 1   Formal and Informal Channels

signed. Informal mechanisms help the organization solve those problems without formal redesign, and without failure. They also protect against the pernicious effects of "goal displacement." [38]

Another maladaptation generating informal responses occurs when the formal structure approaches obsolescence yet continues to be used. Over time the organization's environment changes sufficiently to render a once-adequate formal design inappropriate. For example, a formal structure designed to work on an assumption of low interdependence with other organizations in its environment will begin to make errors when the level of interdependence increases substantially. Landau has suggested that all formal designs have a built-in obsolescence that cannot be circumvented,[39] thus virtually requiring that informal mechanisms be developed if the organization is to continue to prosper. Informal adaptations may endure permanently or may be permitted to fade away as formal responses are made to the altered circumstances. In the latter case, informal adaptations buy the organization sufficient time to make careful changes in its formal structure.

Thus, motivations for developing informal organization fall principally into two categories, having in common the fact that they are related to failures of formal organization. The referent of the first category is the individual or the group. These informalities may facilitate or hinder the goals of the organization as a unit. They may also be intended to hinder the organization as a unit when it impinges on the personal needs of the individual or groups—for example, group resistance to supervision by outsiders.

The other category's referent is the achievement of the larger organizational goals that cannot be met by the formal structure. The problem of coordination is dealt with primarily by informalities falling into this category, which are intended to compensate for formal failures of one sort or another. My attention is therefore directed toward this category of informal mechanisms.

The Multiorganizational Setting

Thus far in discussing informalities and how they achieve ends for formal organizations (as well as for the individuals and groups within those organizations), the frame of reference has been the single organization. My argument has concerned patterns of behavior occurring entirely within the boundaries of one organization. However, this study addresses problems of coordination in multiorganizational systems, so it is vital to understand both the continuities and disjunctures between settings for single and multiple organizations.

There are informal features attached to formal organizations everywhere. But can informal organization develop and be sustained outside the framework of a formal organization? Barnard contends that informal organization "probably cannot persist or become extensive without the emergence of a formal organization."[40] Therefore, in a multiorganizational setting one might wonder at the development and persistence of an informal system at all. There is evidence of the capacity of informal organization to develop and persist for short periods without the prior presence or emergence of formal organization. Some situations call forth more or less spontaneously the existence of informal organizations. Foremost among these are natural catastrophes of a widespread nature such as floods, fires, and earthquakes. Though formal emergency coordination mechanisms are designed "just in case," there are distinctive social processes of adaptation that can be called an "emergency social system." The duration of this system may be "a few hours, a few days, or longer, depending on how rapidly normal social processes can take over the adaptive task."[41] Predominant in this analysis is the idea that some sudden and large change has disrupted the existing social patterns and social roles along with the formal organizations normally responsible for the coordination and provision of service.

In extensive disasters, the capacities of formal organizations to contend with the problems generated are frequently grossly inadequate because of breakdowns in communications systems or lack of knowledge about the nature and extent of the disaster. The disaster simply dwarfs the capacity of existing organizations, or it may cover several jurisdictions. In such situations informal responses typically arise and develop coordination of emergency services at a rapid pace, albeit in a "sporadically improvised fashion." When the disaster is over, the formal organizations continue much as they were before.

But what of the ability of informal organization to persist over longer periods without a supporting or structuring formal organization? Barnard contends that although informal organization may initially result from gregarious impulses, it "will generally be noted that a purely passive or bovine kind of association among men is of short duration";[42] therefore, a concrete object of action is necessary for social satisfaction and the persistence of informal organization. Yet it is his belief that by definition, common or joint purposes are excluded for informal organization. By this reasoning a common purpose is essential to informal organization but cannot be generated by it. One must therefore look to some source outside informal organization.

In the case of the single organization, one need look no further than the formal structure: it provides common purpose. In the multi-organizational case, however, there is no overarching formal structure to provide such a common purpose for the informal organization; the informal organization exists in the interstices between organizations. Nonetheless, in Bay Area public transit one finds a robust and long-lived interorganizational informal structure. How can we explain this apparent contradiction?

The answer is found in the interdependence of the several transit agencies, and the capacity of the informal organization to achieve important ends for the multiorganizational system. As will be seen later in some detail, interdependence provides the commonality of purpose found so important by Barnard. Their interdependence means that cooperation for joint purposes is essential for the transit operators to achieve their individual goals. This informal organization neither supplants nor eliminates the informal organizations *within* each of these organizations; it interacts with them. Thus, the requisite purpose can be provided outside the framework of a single formal organization. Interdependence provides the same commonality of purpose in the multiorganizational case that formal structure provides in the case of the single organization.

Just how little common purpose is actually necessary to sustain stable sets of informal norms is beautifully illustrated by Axelrod's description of trench warfare during World War I. Opposing French and German troops reached informal, tacit agreements about not bombarding each other during certain times (for example, during meals or while removing the dead and wounded). These informal norms persisted despite both high turnover of personnel at the front *and* direct and explicit opposition by commanding generals of both sides.[43] How much more probable is the development and maintenance of informal structures in a multiorganizational setting when the different organizations are not (literally) trying to annihilate one another!

A similar problem arises when we view the multiorganizational situation from another vantage point. I have spent considerable effort elucidating the role of informal mechanisms as compensatory devices for failures of formal organization. In the multiorganizational case there is no formal organization to be inadequate or fail; it simply does not exist. However, just as the absence of certain features in a single formal organization has been treated as a failure (producing pressure for informal mechanisms), the absence of an overarching formal structure in an area where interdependence is present may be treated as a failure.

When a single organization is examined, the individual and group ends that serve to explain the motivation for developing informal mechanisms may overwhelm and obscure the informal features intended to achieve the ends of the organization as a unit. However, in a multiorganizational setting, informal channels (among other informal features) between organizations are difficult to explain in terms of their consequences for individual or group ends. In all probability those ends are achieved by informal structures *within* each of those organizations. If those needs are already being met, one must then look elsewhere for the motivations that explain interorganizational informal systems. The most immediately plausible explanation hinges on the value of those informalities for reducing uncertainty through interorganizational coordination. It is the starting point from which this study proceeds.

Before we proceed, however, a final caveat is in order. It is precisely the focus on informalities whose referents are the individual or group that pushes one to conclude that *all* informalities serve the individual or group, are typically problematic for the organization as a unit, and only on occasion have incidentally positive consequences for the larger organization. If one examines the informalities whose referents are the organization as a unit, a different picture emerges.

The intent of this study is not to develop an empirical distribution of the motivations for and the consequences of informal organization. Instead my intention is to understand better the instrumental value of informalities for dealing with problems of coordination that arise from interorganizational interdependence in the absence of formal coordinating mechanisms. For this reason, I do not investigate all possible ends of informal organization, nor do I contend with those who argue that particular informalities may create serious problems for the larger organization in which they reside. There can be no doubt that at times they do. I do wish to show that some informalities are capable of promoting coordination very effectively, in fact, far more powerfully than has been typically assumed. Furthermore, I intend to demonstrate that such informalities, far from being useful merely as a result of fortuitous happenstance, are often carefully developed and maintained by individuals with the specific goal of coordination in mind. Therefore, there are many aspects of informal organization that are not considered here, and the picture that emerges of informal organization is admittedly incomplete. Only those informal features that bear, directly or indirectly, on the problem of coordination are addressed here. The potential uses of informal structures for other ends are irrelevant to this study's central concerns. It is therefore unimportant whether the modal characteristic of *all* informal features is planning or spontaneity, or whether they have positive or negative effects on the organization as a unit. It is enough to show that under *some* conditions informalities are very powerful coordinating devices indeed.

3

The Problem of Interdependence

Sets of simultaneous equations as a way to
"model" or define a system are, if linear,
tiresome to solve even in the case of a few
variables; if nonlinear, they are unsolvable except in special cases.

—Ludwig von Bertalanffy,
General Systems Theory

At 5:42 A.M. on Monday, the sky is overcast. Philip Wilson
boards an AC Transit bus in the Berkeley hills and pays his fare. In
downtown Berkeley Phil exits the bus and walks into the BART station. He boards a San Francisco–bound train. He exits at the BART
Embarcadero station and walks the four blocks to his office.

An hour later Steve MacFarlane leaves his driveway and parks
at the Tiburon ferry terminal, where he catches a Golden Gate ferry
to San Francisco. On exiting the San Francisco Ferry Terminal he
crosses the street and boards a Muni trolley bound down Market
Street. In a few minutes he exits the trolley and walks a short distance to his office.

At 7:31 A.M. Lila Langtree boards a Muni light-rail vehicle
headed toward downtown San Francisco from her apartment. She
exits the bus to enter a BART station where she catches a train bound
for Daly City. At the BART Daly City station she takes a Samtrans
bus, which drops her at the departures level of the main airline ter-

minal at San Francisco Airport. She catches the daily Pan Am flight to Paris.

About 11:00 A.M. the cloud cover has begun to break. Bill Jones walks from his house in Oakland to the BART station. He boards a train for Berkeley. At the Ashby station he catches a special AC bus bound for Golden Gate Fields Race Track. By 2:00 P.M. he has bet and lost $150 on the first three races.

At 1:06 P.M. the sun is high overhead, the sky is a brilliant blue, and Thad Slimwit has four minutes to get to his organization theory seminar at Cal. Instead, he catches an AC bus to San Francisco. At the Transbay Terminal he boards a Golden Gate bus to Marin County. In San Rafael he transfers to another Golden Gate bus, which will take him to Muir Beach. By 4:17 P.M. he has had one pint of bitter and finished his first dart game at the Pelican Inn.

About the same time, Jim Fratz leaves his Oakland office and descends into the BART 19th Street station where he boards a train for Fremont. At the terminus he walks outside to catch a Santa Clara bus on its way to San Jose. During the trip he disembarks, walks several blocks and meets his girlfriend of many years at their favorite restaurant, where they order drinks and watch the sun recede in a blaze of orange in the western sky.

Taken together these scenarios depict the connectedness of the Bay Area transit operators at the level at which it matters most—that of the passenger. Each trip, because it involves more than one transit operator, creates interdependence, which then raises issues of coordinating bus and train schedules and routes, physical plant layouts, joint fares, "fastpasses," and transfer discounts, along with issues of long-term capital acquisitions and transit planning. The characters and plot lines of these scenarios are, of course, pure fiction, but as John Steinbeck once said of a story he told in *Sweet Thursday,* "There are people who will say that this whole account is a lie, but a thing isn't necessarily a lie even if it didn't necessarily happen."

Basic Premises

My views on interdependence start from two basic premises. Organizations are not autonomous entities; not only are their parts interdependent, but the best laid plans of managers have un-intended consequences and are conditioned or are upset by other so-cial units—other complex organizations or publics—on whom the organization is dependent.[1] Following this premise, the organization cannot be analyzed as a closed system: it is an open system, inter-dependent with its environment.

Although at times we seem to forget this simple point, to speak a language is to follow the system of organization and classification of data that the language itself decrees.[2] We focus on some things as our central concerns and ignore others as irrelevant, using the cues of language as guidelines. By the nature of the language involved, an open-system model of organization points the researcher in direc-tions the use of a closed-system model would not. Drawn from biol-ogy, the open-system model directs one to discover the linkages be-tween the organization and its environment: one searches for those factors external to the organization that affect its behavior, those fac-tors that describe its interdependence.[3]

By interdependence, I refer to a condition where two (or more) organizations require each other, are dependent each upon the other. This state is characterized more or less by symmetry among the parties to the relationship. Connections between the organizations involved are nonrandom. However, there is *no* implication of subordinate status for any of them. It is further recognized that interdependence causes uncertainty for the focal organization. I take uncertainty to mean a "lack of information about future events so that alternatives and their outcomes are unpredictable,"[4] where "events" are under-stood as actions by other organizations in the focal organization's en-vironment. What distinguishes relevant uncertainty from the larger universe is threat to the organization, where "threat" is defined as something likely to injure—to be a source of danger, to endanger actively.[5]

Thus, the behavior of a particular organization in a state of inter-dependence cannot be understood in isolation: its behavior is affected by and in turn affects the behaviors of those involved in the relation-ship. Therefore, to say that a set of organizations is described by interdependence is to claim that the set possesses systemic properties such that it is not immediately decomposable into the individual units of which it is comprised.

More specifically, following Lindblom, I define interdependence this way:

> Within the set, each decision-maker is in such a relation to each other decision-maker that unless he deliberately avoids doing so (which may or may not be possible), he interferes with or contributes to the goal achievement of each other decision-maker, either by direct impact or through a chain of effects that reach any given decision-maker only through effects on others.[6]

An organization's interdependence with other organizations in its environment causes uncertainty for it in two ways. Cause-and-effect relations between these units and itself may not be well understood because of insufficient knowledge. Even if the organization achieves an understanding of such relations, it may not then be able to control them to its satisfaction. It will have to discover through research those factors in the environment that cause it uncertainty, and then seek ways to contend with those that threaten it.

Following Thompson, the central problem for complex organizations is one of coping with uncertainty.[7] Although there are obviously many other potential sources of uncertainty, such as mechanical failure or technological innovation, I focus here on the uncertainty that results from an organization's interdependence with other organizations in its environment.

When another premise is added—that organizations are strongly motivated to achieve what Thompson calls "norms of rationality"— "it becomes abundantly clear why organizations seek to understand and then manage or eliminate the factors in the environment which pose uncertainty for it."[8] Interdependence with other organizations gives rise to uncertainty, which the organization seeks to reduce or eliminate while operating under norms of rationality. The central problem arising from a state of interdependence is to reduce uncertainty (particularly that which threatens the organization) to an acceptable level by ordering the behaviors of all relevant organizations to lessen the extent to which they impinge on each other's behavior and increase the benefits from their behaviors. Organizations attempt to reduce uncertainty in various ways—through expansion and merger, consolidation and centralization, government regulation, lateral coordination, and warfare.

Policy makers and academics who demand better coordination between and among a given set of organizations implicitly assume the existence of some form of nontrivial interdependence. And they assume that the best if not the only way to deal with it is through centralization. However, given the costs of reorganization and formal hierarchical approaches to coordination, and given Simon's argument about the typical decomposability of most systems,[9] simple assumptions about interdependence and integration are risky, and the cost of error may be high.

Any analysis that seeks to discover the need for coordination within a given set of organizations and then to make an evaluation of how well that need is being met by existing institutional arrangements must assess first whether any interdependence exists at all, and must then ascertain the extent and character of that interdependence. Only then can we consider what constitutes an appropriate organizational design for handling the particular problems of coordination raised by the actual interdependence (which may include recommending remedies for the deficiencies).

A prime danger of designs not founded on such knowledge is that a formal coordinating structure so developed may itself intensify existing problems of coordination: new problems of coordination may themselves be artifacts of organizational reform. The organizational structure may also be so poorly adapted to the specific problems of coordination it is intended to address that it is incapable of solving them while simultaneously creating additional problems. Such an approach is obviously inconsistent with the view that organizations are rational instruments that must be carefully designed for achieving specific ends under particular circumstances. And yet it occurs all too often. Consolidation plans for the Los Angeles and San Francisco Bay Area public transit systems are merely two of the most recent significant examples.

Operations, Services, and Planning in Bay Area Public Transit

We must first establish the contours of the Bay Area transit system's interdependence [10] before rendering a judgment on the suitability of existing institutional arrangements. Where does one look for relationships of interdependence? One practical approach is to begin wherever two organizations have any sort of exchange. For Bay Area public transit several different areas must be examined: where formal jurisdictions of the different organizations are contiguous, where they overlap, or where the organizations in the set interact in common arenas (such as the Metropolitan Transportation Commission or MTC).

Map 1 shows the jurisdictions of the major transit agencies of the Bay Area, including the six operators constituting (with the MTC) the set of organizations under consideration: Alameda–Contra Costa County Transit District (AC); Bay Area Rapid Transit District (BART); the Golden Gate Bridge, Highway, and Transportation District (Golden Gate), San Francisco Municipal Railway (Muni); San Mateo County Transit District (Samtrans); and Santa Clara County Transportation Agency (Santa Clara).[11]

BART's jurisdiction includes Alameda, Contra Costa, and San Francisco counties, thus containing completely within its bounds areas also served by AC and Muni. AC and Muni touch boundaries in San Francisco. Golden Gate's jurisdiction includes, among others, Sonoma, Marin, and San Francisco counties, thus overlapping with the Muni, with BART, and touching the boundaries of AC. Santa Clara touches BART and Samtrans. Samtrans overlaps geographically with BART and touches the Muni. Where service territories of organizations touch or overlap with others we would expect to find the potential for interdependence.

Interdependence is found in three areas: *operations, services,* and *planning.* Because problems of coordination require resolution of what may seem to some rather small details, I hope the reader will bear with the ensuing discussion of the finer technical aspects of interdependence in public transit. The picture drawn here is reasonably accurate and complete for the period of this study (1978–80) but undoubtedly looked somewhat different before and looks different today.

In San Francisco, three operators use the same streets simultaneously: Muni in the conduct of its entire operations, and Golden Gate and Samtrans in the course of delivering and picking up passengers in the downtown area to and from outlying counties. Using the same streets creates several problems. There is the potential for traffic congestion, a problem Muni considered sufficiently serious in 1958 to

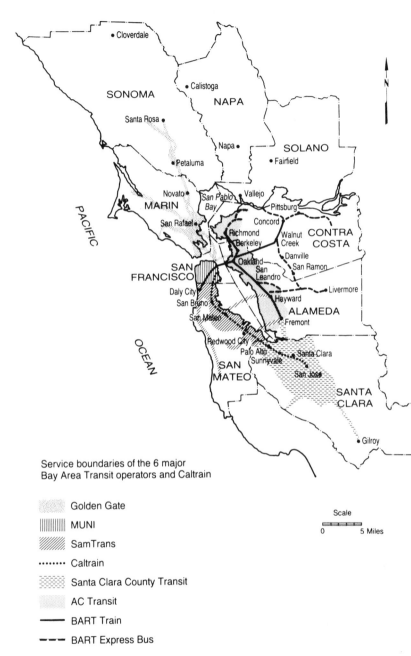

Service boundaries of the 6 major
Bay Area Transit operators and Caltrain

	Golden Gate
	MUNI
	SamTrans
·······	Caltrain
	Santa Clara County Transit
	AC Transit
——	BART Train
———	BART Express Bus

Scale

0   5 Miles

Map 1   Jurisdictions of the Six Major Operators and Caltrain

have a section of the Police Code amended to place certain areas of San Francisco off limits to all operators but Muni. There is the matter of limited space and the siting of bus stops and buspads. The type of service to be offered by each operator has also come into question: Can Golden Gate and Samtrans offer local service similar to that of Muni? Muni has vigorously resisted what it considers encroachment on its territory and has come into considerable conflict with Samtrans on the issue, because it believes that its passenger load (and therefore its revenues) is affected by services provided by these two operators. Samtrans and Santa Clara operate on the same streets (although in a less extensive way than in the San Francisco case) in the area in and around Palo Alto.

Joint use of facilities has resulted in interdependence similar to the joint use of streets, the Transbay Terminal in San Francisco being the most important instance. AC, Golden Gate, Samtrans, and Muni all use the terminal, administered by the California Department of Transportation, to load and unload passengers. Problems of access, traffic flow, buspad numbers and siting, parking space, sales, and advertising have arisen. With some private operators also using the terminal, in competition for space with the public operators, there have been additional facilities-related conflicts.

Facilities-related interdependence also results from the use of particular BART stations by more than one bus operator for passenger loading and unloading. Both Samtrans and Muni have bus lines with stops at the Daly City BART station. AC and Santa Clara use the Fremont BART station. AC shares the Hayward BART station with Samtrans. The issues typically involve the number and physical location of buspads at the stations. Conflicts on these issues have occurred at the Daly City station between Muni and Samtrans. Issues of access, signing, location of buspads, and the like occur even where only one bus operator uses a BART station.

Another facilities-related interdependency results from the joint use of a number of rail stations in San Francisco by BART and Muni. BART's trains run in tunnels at a lower level while the Muni Metro (a light-rail system that supplements the old surface streetcar system) uses tracks in an upper set of tunnels. BART constructed the stations and owns them. Important issues have included security, maintenance, allocation of space, and dispensing passenger information.

The second category concerns services-related interdepenence.

To From	AC	Golden Gate	Muni	Sam- trans	Santa Clara	BART
AC	•	290	6,900	250	≅45	14,300
Golden Gate	290	•	≅1,600	≅30	•	≅30
Muni	6,900	≅1,600	•	470-840	•	13,000
Sam- trans	250	≅30	470-840	•	≅300	≅3,200
Santa Clara	≅45	•	•	≅300	•	≅330
BART	18,300	≅30	13,800	≅3,200	≅330	•

Figure 2   Interoperator Transfers, All Trips, Weekdays

Source: Wolfgang S. Homburger and James A. Desveaux, *Joint Transit Fares in a Multi-Operator Region: A Conceptual Plan for the San Francisco Bay* Area (Berkeley: University of California, Institute of Transportation Studies, 1980), p. 18.

Because no single operator's jurisdiction encompasses all possible travel patterns originating or terminating within it, patrons daily make trips that involve more than one operator. Figure 2 shows the extent of interoperator trips on weekdays among the six major operators. Interoperator transfers create interdependence between pairs of operators: problems of passenger load, the routing of the bus lines, and the physical location of transfers become issues, as well as financial questions involving joint fares and transfers and schedules for buses and trains. How many should run and at what times? Will the operators involved have signaling devices to indicate to each other when loads of passengers are about to arrive?

Decisions by any one operator on any or all of these issues affect the ridership of other operators with which it shares patronage. Issues concerning transfers send financial reverberations through the operators involved. Figure 2 shows some transfer traffic between AC and BART, AC and Muni, BART and Muni, Samtrans and BART, and Golden Gate and Muni. Figure 2 does not indicate transfer traffic between Southern Pacific (now Caltrain) commuter trains on the peninsula and Samtrans, Santa Clara, and Muni; but that traffic is also significant.

Overlap in transit services creates a second set of interdependencies in the service area. If we assume a basically fixed market size or at least a slowly growing market, decisions on fare structures and other services to be offered by one operator directly affect other operators by changing their shares of the market. The transbay travel corridor is the most important instance of this type of interdependence. BART and AC both provide service from several areas in the East Bay to San Francisco. To a lesser extent, BART and AC provide competing services along a north-south corridor in the East Bay from Richmond to Fremont. In San Francisco, BART and Muni offer similar services in some areas, while BART and Samtrans duplicate each other's services on part of the northern peninsula travel routes.

In each area of overlap the interdependent character of operator relationships has become readily apparent when one has altered fares (the AC-BART transbay fare issue has been especially noteworthy), altered headways, changed hours of operation, rerouted its service, or in other ways changed the attractiveness of its services relative to those of other operators. The depth of interdependence on the transbay corridor is never more evident than when through catastrophe or labor-management dispute one operator is unable to provide its regular service.

Another area of interdependence became evident when the imminent termination of a set of transit services threatened to place difficult burdens on several operators and, in general, harm the quality of public transit. For many years Southern Pacific provided commuter service to and from San Francisco along the peninsula corridor running south toward San Jose. If this service was terminated, Muni, Samtrans, and Santa Clara would all be affected in terms of transfer traffic and primary passenger loads. In the late 1970s Southern Pacific sought to withdraw commuter service because of its increasing unprofitability, making clear to these operators its importance to their own operations. There are also several cases in which interdependence in the services area has been created by contractual arrangement for provision of services by one operator for another. Once established, contractual arrangements acquire lives of their own: where no interdependence existed, it now does. AC runs express buses for BART that serve as extensions of rail service in BART's jurisdiction where rail service is not yet available. This contract service creates many questions about routing, schedules, labor agreements, insurance, maintenance, and bus specifications. In a similar case, BART was engaged by Muni to maintain the tracks and tunnels of Muni Metro (the light-rail system), which raised issues of labor agreements and recruiting, specific responsibilities, and payment schedules. And Golden Gate rented shortened buses from AC for use in weekend service on Mount Tamalpais. Issues included timing and method of bus pickup and return, emptying the fareboxes, and methods of payment.

Another instance of interdependence in the services area also has to do with contractual arrangements. Under the dual rationales that when one operator loses passengers to a service breakdown all public transit suffers and that one operator is obligated to assist another in times of emergency,[12] "mutual-assistance" agreements were forged between AC and BART and between Muni and BART. Should either party to the agreement suffer a temporary service breakdown, the other provides service to fill in until the situation has been remedied.

The operators have also come together to exploit "efficiencies" resulting from economies of scale. Economies of scale and sharing of expenses cover a wide range of activities. Through the Regional Transit Association (RTA), various items have been obtained at lower cost than any single operator could secure on its own. Other joint activities have included bus "roadeos," marketing research projects, and a Bay Area transit information center. Another program jointly administered by the six operators is an elderly and handicapped discount identification card.

A final set of interdependencies falls into the general category of planning. As with the operations and services areas, planning interdependence is multifaceted. Interdependence in this area stems from several independent factors that have interactive effects beyond their simple additive properties. AC, BART, Golden Gate, Muni, Samtrans, and Santa Clara all fall within the jurisdiction of the MTC, which was established in 1970. Among its major responsibilities, MTC is to provide a long-range plan for all transportation modes for the nine counties of the San Francisco Bay Area and is responsible for seeing that the transit operators participate in that plan as they develop plans of their own; the operators' decisions must also adhere to the overall plan as it is completed. Additionally MTC administers all federal and state grants and some local transit tax monies. By 1986, this amounted to over $500 million. Its role includes ensuring that recipients—the local operators—adhere to federal, state, and local guidelines, which have often included requirements for standardized procedures and increased interaction among the operators.

Placement under the jurisdiction of a single transportation planning organization affects interdependence among the transit operators in several ways. Although federal and state monies have always amounted to less than the total of the desires of all operators, the fact of MTC placed them in direct competition with each other for funds by virtue of a common arena for application and evaluation. Several factors combined to heighten interdependence from the competition.

First, the statewide ballot initiative, known as Proposition 13, which passed in June 1978, greatly eroded the tax revenues available to local governments (including transit agencies) by placing strict limitations on real property tax rates. Such taxes were the principal tax base for many transit operators. AC, for example, depended on property taxes to make up the bulk of its operating losses. In general, the passage of Proposition 13 meant increased dependence of transit operators on federal and state subsidies.

Second, in the face of increasing demand, intensified by dramatic increases in petroleum prices beginning in 1973–74, the transit operators have attempted to provide expanded services, requiring larger subsidies. Applications by one operator for grant monies affect the abilities of other operators to attain their goals. If each operator had an independent source of revenue sufficient to support its operations, this concern would be irrelevant; but such self-sufficiency is a thing of the past. For example, in Marin County, if certain funds administered by MTC were allocated to Marin County Transit District (MCTD), they are invested in local service. If those funds went to Golden Gate, they were put into long-haul service. Outcomes differed, depending on the actions of each operator. No operator can afford to ignore the actions of others.

Two related factors serve to increase interdependence in the planning area. The fact of a common arena (MTC) invites direct comparisons among the operators across a broad range of subjects, from planning departments to the quality of maintenance schedules for buses. Such comparisons, made only indirectly and much less frequently prior to MTC, are now made directly and regularly. The operators can no longer act in isolation. The mere presence of a single transportation planning organization has provoked demands for consistency of approach in all kinds of areas. For example, when one operator moves to change its fares, that move is felt by other operators and monitored by the MTC. There have been and continue to be pressures for a unified regional fare structure.

Similarly, the operators must comply with the components of the regional transit plan, as well as with state and federal guidelines, as a condition for receiving federal and state monies. For example, Muni did not have a planning unit, nor was it interested in establishing one on its own. But because of federal and state guidelines, MTC refused to release certain funds to Muni until Muni created such a planning unit. Muni reluctantly complied. These factors have combined to increase interdependence among the transit operators over the decade 1972–82.

Bilateral and Multilateral Interdependence

How can we summarize interdependence in these three areas in a way that will help decide the appropriate machinery for coordination? Given that the complexity of problems heightens with increases in the number of actors involved, it is sensible to start with numbers. How many organizations are involved in any given instance of interdependence? Is it bilateral or multilateral?

The relevance of these questions lies in the attempt to discover exactly how loosely or tightly coupled a given system of organizations might be. Table 3 shows the interdependence of the operators distributed into bilateral (simpler cases) and multilateral (more complex cases) categories.

The rationale for making this distinction hinges on an idea sparked by Thompson's brief discussion of "localizing interdependence," [13] Bertalanffy's arguments about the complexity of systems, and Simon's contention that most systems are decomposable. [14] Thompson suggests that interdependence within single organizations can be localized by the creation of departments along functional lines, thus reducing costs of coordination by locating highly interdependent functions of an organization close together.

*Table 3   Bilateral and Multilateral Interdependence in Bay Area
Public Transit*

Bilateral	Multilateral
AC-Muni transfers	Transbay Terminal
AC-BART transfers	San Francisco streets
BART-Muni transfers	BART stations with bus stops
Muni–Golden Gate transfers	Competition for grants
BART-Samtrans transfers	Capital
Muni–Golden Gate ferries transfers	Operating
BART-Muni metro stations	Conformity to regional plan
Samtrans–Santa Clara streets	Development of individual plans
BART stations with bus stops	Conformity to federal guidelines
AC-BART busbridge	Conformity to state guidelines
Muni-BART busbridge	Southern Pacific service
AC-BART express buses	Economies of scale
Muni-BART tracks and tunnels	Purchasing
BART-AC eastbay overlap	Joint ventures
BART-AC transbay overlap	RTA membership
BART-Muni San Francisco overlap	
BART-Samtrans overlap	

As opposed to localizing highly interdependent parts of an organization, can different areas of interdependence be isolated from each
other in the multiorganizational context? If one interdependency
exists between two organizations and another interdependency exists
between one of those organizations and a third organization, are these
two different interdependencies connected? Must the first instance be
treated as a single occurrence of multilateral interdependence or can it
be treated as two separate cases of bilateral interdependence?

Following Simon's assertions about decomposability, the set of relationships among the three organizations is probably less complex
than appearances might indicate. Can we specify the conditions
under which they will be connected and the conditions under which
they will be separate? More concretely, are the interdependencies so
structured that decision makers can isolate one from another in their
decision-making processes, thereby simplifying the problems? If so,
we should be able to employ simpler coordination mechanisms than a
first glance might suggest.

Localizing interdependence improves the likelihood of finding a solution. Treatment as an instance of two bilateral interdependencies lessens cognitive complexity. As Hardin notes in his discussion of contract by convention,

> the more people whose behavior one must know well enough to consider it predictable, the less one will be able to know about each of them on average. Hence, the prospects for successful contract by convention decline as group size increases.[15]

Simultaneously such treatment reduces the minimum number of parties necessary to its successful resolution, potentially diminishing conflict over values as well. Another way to approach this question is to think of solving a set of problems sequentially or serially instead of attempting simultaneous solutions or setting the solution of one problem as a precondition for the solution to another. Localizing interdependence permits fuller enjoyment of the fruits of coordination by reducing the complexity of any single problem, thereby permitting the use of simpler mechanisms for coordination.

The capacity of this approach for reducing the difficulty of coordination is clearly seen in an example from the Bay Area. Several thousand passengers per day use both Samtrans and BART to make a single trip. Close to fifteen thousand trips are made daily using both AC and BART. Yet there is virtually no linkage between AC and Samtrans—perhaps two hundred and fifty trips per day. Is this a single instance of multilateral interdependence or are there two instances of bilateral interdependence that involve one organization in common? Do actions of AC affect the goal achievement of Samtrans and vice versa? Do decisions made by BART concerning its links with AC affect goal achievement at Samtrans? The response to each question is no.

The ratio of total daily trips on BART to those trips involving transfers with either AC or Samtrans is very high. Such transfer trips, although significant, remain a small portion of BART's overall business (about 10 to 15 percent), and AC and Samtrans have such a low direct transfer rate between them that their interdependence in this area is negligible. Because BART runs constant headways instead of a fixed time schedule for its trains (although it does publish a schedule), there is little sense in trying to arrange specific train-bus "meets," thus eliminating one complication. The stations at which

AC transit and Samtrans meet BART are mutually exclusive (with the exception of the Hayward station). Problems arising from the shared use of facilities by AC and Samtrans are not significant.

Because of these facts, on the surface what appears to be a case of multilateral interdependence is in fact two instances of bilateral interdependence. BART can (and does) treat its relations with AC and its relations with Samtrans as two distinct problems. These conditions also permit AC and Samtrans to deal with BART without either having to worry about the actions of the other. Furthermore, there is no incentive for any of the actors involved to treat the situation as a multilateral interdependency. If, however, the percentage of BART's total passengers transferring to and from AC and Samtrans increased dramatically, or if the number of stations at which AC and Samtrans both transfer passengers to BART increased, or if BART changed to a fixed schedule, or if some combination of these three changes occurred, then it might become a situation of multilateral interdependence, with correspondingly more complex issues and more difficult solutions.

Similarly, can one interdependency between two organizations be separated from another interdependency between the same two organizations? Isolating interdependencies between the same two organizations lessens the spillover effect from one to the other. The most "dangerous" problem posed by spillover from one area of interdependence to another, described by Schelling, involves two types of bargaining, each distinguished by the nature of the interdependence involved. There is "what might be called the 'distributional' aspect of bargaining: the situations in which more for one means less for the other. . . . When two dynamite trucks meet on a road wide enough for one, who backs up? The other aspect of bargaining consists of exploring for mutually profitable adjustments, and that might be called the 'efficiency' aspect of bargaining." [16]

AC and BART both provide transbay service. The most lucrative lines for AC have historically proved to be its transbay routes. When BART was in the planning stage and during the early days of operations (which included transbay service), it pushed AC to drop its transbay lines and become solely a feeder service for BART. AC resisted successfully, and the two operators remain competitors for that market. Fierce at times though it may be, this competition has not precluded coordination in a second area of interdependence. One way of making AC and BART more effective transit operators is to simplify transfers from one mode to the other. AC and BART have worked out transfer arrangements comparable with and surpassing in certain respects the arrangements for rail-bus transfers at the Washington Metro, a unified rail and bus agency. BART and AC have been able to put the conflict over transbay service on hold, agreeing to disagree on that point, thus isolating it from the interdependency that has the promise of mutual gain (intermodal transfers). And there have been no quid-pro-quo discussions of concessions in one area in return for concessions in the other.

Although the confounding of any one area of interdependence with any other makes the situation more complex intellectually and politically, a special potential for difficulty exists when a "distributional" problem is linked with a problem of "efficiency." Competition for transbay patronage is an example of the "distributional" element, whereas interoperator transfers represent the "efficiency" aspect. Keeping the two areas independent of each other, as in the AC-BART example, illustrates the positive benefits of localizing interdependence. Under these conditions, we would certainly prefer to employ coordination mechanisms that permit the separation of these different types of interdependence.[17]

What explains the AC-BART situation? It is characterized by a high degree of conflict in an area of interdependence where the probability of a clear winner and a clear loser is high. BART seeks to change the status quo and eliminate AC from competiton for the transbay market. At the same time, BART needs AC's feeder service to and from BART. There is no reason why the two interdependencies need be treated as one, and there is no political incentive for BART to accept such an arrangement. There is an incentive for AC to make the link, however. It has not done so, largely because BART has lessened its demands.

Scott notes that greater interdependence is associated with more elaborate coordination structures.[18] He suggests that higher levels of interdependence necessitate more extensive and complicated coordination mechanisms, an argument similar to the one made here. However, if this statement were turned on its head, it would be interpreted to mean that more elaborate coordination structures precipitate higher and more complex levels of interdependence. By increasing the requirements for successful coordination, the level of interdependence among the components of the system may be artificially increased as an unintended consequence. Under these conditions, coordination requires greater agreement across a broader range of values and the solution of cognitively more complex problems. This appears to be so in the Washington Metro transit system, where issues whose analogues are but loosely connected in the Bay Area are tightly linked together. In general, the relatively lower capacity of the Metro to localize interdependence, as compared with the Bay Area agencies, appears to result from the fact of a unitary, centralized decision-making body—a single arena for resolving all issues.

Metro is a unified operating authority whose jurisdiction includes parts of the states of Maryland and Virginia and the whole of the District of Columbia. Real differences in interest and ideological perspective mark the seven local jurisdictions that are members of Metro. Issues of rail construction finance, rail construction schedules, fare levels, bus and rail subsidy costs, and transfer policies all arise on a regular basis. However, rather than treating them as separate issues whenever possible and solving them independently, at Metro these issues tend to become intertwined. Consequently, separating different areas of interdependence between the same two members at Metro is exceptionally difficult. Similarly, areas of interdependence that in this study would be characterized as bilateral tend to be treated as multilateral, with the dual results of increasing conflict within Metro and rendering coordination solutions correspondingly more difficult and costly. Not only are distributional aspects such as bus subsidy allocations tied to efficiency aspects such as transfers, but issues that need involve only two members typically find their way into the common arena for resolution, where more actors become involved.

Furthermore, if problems of interdependence can be dealt with separately, the quest for consistency becomes less fervent. Discretely arranging coordination solutions for problems of interdependence is more readily accomplished when a push for consistency among those solutions is absent. Consistency is a far more mischievous hobgoblin in Washington Metro than in Bay Area transit, resulting, I contend, from the institutional arrangements.[19]

The need for coordination has so far been considered as deriving directly from a state of interdependence. With interdependence, positive benefits may be gained from some sort of coordination, or negative consequences may be avoided—uncertainty and conflict may be reduced. However, when mechanisms for coordination are overly complex relative to the extent and type of interdependence, the causal flow may be reversed, with the mechanisms themselves creating higher levels of interdependence, linking organizations more tightly than before, and necessitating more complex and less readily achieved solutions.

Origins of Bilateral and Multilateral Interdependence

I began the search for patterns in interdependence by distinguishing multilateral from bilateral cases. I continue that search by looking for differences in its origins. Three general origins can be distinguished. Interdependence occurs naturally when a variety of forces beyond the control of the organizations immediately involved come together to cause them to become connected. This is the type most often considered (explicitly or implicitly) in discussions of interdependence. For example, whenever a significant number of patrons elect to take trips involving more than one transit operator, interdependence is naturally created. The scenarios presented at the beginning of this chapter are all cases of natural interdependence. In response the operators may do nothing or may actively encourage or discourage such travel. But whatever they do, they remain linked through these "naturally" occurring external factors. The behavior of one affects the goal achievement of the other.

Instead of being caused by a natural series of events or a compendium of individual actions, interdependence may result from deliberate efforts of an outside party to link two or more organizations for some purposes of its own (which may have little to do with the goals or interests of those two organizations). Call this "artificial" interdependence (in the sense of artificial organization versus natural organization). The actions of MTC in Bay Area transit illustrate this type of interdependence. Operators applying for capital or operating subsidies are forced into interdependence through demands by MTC for conformity to various standards and plans of its own construction.

Interdependence also results when organizations voluntarily enter into arrangements to realize some array of mutual benefits, as when one operator seeks to have another perform services on a contractual basis. Contractual arrangements of this sort are extensive in the Bay Area and are of two types. In the first, one operator performs services for another for compensation. The second type involves coordinated joint action to secure the benefits of scale economies. Over time these arrangements acquire an institutionalized presence, so that interdependence develops between the organizations that does not hinge on external circumstances. This interdependence goes beyond simple interlocking effects of decisions concerning the contracted service. Simply observe the effects of cancellation of such service on both organizations. Call this "voluntary" interdependence. In natural interdependence, coordination follows interdependence. In voluntary interdependence, the converse is true. However, this is to be distinguished from a situation where use of an inappropriate device for coordination leads to increased complexity of the interdependence. Table 4 shows the interdependencies of Bay Area transit categorized by their origins.

Bay Area transit is characterized by both bilateral and multilateral interdependence, with most interdependence taking the bilateral form. There are several important differences in the origins of bilateral and multilateral interdependence, as shown in Table 5. Naturally occurring interdependence is, with one exception, bilateral, whereas no bilateral interdependence is of the artificial type. Without external intervention, naturally occurring patterns of interdependence take the bilateral form: they are relatively simple in character. Conversely, without exception, the artificially developed interdependence in the Bay Area is of the multilateral type. Voluntary interdependence falls into both bilateral and multilateral categories.

Figure 3A shows the character of the Bay Area transit system, when natural, artificial, and voluntary origins of interdependence are considered together. The number of lines connecting any pair of operators indicates roughly their degree of interdependence. The six major operators are linked together in a system characterized by multilateral interdependence, such that decisions by one operator affect all the others, both directly and indirectly. But a very different picture emerges when only natural interdependence is taken into account, as shown in Figure 3B. Instead of a tightly coupled system of

*Table 4   Natural, Artificial, and Voluntary Interdependence
in Bay Area Public Transit*

Natural	Artificial	Voluntary
AC-Muni transfers	Competition for	Transbay Terminal
AC-BART transfers	grants	Samtrans–Santa Clara
BART-Muni	Capital	stations
transfers	Operating	BART stations with bus
Muni–Golden Gate	Development of	stops
transfers	plans	Southern Pacific service
BART-Samtrans	Conformity to re-	AC-BART express buses
transfers	gional plan	BART-Muni tracks and
San Francisco	Conformity to fed-	tunnels
streets	eral guidelines	BART-Muni metro
Samtrans–Santa	Conformity to state	stations
Clara streets	guidelines	AC-BART busbridge
Muni–Golden Gate		Muni-BART busbridge
ferries transfers		Economies of scale
		Purchasing
		Joint ventures
		RTA membership
		AC-BART transbay
		overlap
		AC-BART eastbay
		overlap
		BART-Muni San
		Francisco overlap
		BART-Samtrans overlap

multilateral interdependencies, Bay Area transit appears to be a more
readily decomposable system. It is more loosely coupled and characterized by a series of bilateral interdependencies that include overlapping sets of operators. Even when voluntary interdependence is considered with the natural type, the picture is not greatly complicated;
the predominant character of the system is bilateral. One concludes
that, in good measure, the current complexity of Bay Area transit
results from the coordinative arrangements employed there, especially from actions by the MTC.

*Table 5   Origins of Bilateral and Multilateral Interdependence
in Bay Area Public Transit*

	Bilateral	Multilateral
Natural	AC-Muni transfers AC-BART transfers BART-Muni transfers Muni–Golden Gate transfers Muni–Golden Gate ferries Samtrans–Santa Clara transfers	San Francisco streets
Artificial	None	Competition for grants Capital Operating Development of individual plans Conformity to regional plan Conformity to federal guidelines Conformity to state guidelines
Voluntary	BART-Muni metro stations BART-Muni tracks and tunnels AC-BART express buses Samtrans–Santa Clara stations BART stations with bus stops BART-AC transbay overlap BART-AC eastbay overlap BART-Samtrans overlap BART-Muni San Francisco overlap BART-Muni busbridge BART-AC busbridge	Transbay Terminal Southern Pacific service Economies of scale Purchasing Joint ventures RTA membership BART stations with bus stops

A. Assumed: Multilateral

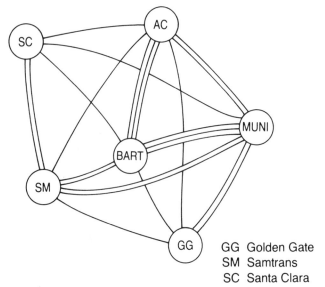

GG Golden Gate
SM Samtrans
SC Santa Clara

B. Actual: Bilateral

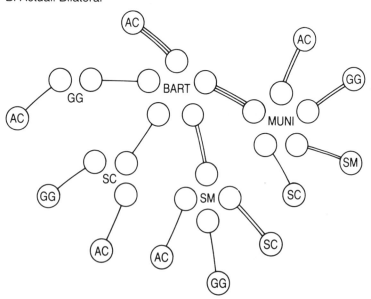

Figure 3   Interdependence in Bay Area Public Transit

Conclusion

In general most systems are decomposable. Empirically, it has been shown that for the most part, naturally occurring interdependence in the Bay Area is relatively simple, taking a bilateral form, permitting the transit system to be considered as a series of smaller problems of coordination—that is, it *can* be decomposed.[20] More complex multilateral interdependence has resulted from voluntary action of the operators themselves or has been forced on them by external parties such as MTC.

Because the ability to comprehend a system decreases as the number of components and the complexity of their interactions increase—coordination structures may themselves increase complexity and decrease comprehension—and because the distributional and efficiency aspects of bargaining and the danger of spillover remain distinct, great caution should be exercised when altering institutional arrangements of *any* multiorganizational system such as Bay Area transit. It will likely serve to increase interdependence in the system without guaranteeing significantly better coordination. Furthermore it is foolish to impose coordinative arrangements predicated on high levels of multilateral interdependence on a system actually described by a series of bilateral interdependencies, which themselves do not affect the individual transit agencies greatly. In this case, following the rule of the lowest common denominator is probably the most effective strategy: use the minimum mechanisms necessary to achieve a satisfactory level of coordination.

4

Informal Coordinative Mechanisms

> If individuals act without first establishing arrangements with those whom their actions affect and who affect them, each is likely to be sorry when he sees the price all will pay.
> —Philip B. Heymann, "The Problem of Coordination: Bargaining and Rules"

I turn now toward the heart of the matter: understanding informal organizational features—how they work and how they facilitate coordination. My intention is to work backward, using public transit as a vehicle for generating broader generalizations about the problems of coordination inherent in multiorganizational systems and the role of informal mechanisms therein.

Where the modal tendency of contemporary discussions of coordination problems has been to assess the interests of the several actors involved and then to evaluate the attractiveness to each actor of various alternative solutions in light of the costs and benefits involved as a precursor to predicting behavior, here I focus on the mechanisms through which communications take place and solutions are sought and implemented. In this sense, the center of attention in this research has shifted from concerns about motivation and interests to actual observed behavior and processes of coordination.

The argument in this chapter complements rather than competes with theories of rational choice. However, where rational choice theories have largely assumed that near-perfect information is available to all relevant actors and that clear communication is not problematic, the approach adopted here treats these as questionable factors whose presence cannot be assumed;[1] thus some sort of redress may be required for coordination to occur. Informal channels, in particular, are the conduits through which bargaining and negotiation take place, while informal norms provide foundations for coordination activities, and informal bargains and agreements are frequently their products. Some theorists of rational choice, such as Axelrod and Hardin,[2] have begun to examine closely the development of informal norms and conventions and their effects on problems of coordinating multiple independent actors. Although the strategy employed here differs significantly from theirs, the conclusions reached appear to be rather similar.

Formal Failures and Informal Channels

The development of informal mechanisms is associated with inadequacies and failures of key aspects of formal organization. One such inadequacy is slowness. Although formal channels provide perfectly expeditious solutions to pressing problems in many cases, sometimes they are too slow to facilitate timely solutions. Or two organizations might benefit by solving a problem more quickly than a formal approach would allow. As one transit manager noted, where fast response is important, formal lines may take so long as to prevent essential action:

> When it comes down to the short hairs, you go to the people you have known. You go the shortest distance necessary to get the information. I hate to ask a question and have the person wait to clear through twelve people before he can respond.[3]

Informal lines of communication work more quickly than their formal counterparts because time-consuming formal constraints and ambiguity about who is responsible for a problem are eliminated.

Informal contacts are used regularly in the grant application process to check on progress of proposals through the formal machinery as well as to push for greater speed. A planner at BART who has two friends at UMTA notes that "when funding is slow going through UMTA, I call them up to accelerate things a bit."[4]

Informal channels also work more rapidly than their formal analogues because of a reservoir of mutual trust between the individuals involved. They go out of their way to act expeditiously as a return on prior obligations.[5] Of course, such favors can exhaust the reservoir. "Hurry-up" favors cannot be asked in unlimited quantity. Nowhere does this show more clearly than in the execution of the express bus contract between BART and AC. Formally, BART sets the broad parameters, and AC works out the details in a two-stage procedure. Informally, however, the process is one of greater interaction:

> A senior staff member at AC whom we shall designate as "S" maintains a continuing and close tie with a senior staffer at BART, who we shall refer to as "C." Both operate in "fairly unconventional ways" and bypass official channels easily. They originally got to know each other through their official tasks in connection with the express bus service that AC runs for BART. . . . For AC to establish a new express route by request takes some three months. Requests are routed to the office of scheduling, then referred to AC planning for study, then back to scheduling. In late August 1979, "C" called "S" to inquire about the possibility of a new route in Martinez. "S" immediately invited "C" to join him in a test of the proposed route. Securing a bus, they made a run to check out the availability of stops, potential traffic problems, the ability of an AC bus to negotiate hills and curves, etc. Both decided the route was feasible. On the same day they met with the public works director of Martinez and fixed the route. "S" then presented the request to the director of scheduling along with the necessary technical support. The new service route was established in less than five weeks.[6]

Insofar as this channel is used regularly and successfully, the formal channel may in time become little more than a pro forma validation of what has been worked out informally. Or the informal channel may retain its role as a backup for the formal in that subset of situations where the formal is too slow.

Informal channels and procedures are also used where formal channels are not simply sluggish but actually blocked, perhaps because of organizational politics or because the person with the formal responsibility is reluctant to make a decision. At AC transit, a number of standard length (forty feet) buses were sectioned and short-ened (to about 30 feet) to use on routes with hills, tight-radius turns, or light passenger loads. The buses were considered successful from the perspectives of both engineering and use. On weekends, Golden Gate runs some buses on narrow two-lane roads with curves difficult for standard-length buses to negotiate safely. After some mishaps, and knowing of the AC success with the shortened buses, a Golden Gate manager "A" wrote to the appropriate AC official "B," pro-posing that Golden Gate purchase or rent the buses for use on the weekends. Weeks passed with no response. "A" then called "C," an informal contact at AC, and asked him to look into the matter. "C" discovered that "B" had had a difficult time deciding but thought he had responded to Golden Gate. A check of the files indicated in the negative. "C" then brought Golden Gate's proposal to the AC gen-eral manager, noting that AC had no use for the shortened buses on the weekends. On the spot, the general manager agreed to rent buses to Golden Gate.[7] In this case the informal channel served a backup function for the formal channel, ensuring that contact would be made, and some sort of decision reached.

Clearly, organizational actors think of informal contacts in terms of their backup role for formal channels. A Golden Gate planner maintains a good informal relationship (developed through work contact) with a district manager at the California Department of Transportation (Caltrans). He calls and talks with him from time to time, but "since Caltrans has a professional information office, I can call them for my information needs, and since they have proven reli-able, I call him less than I might."[8] The formal channel works well enough that the informal channel stays mostly dormant. It is not usu-ally needed but remains available.

Another difficulty is created when formal channels do not exist in a form appropriate to the problem at hand, a failure that is both inevi-table and not specifically predictable. Our knowledge is usually in-sufficient to permit the design of organizations capable of coping with all the problems they will ultimately have to face. Even if we could, economics would preclude us from doing so. It is also true that formal organizations are designed to operate under a specific set of conditions; but conditions rarely remain constant. A formal struc-ture predicated to function effectively under conditions at Time 1 will be ineffective at Time 2 when other conditions obtain.

In the short run, however, it is the fact of anomaly that pushes informal channels to the forefront. For example, on the first occasion that BART and AC were to provide service simultaneously for the California versus Stanford football game, no formal procedures had previously been devised. No specific information about the particular problems involved was in hand. The BART and AC planners informally worked out the number of trains and buses necessary and the bus routes AC should emphasize. Because they had no prior experience, they just had to "wing it," [9] operating pragmatically and experimentally.

Coordination also requires accurate information. As both Devons and Sapolsky have noted, formal channels often tend to be ineffective when information is sensitive or politically charged: formal counterparts do not trust each other; there are sanctions against the transmission of such information; or there are no formal channels between the person who wants the information and the person who has it. Informal channels are not so constrained.

In one case I observed during the course of my research, the various transit agencies disagreed over the specific form and application of a proposed Bay Area elderly and handicapped fare-discount card. During negotiations, one operator sought to make an end run past another by surreptitiously building an opposition coalition. Through an informal channel (which was confidential) an employee of a third operator apprised a contact at the target agency of the effort. This allowed the latter to prevent the coalescence of a formidable opposition. Whether formal channels could have been used to make such warning is doubtful because of their open, visible nature. The political costs are too high.

In other cases, however, lack of information reliability is due not to any limitation inherent in formal channels but to the politics that typify the relationship of two organizations. Mutual distrust characteristic of the relationships between Bay Area transit agencies and MTC lays a foundation rendering information passed through formal channels nearly always suspect. At MTC, one section manager commented, referring to transit personnel, "they don't trust me completely, and I am never quite sure of how accurate or complete the information I get from them is." [10] This manager's solution was to develop personal relationships founded on mutual trust and reciprocity with personnel at each operator.

When formal channels fail to provide parties in negotiation with an accurate perception of the reactions of other relevant organizations to their proposals,[11] informal channels often supply the information. Says one Golden Gate planner:

> Muni is a place where formal responsibility for policies cannot be discerned. If I have a plan in mind I go to a fellow I know real well since he used to work at Golden Gate, to see if he can do anything about it directly. I am then able to tailor my proposals to the idiosyncrasies of Muni.[12]

Organizational actors also use informal channels to let their counterparts know the importance of a particular proposal that has been (or is about to be) transmitted formally. The intention to ensure that some response is made, not necessarily to stimulate a particular response.[13] However, such informal communication of importance can only be made on a portion of coordination proposals; otherwise its currency is diluted.

Thus, informal channels perform important primary functions in the face of both permanent and episodic failures of formal mechanisms. Other important failures of formal designs with consequences for coordination are redressed by informal conventions and norms. I turn to that topic after first considering the contours of informal channels in the Bay Area public transit system.

Informal Channels and Informal Networks

Informal channels based on personal relationships between pairs of individuals are the most frequent and direct contributors to coordination in Bay Area transit. They have developed on an as-needed basis and have proved surprisingly flexible, adaptive, and effective as devices for coordination. They are predicated on personal relationships and exist independently of formal responsibility or position.

How can an informal channel be recognized when it is present? In this study, I proceeded to interview officials of many kinds and at levels ranging from transportation supervisors to general managers, with the interviews varying in length from about one to more than four hours, the average being about two hours. Although formal position was a factor in the selection of interviewees, it was not the sole determinant. In fact, in many instances the precise formal title of the individual was not known until the interview. More important, in the selection of those to be interviewed I depended on responses of the interviewees themselves. In seeking to trace out the informal network of relationships among the personnel at the various operators and MTC, I asked the individuals interviewed: "To whom would you go if you needed to resolve an interorganizational problem, or to whom would you speak if you needed absolutely reliable information about some problem?" Those persons so named were then interviewed and asked the same questions. This procedure permitted verification of the statements made by one individual about a relationship with another.

For the purposes of this research, an informal relationship was reckoned to exist when each person named the other, irrespective of formal position, as someone to whom he would go with a problem, when reliable information was needed, or when he wished to transmit information to the other organization. This question was followed with queries about the specific character of the interactions as a check upon the extent of the relationship. Given that the research focused on links between problems of coordination and informal mechanisms, I did not want to include purely social relationships, so the questions focused specifically upon contacts that were directed toward solving work-related problems. However, expressions of friendship were also considered in the evaluations, as were social contacts outside the workplace, as additional evidence of an informal relationship.

On occasion, a pairing was included as an informal relationship where only one person named the other, if it was clear that the two carried on business with each other regularly. If an individual could not name an informal contact at another organization, I did not pressure him to do so. By following these procedures, I believe that I effectively safeguarded against including pairings where no informal relationship existed, preferring to err on the side of underinclusion.

Other approaches to establishing the presence of informal ties between individuals have included asking respondents to name people with whom they personally and frequently communicate, usually being defined operationally as three times per year (in two studies on social networks among academic researchers).[14] I did not use this procedure as I was not sure what the meaning of any particular frequency of contact might be and wished to avoid an arbitrary threshold for inclusion as an informal channel. Nor did it seem particularly useful to ask the respondents to make a subjective estimate of the proportion of their work activities that involved such informal contacts.

The interviewing process can thus be best described as a series of branching actions, with succeeding interviews dependent on responses in ongoing interviews. This procedure permitted discovery of the presence of informal channels without imposing a priori theoretical views on the way they might look. Confidence grew that the informal channels of the Bay Area transit system had been encompassed as fewer and fewer new names were obtained in succeeding interviews.

However, this method runs the risk of omitting informal relationships that do exist, because it depends for its effectiveness on tapping into the informal network[15] initially. Where subsets of an informal network exist, and the subsets are relatively insulated from one another, an entire subset might be missed; thus, more informal channels might exist than were discovered. However, for reasons to be discussed I am confident that no gross errors were made in this regard.

Although multiple subsets of the informal network were discovered in the Bay Area transit system, I also found that they overlap with one another. Thus, if I successfully tapped into one subset, sooner or later I found my way into the others. Furthermore, individuals were asked to name others within their own organizations they thought should be interviewed—for example, planners were asked about people in their respective operations and maintenance sections.

In any case, given the questions of central concern in this study— Can informal mechanisms be instrumental for coordination of interdependent organizations, and are they in fact?—it is acceptable if considerable evidence is found for the existence of informal channels and their importance for coordination. I therefore preferred to err in a conservative direction: I deemed it better to miss some informal channels that were there than to assume the existence of some that were not. I am convinced, furthermore, that the description of the informal network among the Bay Area transit operators, although incomplete, is nonetheless an accurate representation of those that do exist. Those informal channels that were found are so wide-ranging and so clearly important for coordination among the transit organizations that incompleteness does not weaken the hypothesis.

If informal organizational features arise when formal designs are either nonexistent or inadequate for one reason or another and if interdependence between two or more organizations creates uncertainty, thus giving rise to pressures for coordination, the expectation is that where there is pressure for coordination and no formal mechanisms to deal with that pressure, a more extensive set of informal relationships will develop than where there is no pressure. Thus, I examined informal ties between personnel at pairs of transit operators whose relationships are characterized by varying degrees of interdependence. Informal channels in Bay Area transit meet the expectations rather closely, with some exceptions.

Figure 4 schematically depicts the contours of informal channels in the Bay Area transit system. Existence of an informal relationship between two individuals from different organizations is represented by a dot at the intersection of their respective coordinates. Only direct informal relationships are included. Indirect two-step or three-step relationships are not considered. Figure 5 summarizes the frequencies of informal relationships observed for each pair of organizations.

Although the pattern of informal relationships is relatively stable, it does undergo change. The picture presented in Figures 4 and 5 is therefore not immutable: it is accurate for the 1978–80 period, but undoubtedly looked somewhat different before and looks somewhat different today. The contours change less and more slowly than the personnel involved, because the patterns of channels depend on the patterns of interdependence in the system.[16] That is, one finds that the same kinds of informal relationships tend to persist despite turnover of personnel, as long as the pattern of interdependence characterizing the relevant organizations remains stable. This suggests that "role" within the system may have an effect independent of other individual traits.[17]

Figure 6 shows the natural and voluntary interdependence in the Bay Area transit system (as so classified in Chapter 3) by pairs of operators. The two agencies with the greatest interdependence, AC and BART, display a well-developed set of informal relationships. Informal relationships are especially strong between the planning staffs, and quite durable between management personnel, and between certain operations people. Muni and BART also enjoy a relatively high level of interdependence and reveal a similar set of informal channels. Golden Gate and Muni are well connected informally although their interdependence is very low. AC and Muni touch only at the Transbay Terminal operationally and, as expected, have a less well-developed set of informal channels than pairs of operators with greater interdependence. Golden Gate and BART have virtually no interdependence, and their informal contacts are correspondingly limited. The same holds for Golden Gate and Samtrans, which, like AC and Muni, touch only at the Transbay Terminal. They also share some San Francisco streets but have virtually no overlap in passenger clientele. Golden Gate and Santa Clara have no interdependence at all and show far fewer informal channels than AC and BART. AC and Samtrans show little informal contact when compared with AC and BART or BART and Muni. This finding was anticipated because the two agencies touch only at the Transbay Terminal and share no surface streets. BART and Samtrans are linked through contact at the BART Daly City station and show a commensurate set of informal ties. Santa Clara and Samtrans are connected less than would be anticipated from their level of interdependence. BART and Santa Clara connect at two BART stations, but have little overlap in passenger clientele. Muni and Santa Clara show only slight informal contact, reflecting their low level of interdependence.

Because of the size of its jurisdiction, the extent of its operations, and the fact that it depends on the bus operators to provide feeder service for its rail lines, of all the agencies, BART shows the most extensive set of informal interorganizational ties and channels. Conversely, Santa Clara shows the least informal contact with other transit companies, as would be expected from its geographic isolation and low level of interdependence.

Analysis of these informal relationships must be tempered by the recognition that reliance on sheer numbers as a method of comparison of the extent and importance of informal channels between one pair of operators as opposed to another pair is problematic for two reasons. Bay Area transit organizations vary considerably in the size of their operations, personnel, equipment, budgets, and numbers of passengers carried. Santa Clara and Samtrans are small when compared with the other agencies. Golden Gate is smaller than AC or

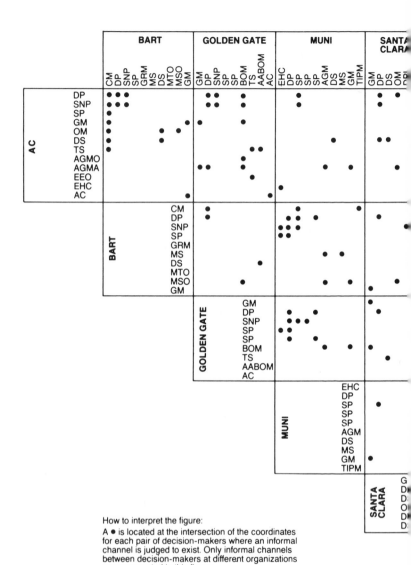

*Figure 4   Interorganizational Informal Channels in the Bay Area
Public Transit System (1978–80)*

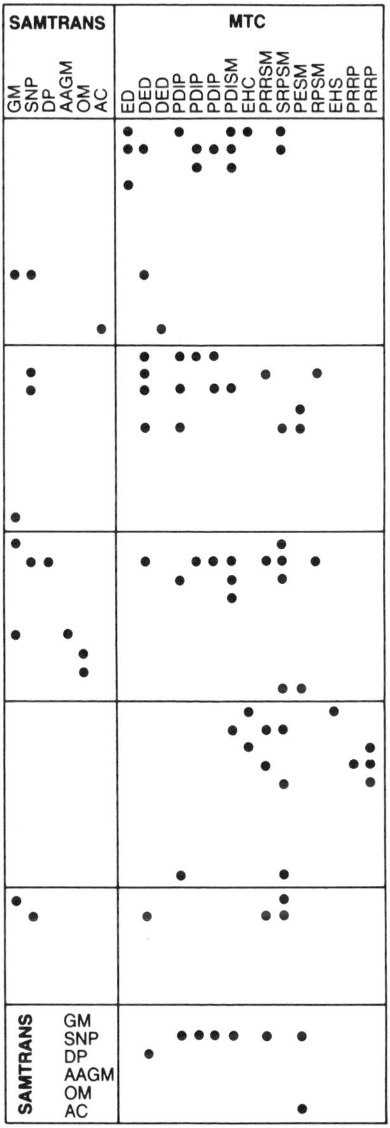

This matrix cross-references SAMTRANS roles (rows in lower block / columns) against MTC roles (columns). Columns are labeled left-to-right by the abbreviations printed at top.

SAMTRANS columns: GM, SNP, DP, AAGM, OM, AC

MTC columns (left to right): ED, DED, DED, PDIP, PDIP, PDISM, EHC, PRRSM, SRPSM, PESM, RPSM, EHS, PRRP, PRRP

Upper matrix — SAMTRANS rows (GM, SNP, DP, AAGM, OM, AC) × MTC columns:

SAMTRANS row	GM	SNP	DP	AAGM	OM	AC	ED	DED	DED	PDIP	PDIP	PDISM	EHC	PRRSM	SRPSM	PESM	RPSM	EHS	PRRP	PRRP
							•						•	•					•	
							•	•			•	•	•			•				
											•		•							
							•													
	•	•									•									
				•							•									

SAMTRANS row	GM	SNP	DP	AAGM	OM	AC	ED	DED	DED	PDIP	PDIP	PDISM	EHC	PRRSM	SRPSM	PESM	RPSM	EHS	PRRP	PRRP
								•		•	•	•				•				
		•						•					•			•			•	
		•						•				•	•	•						
								•		•							•	•		
	•																			
	•														•					
		•	•					•		•	•	•	•		•	•	•		•	
											•		•			•	•			
													•							
	•																			
			•															•		
			•																	

SAMTRANS row	GM	SNP	DP	AAGM	OM	AC	ED	DED	DED	PDIP	PDIP	PDISM	EHC	PRRSM	SRPSM	PESM	RPSM	EHS	PRRP	PRRP
													•			•				
											•		•	•						
													•							
													•						•	•
													•							

SAMTRANS row	GM	SNP	DP	AAGM	OM	AC	ED	DED	DED	PDIP	PDIP	PDISM	EHC	PRRSM	SRPSM	PESM	RPSM	EHS	PRRP	PRRP
											•		•							
	•										•		•							
		•																		

Lower block — SAMTRANS rows labeled GM, SNP, DP, AAGM, OM, AC:

SAMTRANS	GM	SNP	DP	AAGM	OM	AC	ED	DED	DED	PDIP	PDIP	PDISM	EHC	PRRSM	SRPSM	PESM	RPSM	EHS	PRRP	PRRP
GM									•	•	•	•		•			•			
SNP																				
DP							•													
AAGM																				
OM																				
AC														•						

Key to Abbreviations:

AABOM	Admin. Asst. to Bus Ops. Manager
AAGM	Admin. Asst. to General Manager
AC	Auditor-Controller
AGM	Assistant General Manager
AGMA	Asst. Gen. Mgr. for Administration
AGMO	Asst. Gen. Mgr. for Operations
BOM	Bus Operations Manager
CM	Contracts Manager
DED	Deputy Executive Director
DP	Director of Planning
DPI	Director of Public Information
DS	Director of Scheduling
DST	Director of Safety and Training
ED	Executive Director
EEO	Equal Employment Oppr. Officer
EHC	Elderly and Handicapped Coord.
EHS	Elderly and Handicapped Staff
GM	General Manager
GRM	Grants Manager
MS	Maintenance Supervisor
MSO	Manager of Station Operations
MTO	Manager of Train Operations
OM	Operations Manager
PDIP	Policy Dev. and Impl. Planner
PDISM	Policy Dev. and Impl. Section Mgr.
PESM	Policy Evaluation Section Manager
PRRP	Policy Review and Research Planner
PRRSM	Policy Review and Research Sec. Mgr.
RPSM	Regional Planning Section Manager
SNP	Senior Planner
SP	Staff Planner
SRPSM	Sub-regional Plan. Section Manager
TIPM	Transit Improvement Project Manager
TS	Transportation Superintendent

NOTE: The titles listed above are standardized references to job function. The actual job titles vary somewhat from organization to organization.

	BART	Golden Gate	Muni	Santa Clara	Sam-trans	MTC
AC	16	16	6	6	3	16
	BART	4	15	4	3	16
		Golden Gate	11	5	7	4
			Muni	2	0	14
				Santa Clara	2	4
					Sam-trans	8

Mean frequency of informal relationships, by pairs of organizations, including MTC: 8.2; based upon 21 pairs of organizations, 172 informal relationships, and 68 actors.

Mean frequency of informal relationships, by pairs of organizations, excluding MTC: 6.7; based upon 15 pairs of organizations, 100 informal relationships, and 53 actors.

Figure 5   Frequencies of Informal Relationships by Pairs of Operators

Muni. Sufficient informal contact with smaller operators requires knowing fewer people.

Furthermore, the importance of one informal channel for problems of coordination is not easily calculated in comparison with others. It would be incorrect to assume that all informal channels are created equal, because the importance of business conducted through one channel as opposed to another is not amenable to quantitative measurement (at least at our present state of knowledge). From this perspective, one informal channel may be more valuable than two or more others. In light of these considerations, one ought not assume automatically that informal connections should be equally extensive for two different pairs of organizations subject to similar levels of interdependence. Still, I found more extensive informal channels as interdependence increased.

There are several exceptions to the expected levels of informal contact between pairs of agencies. Muni and Samtrans are opera-

	BART	GOLDEN GATE	MUNI	SANTA CLARA	SAMTRANS

AC	Transfers
	Express buses
	Competition
	  a. East Bay
	  b. Transbay
	RTA
	Funding
		Transbay Terminal
		RTA
			Transfers
			Transbay Terminal
			RTA
				RTA	Transbay Terminal
					RTA

BART		RTA	Transfers Metro Stations Metro Track and Tunnel Maintenance S.F. Overlap RTA	RTA	Transfers Peninsula Overlap RTA

GOLDEN GATE			Transfers
			  a. bus
			  b. ferry
			S.F. Streets
			Transbay Terminal
			RTA
				RTA	Transfers
					S.F. Streets
					Transbay Terminal
					S.P. Peninsula Service
					RTA

MUNI				S.P. Peninsula Service RTA	Transfers S.P. Peninsula Service S.F. Streets Transbay Terminal RTA
SANTA CLARA					Transfers S.P. Peninsula Service RTA

Figure 6   Natural and Voluntary Interdependence in Bay Area Public Transit

tionally linked in a number of ways. However, there is a competi-
tiveness and animosity between their personnel that had, at least at
the time of this research, effectively precluded development of informal relationships between them. Despite their level of interdependence, no informal channels existed; the systems appeared to be
at war.

Conversely, Golden Gate and AC transit display a more well-
developed set of informal ties than their virtually nonexistent interdependence would lead one to expect. This is explained largely by
the movement of personnel from AC to Golden Gate at the time the
latter commenced bus operations.[18] Similarly, AC and Santa Clara
have more extensive informal ties than would be anticipated from
their slight interdependence, principally because AC provided con-
sulting services for Santa Clara when it began bus operations. More
generally, contact through the RTA and MTC has increased the overall level of informal ties for the Bay Area beyond what would be anticipated from the level of interdependence.

Informal ties between the transit companies and MTC are extensive, matching the importance of the grants and planning processes
to the operators. MTC personnel need and want reliable information
about the operators: by 1980, the operators were officially required to
submit over twenty reports per year to MTC. The agencies also need
and want accurate information about the application of federal and
state guidelines, the intentions behind new laws, and information
about the availability of grants and other monies. Informal channels
meet these needs and also make possible informal consultations and
negotiations between the operators and MTC. MTC personnel have
most of their informal contact with the planning sections of the transit companies. The most extensive informal connections appear to be
between MTC and AC, MTC and BART, and MTC and Muni, with
Golden Gate following close behind. Santa Clara and Samtrans are
less well informally connected with MTC.

Informal Network and Subsets

Although informal channels are best described as links between pairs of individuals, and have thus far been analyzed in the
context of pairs of interdependent organizations, I also found it

useful to group the channels observed on the basis of shared characteristics, in the belief that understanding the informal network in the
Bay Area transit system would be enhanced by comprehending the
different subsets of informal channels of which it is composed.[19]

Social networks have been studied through a variety of methods,
and a significant body of "network analysis" literature has developed. In recent years significant strides have been made in our ability
to describe social networks by formal mathematical models. In particular, the work of Lorrain and White and their colleagues has added
considerably to our understanding of patterns and arrangements of
social relations.[20] Although my use of "network" is consistent with
theirs, and my approach resembles that of graph theory, both the
goals of this research and the methodology employed here are simpler.
My interest in network morphology has no intrinsic basis; it results
entirely from a concern with the extent to which informal network
development varies with observed interorganizational interdependence. Whereas social network researchers are often preoccupied
with assessing personal or organizational influence within networks,
the development of cliques, the structural equivalence of individuals,
or the social structure of a total system, my aims are more modest.
I am concerned with informal channels and networks only as they
arise and are used to address certain problems of coordination created by interorganizational interdependence.

Furthermore, whereas sociologists have been concerned with
various relational types,[21] the research reported here focuses solely
on informal relationships predicated upon and used for the conduct
of work-related activities—communications relations and instrumental relations. Communications relations are understood to mean
linkages between actors in the form of channels by which messages
may be transmitted from one actor to another. Instrumental relations
involve contact between actors in efforts to secure valuable goods,
services, or information.[22] Differences in channels stem from variations in the principal kind of business conducted through them.

If we examined the universe of Bay Area transit organization personnel and the ties between pairs of them, we would discover subsets
of the larger universe of informal channels. In operational terms,
subset is understood to mean a discrete clustering of channels among
individuals, who, as a group, communicate informally with each
other more often than they communicate informally with those out-

side the group. In the simplest case, members of one subset would have informal relationships only with those within their subset and no such relationships with others outside.[23] I determined subset boundaries empirically by questioning individuals about those to whom they speak, moving to question that next set of individuals, and so forth, until no more new names are mentioned—the so-called snowballing technique.[24] However, as I was interested solely in direct first-step informal relationships, the question of where to stop moving outward from the initial sample was not a problem. Furthermore, unlike more broadly cast studies of social networks, the universe of potential actors was clearly limited to members of the relevant organizations. The structure of any subset is composed of the individuals (or nodes) and the channels between them.[25]

The Bay Area transit system is described by several such informal subsets. The subsets are accurately considered as separate entities, but share some members in common. The kind of business transacted in different subsets varies significantly.[26] Although exchange of expertise, exchange of factual information, and informal negotiation occur at one time or another in each, one or two activities tend to predominate in any one subset. Thus, there appears to be not only specialization of informal channels, but specialization of entire subsets of channels.

Three informal subsets were observed within the larger informal network of the Bay Area transit system: operations/maintenance, planning, and management. These subsets are portrayed diagrammatically in Figure 7. Although interactions among the management personnel and among planning staffs at the different operators were expected, those among the operations/maintenance subset were not.

Among the operations/maintenance personnel, exchanges of expertise and factual information were the dominant types of informal communication. For example, the bus operations manager at Golden Gate supplied expert advice to Samtrans on the design of a fare-collection system.[27] One of the maintenance personnel at Golden Gate discovered that four small batteries could replace the single large battery typically in use on buses, resulting in savings when cells in the battery died. He passed the word along to his informal contacts at several other transit agencies.[28]

Maintenance personnel at AC and Golden Gate worked together informally to solve a problem with the rear doors of the (then) new articulated buses that both properties had purchased.[29] Although this type of communication constitutes the bulk of informal interactions among the operations/maintenance personnel, significant coordination has also been achieved through this subset.

Operations people at AC and Golden Gate were responsible for designing and implementing arrangements for weekend loans of shortened AC buses to Golden Gate. More important, all negotiations and arrangements for the AC-BART busbridge agreement were worked out by operations personnel. Even where exchange of expertise does not directly affect the course of coordination, it contributes indirectly by making future interorganizational cooperation easier by promoting similar decision premises at the agencies involved. It also provides opportunity for initial (in some cases) or continued (more often) contact between two individuals, making possible the development of mutual trust, and a chance for the norm of reciprocity to come into play.[30]

In the planning subset, direct coordination efforts appear to be the modal activity, although exchange of expertise also occurs. AC provided Golden Gate with expert advice on changes in bus-stop lengths and locations along with driver training changes necessary for successful use of the articulated buses. The planning director at Golden Gate called an informal contact at AC planning, who put him in touch with someone in AC's training department. Knowledge AC had acquired through trial and error was thereby transferred informally to Golden Gate.[31]

Informal communications in the planning cluster often revolve around formal tasks of coordination that have been assigned to the planners. These problems range from fairly high-level discussions to ironing out specific details for implementing coordination. At the higher level, there might be negotiations on problems of a joint fast-pass, involving issues of financial equity and mechanical compatibility. There are also continuing informal contacts over common technical problems of coordination, such as the express bus service that AC operated for BART.

The management subset is composed of fewer individuals than either the operations/maintenance or planning networks. This subset typically involves high-level discussions of policy issues, although exchange of technical expertise is not unknown. Sometimes these informal channels are simply used to communicate the importance of a

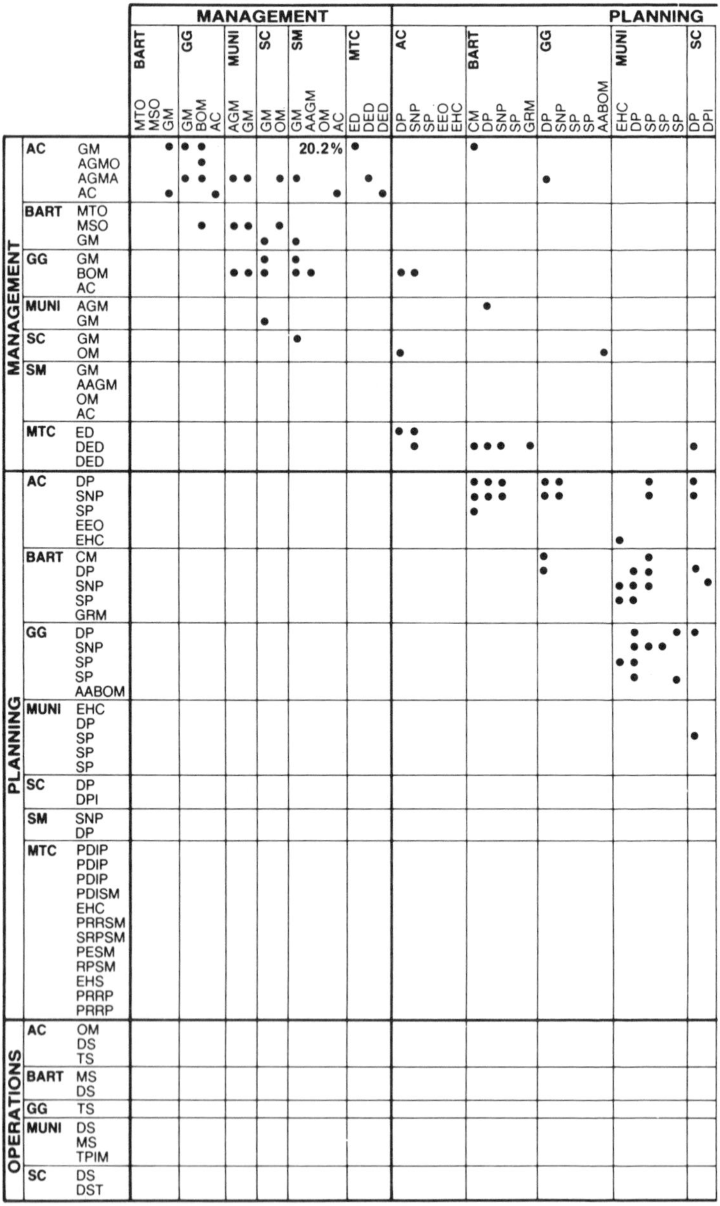

MANAGEMENT | **PLANNING**

			BART	GG	MUNI	SC	SM	MTC	AC	BART	GG	MUNI	SC
			MTO MSO GM	GM BOM AC	AGM GM	GM OM	GM AAGM OM AC	ED DED DED	DP SNP SP EEO EHC	CM DP SNP SP GRM	DP SNP SP SP AABOM	EHC DP SP SP SP	DP DPI

Figure 7   Subsets of the Informal Network

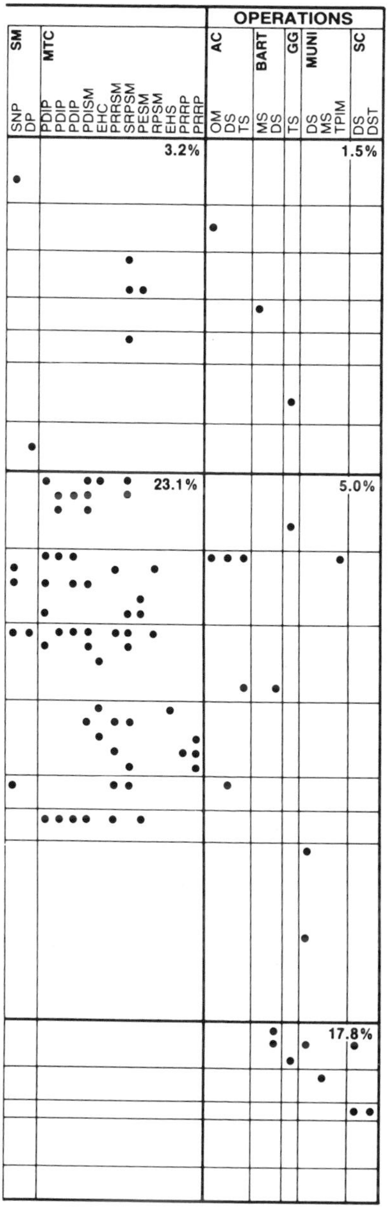

		OPERATIONS				

Column headers (left group): SM | MTC ... with sub-labels: SNP DP | PDIP PDIP PDISM EHC PRRSM SRPSM PESM RPSM EHS PRRP PRRP

Operations group: AC (OM DS TS) | BART (MS DS) | GG (TS) | MUNI (DS MS TPIM) | SC (DS DST)

Percentages shown in figure: 3.2% ... 1.5% ... 23.1% ... 5.0% ... 17.8%

Key to Abbreviations:

AABOM	Admin. Asst. to Bus Ops. Manager
AAGM	Admin. Asst. to General Manager
AC	Auditor-Controller
AGM	Assistant General Manager
AGMA	Asst. Gen. Mgr. for Administration
AGMO	Asst. Gen. Mgr. for Operations
BOM	Bus Operations Manager
CM	Contracts Manager
DED	Deputy Executive Director
DP	Director of Planning
DPI	Director of Public Information
DS	Director of Scheduling
DST	Director of Safety and Training
ED	Executive Director
EEO	Equal Employment Oppr. Officer
EHC	Elderly and Handicapped Coord.
EHS	Elderly and Handicapped Staff
GM	General Manager
GRM	Grants Manager
MS	Maintenance Supervisor
MSO	Manager of Station Operations
MTO	Manager of Train Operations
OM	Operations Manager
PDIP	Policy Dev. and Impl. Planner
PDISM	Policy Dev. and Impl. Section Mgr.
PESM	Policy Evaluation Section Manager
PRRP	Policy Review and Research Planner
PRRSM	Policy Review and Research Sec. Mgr.
RPSM	Regional Planning Section Manager
SNP	Senior Planner
SP	Staff Planner
SRPSM	Sub-regional Plan. Section Manager
TIPM	Transit Improvement Project Manager
TS	Transportation Superintendent

NOTE: The titles listed above are standardized references to job function. The actual job titles vary somewhat from organization to organization.

How to interpret the figure:

A ● is located at the intersection of the coordinates for each pair of decision-makers where an informal channel is judged to exist. Only informal channels between decision-makers at different organizations are represented in this figure.

particular issue from one agency to another, with its resolution left to subordinates.

However, these subsets are not entirely independent of one another. The management subset intersects with both the operations/maintenance subset and the planning subset (although the planning and operations/maintenance subsets do not appear to connect significantly). These relationships develop because management concerns overlap with concerns in each of those areas, and because in many cases managers were promoted from within those sections, taking with them contacts from their old positions to their new ones.

Several generalizations can be made about patterns of informal ties between personnel at different agencies. Type of informal tie is closely linked to function. For example, if it is used primarily as an advisory channel for exchange of expertise, the tie tends to be between individuals of equivalent formal status and similar area of activity.[32] Thus, general managers talk to general managers, controllers talk to controllers, schedulers talk to schedulers, and maintenance supervisors talk to maintenance supervisors.

Conversely, for informal channels used primarily to exchange sensitive information, or for bypassing formal channels, ties are often between people of different formal status within their respective organizations. Apparently, mutual trust is more important than equal rank. These channels tend to retain the elements of a primary, intrinsically valuable relationship, though they are used for essentially instrumental reasons.[33]

Earlier I expressed surprise that the operations/maintenance subset not only trades expertise but actually coordinates as well. Why? J. D. Thompson has argued persuasively that in most organizations some differentiation of function occurs, referring not to technical specialization in the production of a good or service, but to components of the organization such as the technical core and the buffer. The latter exists to protect the former from changes in the organization's task environment that might disrupt production. While as a whole the organization may be an open system, an adequate buffer permits the technical core to approximate a closed system, thereby improving the effectiveness of production.[34]

I therefore expected to find that at any particular transit operator a specialized subunit would perform the buffer function for the technical core, in this case rail or bus operations, or both. External communications of all kinds would be conducted by this subunit, allowing bus and rail operations to be run as a closed system, even though interdependence compels the organization as a whole to be treated as an open system. To be sure, the planning sections appear to perform this function.

Against the perspective of Thompson's theory, however, I found extensive contact between the technical cores of the different transit agencies. The cores appear to be far more permeable than Thompson's theory would lead one to expect. It might be countered that his theory does not preclude contact between the technical core of an organization and its environment, that the buffer simply shields the core from unwanted intrusions. But in the Bay Area, the technical cores directly negotiate agreements among themselves to reduce uncertainty and, as I shall show, sometimes intentionally circumvent their own buffers.

Development of extensive interorganizational informal networks means that many more organizational actors become boundary spanners than an analysis of formal responsibilities would suggest. This helps explain the apparent contradiction of Thompson's theory; although he treats organizations as open systems, he considers only formal structure in his analysis of buffer functions. Had he included interorganizational informal mechanisms, he might well have come to a different conclusion.

Informal Conventions and Norms

An important part of coordination is to establish processes for decision making that are essentially continuous, stable, and enduring. Sometimes these processes are spelled out in the formal designs of organizations, often they are not. Even when they are, they are inevitably incomplete, so that effective coordination always depends, at least in part, on the development of informal norms and conventions through group interaction, socialization, and experimentation. Such informal conventions limit the scope of conflict and the range of issues to be considered, establish expectations of behavior on the part of participants, and set out the kinds of factors to be considered in decisions. In short, they provide a ready foundation and a context for coordination. Heymann argues that without general understandings, there are several reasons why we cannot expect coordination on an ad hoc basis even when a group of parties might see benefits from working together. Some sort of conventions or general rules are essential. Heymann emphasizes rules that are not legally enforceable; he supposes that coordination is at least as dependent upon such rules as it is on formal law itself.[35] In this sense, motivation for coordination (for example, commonality of interest) is a necessary but not a sufficient condition for coordination to take place. The other necessary condition is the actual capability for coordination, which is provided by informal conventions and norms (as well as informal channels). Public choice theorists have sometimes missed this key point by focusing almost exclusively on differences and commonalities of interest of the parties involved.

Following Lewis, I understand informal norm or convention (I use the terms interchangeably) as follows:

> A regularity R in the behavior of members of a population P when they are agents in a recurrent situation S is a *convention* if and only if it is true that, and it is common knowledge in P that, in almost any instance of S among members of P,
>
> 1. almost everyone conforms to R;
> 2. almost everyone expects everyone else to conform to R;
> 3. almost everyone has approximately the same preferences regarding all combinations of actions;
> 4. almost everyone would prefer that any one more [person] conform to R, on condition that almost everyone conform to R;
> 5. almost everyone would prefer that any one more [person] conform to R', on condition that almost everyone conform to R', where R' is some possible regularity in the behavior of members of P in S, such that almost no one in almost any instance of S among members of P could conform both to R' and to R.[36]

Informally derived norms are essential even where the formal organization structure is specified in great detail: not all important factors can be taken into account ahead of time, and the character of some vital procedures is such that they are not easily formalized.

When the formal organization is less well specified, informal norms assume greater importance:

> The early months of the Economic Cooperation Administration provide a striking example of the ratification of informal relations. Between April 1948, when the agency was established, and about July 15, when it already had some six hundred employees, it operated without any formal plan for its internal structure even so elaborate as an organization chart showing its principal divisions. . . . The real core of this organization, which was in full operation before May 1, lay in a complex set of behaviors and understandings that had grown up almost spontaneously. The formal plans that were finally issued in July and subsequently were in very large part ratifications of this informal scheme.[37]

My own research on the California Coastal Zone Conservation Commission in 1976 produced similar findings. Few formal structures and procedures were found within the central commission staff, yet there was little confusion as to which persons had which responsibilities and which procedures were to be followed. These functions were all performed by an extensive set of informal conventions that were widely understood by the staff. In response to a query about an organization chart, one staff member replied: "We had one somewhere, but no one pays any attention to it."[38] Kagan's work on the administration of wage and price controls during the Nixon and Ford presidencies produced similar findings.[39]

In the case of new organizations, much time must be given to development of informal procedures. Critics expecting immediate substantive results from new organizations often fail to recognize the time and resources required to develop informal norms and procedures. The problem becomes acute when multiple independent organizations come together for the purpose of coordination, because no coercive mechanisms are available to enforce compliance (as there are within single organizations). A complex process of negotiation and accommodation is necessary. The situation is further complicated where no precedent exists on which to base informal procedures.

The RTA illustrates both complications.[40] Before RTA could produce tangible results on problems of coordination, it had to establish procedures and mechanisms by which it could deal with them.

Much time in early RTA staff-level committee meetings was spent establishing what issues would be considered and how they would be considered. Sometimes these procedures were explicitly specified. The Management Systems Committee tried in its first six months to come up with a viable set of objectives and was finally successful on the third attempt. In other committees, such as Joint Procurement, trial-and-error processes led to an informal procedure for letting out procurement bids. Developing these procedures involved contending with differences in interest and operating procedures among the member agencies. Yet once the procedures were established, they were adhered to closely.[41]

Washington Metro provides another illustration of the importance of informal norms for establishing decision-making procedures. The construction schedule for Metrorail was formally determined by a long-range plan based on projected patronage figures and cost of construction. In actuality, informal norms have been more important in fixing the order of construction. Given participation in Metro of several local jurisdictions, each with its own constituency and representatives, and economic constraints that preclude simultaneous construction on all planned rail lines, Metro's board had to arrive at some way to "allocate construction." It did so informally, taking into account political factors that the formal procedures did not. According to a former board member, "We give each board member enough construction each year to survive politically."[42] There are no formal strictures, yet the norm is well recognized, accepted, and defended. A stable pattern of interaction exists, remaining constant even with changes in board membership.

Informal socialization processes and group pressures for conformity produce adherence to the conventions governing acceptable types of decision.[43] This affects the choice of decision-making style, often excluding conflict-intensifying types, such as unconditional manipulation and prior decision, in favor of bargaining and compensation.[44] Because at Metro, coalitions are expected to vary from issue to issue—"You never know who you might need next"—persuasion and consensus building are emphasized over confrontation and majority votes over minority objections. These norms are well understood by the board members: "When a new member came on board he didn't know the norms; so we sat on him and he learned."[45]

Decision makers and others in the organization community know which approaches are beyond the pale. Manipulation through threats is considered destabilizing and costly to the organizational system. In 1980, Fairfax County began withholding its share of the Metro bus budget, claiming that the agency's irresponsible accounting prevented the county from planning its own budget.[46] The county's primary concern was the rate of increase in operating costs and the general unreliability of estimates of future bus subsidies.[47] Condemnation of Fairfax County by other members of Metro and by the press was nearly universal. After almost nine months of withholding by Fairfax, the *Washington Star* said in an editorial:

> Fairfax all along has had democratic access to the Metro Board to make its points on budgeting methods and other issues. And on questions where all of the participating jurisdictions have similar interests (as on the need for accurate subsidy forecasts) it should not be hard to construct a majority of the board to make a desired change.
>
> The Fairfax tactic of withholding money it clearly owes could not be emulated by all of the local jurisdictions simultaneously, without precipitating the financial collapse of the transit system. That would help no one—certainly not Fairfax riders who have used the subsidized service throughout the boycott.[48]

Besides conformity to group standards, other incentives exist for individuals from various organizations who must work together to adhere to informal conventions: "Where these are not law people may accept them out of the conviction that the stability of the system demands their acceptance."[49] Certainly this is true at Metro.

Cosmopolitanism and Coordination

Some of these same informal processes also led to the development of cosmopolitan attitudes sympathetic to the idea of coordination among multiple organizations. Cosmopolitan attitudes work as lubricants in situations of interdependence where informal mechanisms are already in place. When representatives of the different transit agencies meet more or less regularly to discuss problems, they may eventually reach accommodations to take back to sell to their respective organizations. Processes of group interaction often result in the development of loyalties to other group members that condition behavior of the individual toward his own organization. For example, one San Francisco supervisor who serves on the Metropolitan Transportation Commission is also a member of the governing board of one of the operators. On several occasions he has experienced what might be called "role conflicts" as a result of his overlapping memberships. Two San Francisco mayors have publicly criticized him for misrepresenting or betraying the city's interests in various transit matters before MTC.[50] Through continued exposure to different points of view, he had developed multiple loyalties and simultaneously a more regional or cosmopolitan attitude.

Furthermore, personal loyalties to personnel from other organizations develop through close working relationships over long periods of time. Such bonds strengthen the social cohesion of a group (composed of individuals from various organizations) that has come together to work on problems of interdependence:

> Integrative bonds of social cohesion strengthen the group in pursuit of common goals. Group cohesion promotes the development of consensus on normative standards and the effective enforcement of these shared norms, because integrative ties of fellowship enhance the significance of the informal sanctions of the group, such as disapproval or ostracism, for its individual members. Cohesion, therefore, increases social control and coordination.[51]

Continued participation in RTA staff-level committees has bred identification with other members of the group and with the group qua group. A Golden Gate planner observed that while the RTA representatives clearly brought the views of their respective organizations to RTA meetings, they were probably more oriented toward regional integration (in whatever form) than others at their organizations.[52]

A willingness to engage in coordination processes complements an objective need for coordination—that is, participation in coordination activities helps to develop a positive attitude about coordination. For example, the RTA

> affords an institutionalized forum for discussion of regional as opposed to operator-specific problems. Such discussions serve as socializing media. They make regional considerations legitimate topics of concern instead of utopian or unrealistic dreams, and they increase awareness of the advantages associated with cooperative efforts and lay the basis for future cooperation.[53]

In addition to the development of identification, extraorganizational loyalties, and positive attitudes about coordination, participants in group processes come away with a more thorough understanding of the attitudes of their counterparts and the operating conditions they face. When making proposals for joint action they can better predict the likely responses of their counterparts, thereby improving their chances for success. Thus, informal mechanisms indirectly promote coordination through processes of socialization, knowledge acquisition, and development of extraorganizational loyalties. Members of informal networks and participants in formal coordination efforts develop affiliations with members of other organizations that compete for attention with loyalties to their own organizations. Furthermore, they come to understand coordination problems from a regional perspective rather than from simply the parochial perspective of their own organization. These factors, taken together, work to promote what I call a "cosmopolitan attitude" about coordination.

Following Simon's argument that behavior in organizations is determined by decision premises,[54] one would conclude that two organizations with similar decision premises are likely to exhibit similar behavior, other things being equal. With respect to coordination, similar decision premises correspond to coordination by standardization as described by J. D. Thompson.[55] The difference is that in the multiorganizational case similar decision premises are not mandated by some superior authority to the actors in the system.

Similar premises facilitate coordination both directly and indirectly. They narrow the scope of conflict when two organizations come together, providing a foundation for discussion: some issues are simply removed from contention. Through common histories, shared decision premises may also provide such similar approaches to problems that little or no discussion is required for successful coordination:

> Common background and training, as well as professional traditions, among public administrators will support some common standards to guide agency decisions.[56]

Similar premises constitute a potential for what I will call "latent coordination." If two decision makers, X and Y, at two different organizations, base their decisions on similar premises, then their decisions may be well coordinated even if neither X nor Y makes any consideration of the consequences of his decisions for the other. I suspect, but have no conclusive evidence to support the argument, that similar premises cannot overcome serious differences in interest among organizations. But differences in decision premises may inhibit coordination even in the presence of mutual interests. The strained relationship between Muni and Samtrans results in part from very different decision premises for transit operations.

Thus, the public transit system of the San Francisco Bay Area is marked by the absence of a formal mechanism for coordinating the multiple organizations it contains. Simultaneously, the transit system possesses a stable and extensive network of informal relationships between personnel from different agencies, the density of which positively correlates with increased interdependence. Informal channels redress specific failures of formal mechanisms in particular situations and are powerful devices for coordination in their own right and on a regular basis. They provide the conduits through which coordination can take place, while informal agreements and norms of behavior form the foundation for coordination and, under certain conditions, actually coordinate behavior of different organizations without any direct communication.

5

The Fruits
of Informal
Coordination

It will be important that the separate surface
and rapid transit networks be co-ordinated to
provide, in effect, a complete public transit
service for the Bay Area. This is not to suggest
that the authority which operates the rapid
transit system should also exercise control
over or own and operate the surface transit
systems. But it is to emphasize that an effective means of coordinating rapid transit operation with the public or private operation of surface transit will be essential to the success
of both.

—Regional Rapid Transit:
A Report to the San Francisco
Bay Area Rapid Transit
Commission 1953–55,
Parsons, Brinckerhoff, Halt,
and Macdonald Engineers

Having discussed the general roles of informal channels and
conventions in coordination, I now consider two examples from Bay
Area transit that illustrate the power and versatility of informal features for solving problems of coordination in detail: the grant appli-

cation process and the AC-BART busbridge agreement. I then evaluate the coordination in the Bay Area transit system in 1978–80,
especially as it addressed the various interdependencies outlined in
Chapter 3.

The Grant Application Process and the Busbridge Agreement

The grant application process illustrates the importance of
informal channels in day-to-day activities involving problems of
coordination. The actual grant application process does not very
closely resemble the formal grant application procedure, both with
respect to the timing of events and the character of communications
between the parties involved. For example, MTC should only pass
judgment as to whether grant proposals meet with criteria established
in the Regional Transportation Plan. Typically, however, UMTA
waits for the MTC view on the proposal in general before making its
own decision. Usually MTC receives the grant proposal simultaneously with its delivery to UMTA. Then, after MTC administers
"holy water," [1] the UMTA people discuss the background material
for the proposal with the operator, while simultaneously holding
public hearings on the proposal.

The effects of these informal alterations are twofold: an increase
in MTC's influence on the outcome of the grant process, and a com-
pression of the duration of that process. The former occurs because
MTC is more familiar with the conditions immediately surrounding
the grants than UMTA; the latter expedites the process so that money
flows more quickly.

What about the direct role of informal channels in the grant process? In the Bay Area (and in Washington) it is common for operating personnel to develop and maintain informal contacts at granting
agencies. Questions raised in informal channels typically occur at
several stages of the grant application process. Transit personnel call
to discover the granting agency's priorities: What programs are currently being funded? Information of this type is hard to come by in
published documents, especially as to which programs UMTA administrators have a stake in promoting. What programs are most im-

portant to them, and for which will they be most likely to approve funding?

Transit personnel also frequently call for clarification of criteria required to receive funding. The exact character of these require-ments, especially interpretations of the published criteria by indi-vidual administrators, usually can only be discovered informally.[2] "UMTA theory is difficult to define operationally. It is hard to under-stand and implement. The Transit Systems Management Program is a good example of this problem."[3] After a number of informal inter-actions to ask more precise questions about particular grant applica-tions and the modifications necessary to ensure their success, the local transit personnel become adept at predicting responses of indi-vidual grant administrators to the various types of applications. Cer-tain accommodations are made in the style and substance of the applications that take into account idiosyncrasies of individual ad-ministrators—all without any direct communication:

> Until 1977 there really was no UMTA regional office. The UMTA people in Washington were whom I dealt with because the regional office had no grant approval power until January of this year (1978). This means a change in the UMTA personnel I have to deal with; but it hasn't hurt since I know the regional personnel really well. I can predict the reactions of "Q" to grant proposals and so I put language and details in the proposals to deal with those reactions. Now "Q" has an assistant, "S," who asks harder questions than "Q," so I write the proposals to answer his questions in advance, but not in so much detail that it leads to more questions. I usually leave room for more questions to be asked, though.[4]

Or take the words of the planning director at another operator:

> I have some contacts in the Washington office of UMTA. I usually call "X" at UMTA to see what monies are available, or "X" calls me. Then if it seems appropriate for us to apply, we go through regular MTC channels. I usually use my channels to UMTA for reconnais-sance purposes. Yesterday I received a call from UMTA about a new kind of grant. The discussion involved whether we could fit the criteria. After an in-house discussion of the grant we will proceed through MTC.[5]

There is yet another informal way to expedite the grant process. If a transit agency is in a hurry to begin a project covered by a grant proposal, and UMTA is slow to approve the grant, the transit agency will ask UMTA to write a letter of "no prejudice," explaining that it does not oppose the project. The operator can then proceed with the project using local capital to get the cashflow started. There is no guarantee of UMTA approval, but one operator at least "has never been had."[6]

Informal contact also characterizes interactions between the operators and MTC. Informal consultation has become an integral part of the grant process. Informal communications between the operators and MTC help to ensure that inconsistencies are minimized to the extent possible between:

a. Long-range planning efforts and specific expenditures

b. One operator and another

c. Regional and subregional goals as specified by MTC

The use of "grant managers" at each operator facilitates the use of informal channels in the grant process. Over time they have developed specialized knowledge and informal relationships that dramatically increase the speed and success rate of grant proposals. These channels make possible informal consultation and negotiation as well as the acquisition of sensitive or fugitive information that cannot be gained through formal channels. Informally adopted conventions permit an acceleration of the grant process and the realignment of influence to coincide with the location of expert knowledge.

The development of the AC-BART busbridge emergency agreement and its activation dramatically demonstrate the power of informal channels and informal agreements for producing coordination between organizations. Some background on its development provides a context for its current form and periodic activation.

BART's scheduling director worked originally at several positions at AC, including that of schedule analyst. He was interested in moving on. When a position became available at BART, his former supervisor, who knew the (then) BART director of transportation quite well, let him know and "greased the skids" before sending him over for an interview.[7]

By virtue of his tenure at AC, BART's new scheduling director had two valuable resources at his disposal: an intimate knowledge of the internal processes of AC, which enabled him to predict accurately both individual and organizational responses to various proposals he might make; and a set of strong informal relationships with AC personnel.

Soon after he moved to BART he realized that it had inadequate arrangements for handling emergency situations. Should a portion of the BART rail system be shut down for some reason, there were no backup arrangements to carry its passengers. After receiving approval from BART's general manager to develop an emergency procedure, he called one of his contacts at AC, the operations manager, and in fairly short order they worked out an informal agreement, a sort of "mutual-assistance pact." AC would provide emergency bus service should BART suffer a failure of any portion of its system within AC's jurisdiction.

They *intentionally* kept the agreement on an oral and informal basis out of their concern that if it was put into writing, their respective lawyers "would get hold of it, make it too complex and too restrictive." [8] They wanted it kept flexible, because they could not predict all of the problems that might arise. The two men felt that because they were both members of the "operations fraternity" and knew each other well, they could operate on the basis of mutual trust: the strength of the AC-BART pact derived not from a written contract but from a strong informal relationship.

The busbridge agreement works simply. Once BART personnel determine that a portion of the BART system is likely to be down for a period long enough to warrant a busbridge, BART Central calls the AC dispatcher, who then redirects buses from existing runs or rolls buses from division yards to provide shuttle service around the portions of the BART system affected by the emergency. When BART is again operational, the buses are withdrawn.

For example, in December 1982, a tree blew down on the Richmond-Fremont line near El Cerrito, blocking all stations on that line north of Berkeley. AC quickly provided a busbridge between Berkeley and the three stations blocked by the tree until the line could be cleared and service restored, a matter of several hours. Similar activations of the agreement have occurred several times each year since the agreement was established.

Payment is a simple arrangement. AC charges BART the cost of running the buses as opposed to letting them sit in the yard. This involves a calculation of labor, fuel, and maintenance costs and a small overhead charge. BART has never questioned AC's bills.

Conversely, if AC is unable to run its buses on particular routes, it can request a trainbridge from BART. This happens rarely. The Oakland Bay Bridge was closed once because of a chemical spill, putting AC out of service until late in the evening. AC then sent some forty buses over the San Mateo bridge to the south, as an alternate route, and also requested a trainbridge. Passengers at the Transbay Terminal were directed to the BART Montgomery Street station. BART accepted AC tickets and the passengers were able to catch their regular AC bus upon exiting the BART Oakland West station on the opposite side of the bay. BART billed AC in the same manner as AC bills BART.[9]

The Washington Metro, where bus and rail operate under the same organization, has a similar emergency arrangement. Yet formal arrangements at Metro are in no way more effective than the informal mutual-assistance pact between AC and BART. Because bus and train dispatchers are located next to each other, they simply walk from one room to another. As in the Bay Area, when Metrorail suffers an occasional shutdown of a portion of its lines, it requests a busbridge. It works about the same as between AC and BART; however, although Metrorail and Metrobus are funded separately, Metrobus is not reimbursed for its costs by Metrorail, which has led to resentment on the part of bus personnel.[10]

In the BART-AC case, informal relationships between the two agencies not only facilitated the speedy negotiation of emergency agreements, but through the cement of mutual trust assured that the arrangements would remain highly flexible and adaptive. Flexibility remains essential because the exact nature of the emergency shutdowns cannot be predicted. Through experience the procedures have been refined, and activations of the agreement have gone increasingly smoothly. The BART-AC agreement demonstrates clearly the power of informal mechanisms to provide effective coordination between organizations. The circumstances of the BART transbay tube fire and its aftermath make these points even more strongly.

The Transbay Tube Fire and Its Aftermath

At 6:06 P.M. on 17 January 1979, BART train 117, bound for San Francisco, caught fire about one mile into the transbay tube from the Oakland West BART station.[11] Efforts to evacuate the train's passengers safely and control the fire were poorly organized and nearly resulted in catastrophe. There were severe communications problems between BART and both the Oakland and San Francisco fire departments. These problems were compounded by inadequate oxygen equipment for the firefighters and by the toxic fumes given off by materials in the burning train. However, the passengers were evacuated by 6:58 P.M., and the fire was finally declared under control at 1:31 A.M. the next morning.

But BART's real problems were just beginning. The transbay tube was now closed, and the most optimistic estimates at BART had the tube opening no sooner than several days hence. How were the thousands of BART passengers who use the tube daily to be accommodated? Within an hour after the initial report of the fire, BART Central had called the AC dispatcher to request a busbridge between MacArthur station on the Oakland side of the bay and the Transbay Terminal on the San Francisco side (see Map 2). AC refueled buses coming into the division yards after the evening peak, put the drivers on overtime, and sent the buses into the busbridge.

AC was able to roll a sufficient number of buses for the emergency only because one shift was just ending and the evening peak was almost finished. If the request had come a little later and the drivers had gone home, AC would have had to pull buses from other runs and fewer would have been available. Only at that time did AC have sufficient slack to permit such a maneuver. Furthermore, the BART-AC agreement anticipated a rail shutdown of only a few hours on sections of lines that were not so heavily used. No one envisioned the closure of the tube for days at a time. AC would not have sufficient spare equipment and labor to operate an adequate busbridge for BART in the Friday morning commuter rush, now less than twelve hours away.

AC was able to make some adjustments. The morning commute is

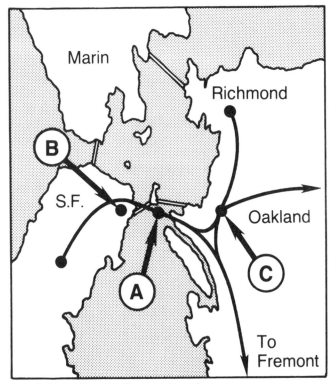

KEY: A. Train 117 catches fire in transbay tube
     B. Transbay bus terminal
     C. BART MacArthur station

Map 2   Location of BART Transbay Tube Fire

easier to deal with than the evening commute because travelers leave
from various locations at different times. In the evening travelers
leave from a concentrated area during a forty-minute period. AC
added buses (about twenty-five) to its regular transbay routes and put
some buses into the MacArthur-Transbay Terminal shuttle for BART
(about ten of its larger-capacity articulated buses). Still this was not
enough.[12] Meanwhile, BART's scheduling director had been called
by BART's assistant general manager for operations and given carte
blanche to do what was needed to arrange buses for the morning. He
came into BART a little before midnight to begin preparations for the

next day. He already knew that BART would need more buses for the shuttle than AC could provide. Once before, during a wildcat strike, the scheduling director had had to resort to several private operators to provide bus service to patrons in areas not served by AC.

But he had no informal contacts at any of these private operators. In fact, he did not know with any certainty how reliable they were. Worse, he had no previous contact with other private operators in the area. He went through the yellow pages of the phone book to get the numbers of relevant companies; the Greyhound night number was not even listed. Somehow, however, he managed to make sufficient arrangements for the next morning.

On the first day after the fire, AC provided a dispatcher to help keep the buses rolling at the MacArthur BART station, and of course at the Transbay Terminal. BART notified the state police (who are responsible for the terminal) and the Bay Bridge authorities of the additional traffic they could expect. This amounted to more than one hundred additional buses, including AC and the private companies.[13] For the next five days BART's scheduling director ordered buses from the private operators for the shuttle. During that time AC increased its role at the MacArthur BART station, putting up signs directing passengers to the correct loading areas, answering questions about service, and loading and dispatching buses. Initially, passengers had to wait ten to twenty minutes for a bus; within a few days the wait had been reduced to three to five minutes.[14]

On 23 January, AC's assistant general manager for operations decided that AC, with its bus expertise, should relieve BART of the responsibility for chartering the private coaches. One of his assistants proposed this to BART's scheduling director, who agreed, but reserved veto power over any decisions AC might make in that regard. He assigned one of his assistants to act as a liaison to AC on the private charters, informed BART's assistant general manager of the new arrangements, and reserved the right to retain the private operators who had responded on the first day; he felt an obligation to them because they had responded on such short notice.[15]

The task of organizing the BART shuttle fell to the AC charter service manager. Having been in the bus business in the Bay Area since 1945, he knew all of the relevant people at the private operators. He ordered buses for each day beginning at 9:00 A.M. the preceding morning. His criteria for chartering the buses included cost per bus, the total number of buses needed, and the availability of other buses. Prior to AC's assumption of the chartering function, BART had contracted with about ten different private operators for buses between 6:00 and 10:00 A.M. and between 2:00 and 10:00 P.M., with prices charged BART varying by as much as $100 per day.

For example, one company provided forty buses per day at $380 each. Another charged over $400 per bus per day. Others were charging only $280 per bus per day, which was in line with what AC deemed appropriate. AC's charter manager instructed the private operators to give him price quotations (which had been a problem in itself), on the basis of which he cut one operator back to twenty buses per day and refused to order buses from another until its price came down. This strategy resulted in savings of several thousands of dollars per day for BART.[16]

When BART first chartered the buses, it had ordered one hundred or more per day. By 1 February, AC was chartering ninety buses per day. Traffic on the Bay Bridge had established a fairly regular pattern and was flowing more smoothly. At first, roundtrips by shuttle buses had taken forty-five to fifty minutes; this eventually dropped to thirty-three to forty minutes, making possible more trips per bus per commute peak. AC also made sure that each bus was fully loaded before departing, thereby increasing the loading factor. By 1 February the shuttle involved about three hundred bus trips per peak period with twelve thousand passengers per peak and two thousand off-peak.[17]

Before 24 January, BART was billed directly by the private companies. Thereafter they billed AC, with the invoices being sent to AC's manager, who approved them and passed them to AC's controller, who then sent them along to the scheduling director at BART. When the scheduling director approved them, BART released the money to AC, which then paid the private operators. BART would not release any money without AC approval; neither did it demur on any payments authorized by AC. AC sent along the original invoices to BART so that it was clear that no "additional" cost had been added. The amounts ran into the millions of dollars.[18]

When it began to look as though the transbay tube would be closed for an extended period, BART's board concurred with an earlier suggestion by BART staff that a fare be charged for the shuttle. Commuters could purchase tickets from booths at the Transbay Terminal or at MacArthur station or from regular BART ticket machines. The bus drivers collected the tickets, turned them over to BART staff who then had AC (literally) weigh them to obtain a count (the same method AC uses to count its transfers). BART's $20,000 to $30,000 cost per day for the shuttle was partially offset by the fares.

AC billed BART separately for its own role in the shuttle. BART was charged for management and overhead costs involving the administration of the private charters and for the extra employees at the Transbay Terminal and the BART MacArthur station. AC's accounting department coordinated the gathering of information on these internal labor and management costs.

AC billed BART for its buses used on the shuttle on the same basis that it bills BART for the express services it runs under contract with BART. This includes actual driver time and cost; mileage costs based on fuel, tires, and maintenance; and an overhead percentage per month. Overall, the costs amounted to slightly less than $0.5 million. BART paid the bills with little discussion, auditing them only afterward.

Neither BART nor AC had ever envisioned that the tube would be closed for longer than a week or so following the fire. But because of the potential for catastrophe that the fire dramatized, the California Public Utilities Commission refused to permit BART to resume tube operations until investigations had been undertaken, hearings held, and changes either made or guaranteed. Given the seriousness of the matter, the number of actors involved, the highly charged political character of the problem, and its general complexity, BART was not permitted to recommence operations through the tube until 5 April 1979, making the total time closed about three and one-half months.

The BART transbay tube fire and closure suggests a number of things about informal organization and the problem of coordination. Even though the original informal busbridge agreement did not anticipate an emergency of the scope or duration of the tube closure, it provided both an immediate set of procedures to follow and the foundation for a series of informal adaptations to deal with the unanticipated consequences. The duration of the closure along with its severity precluded the exclusive use of AC buses, but AC remained actively involved by becoming BART's agent for administering the private coach operation. AC's motivations for this informal expansion of its role certainly were a mix of concern for transit patrons, an opportunity to place BART in its debt, and a recognition that AC personnel possessed the expertise required for efficient operation of the shuttle. BART's motivations for accepting the expanded AC role were a mix of deference to AC's superior bus expertise and a willingness to devolve the responsibility onto AC so that its limited managerial resources could be concentrated on reopening the tube.

Irrespective of motivations, the informal relationships and agreement showed a tremendous capacity for coordination and adaptation. Even though the expanded role of AC involved the administration of millions of dollars for BART, and almost one-half million dollars for AC's efforts, the informal arrangements worked smoothly and effectively. It seems doubtful that a formal arrangement could have improved the quality of coordination. In fact, as BART's director of scheduling long ago contended, a formal agreement on the busbridge may well have decreased the effectiveness of coordination efforts because of its more rigid and constraining character.

Coordination in Operations and Services

The coordinative power of informalities in two specific cases is quite clear, but how well has Bay Area transit interdependence been addressed by informal mechanisms more generally? However extensive informal networks may be, however well understood conventions may be, they are irrelevant to the problem unless coordination is a product. Happily, for a formal organizational structure characterized by "fragmentation," competition, and duplication and overlap, a surprising number of successful coordinative efforts were observed in the Bay Area.

Many informal efforts were directed toward solving the problems of interdependence described in Chapter 3. However, for the most part we cannot prove causation—that informal features are directly and explicitly linked to successful coordination. Because I do not have other cases where the organizational system is similar to the Bay Area transit system (for example, cases where comparable levels of interdependence obtain with a less well-developed informal organization), I cannot, with certainty, state as a general rule that the more fully developed the informal organization, the better the quality of coordination. I have correlation and must infer causation. Because my primary interest is understanding the utility of informal mechanisms for effecting coordination, this is a lesser problem than might first be supposed. I can say that I have found an extensive informal organization and simultaneously broadscale successful efforts at coordination in the absence of a formal structure. And in particular cases I have been able to demonstrate direct links between informal mechanisms and coordination—as in the grant process and the transbay tube fire.

Interdependence created by common use of streets and thoroughfares in San Francisco by Muni, Golden Gate, and Samtrans has been handled largely on an informal, bilateral basis between the pairs of operators involved. The most satisfactory and congenial arrangements appear to have been developed between Muni and Golden Gate. Signing, bus stops, and routing have been worked out so that both operations go smoothly. Golden Gate does not pick up passengers once it enters San Francisco but only drops them off; the converse is true for outbound buses. This resolves the issue of competition for passengers.

The Muni-Samtrans relationship is much less cordial, yet some accommodations have been worked out to coordinate joint use of San Francisco streets. Coordinative efforts have been strained by Samtrans's reluctance to provide service information to Muni and by its attempted end runs around Muni in its dealings with city government.[19]

The Transbay Terminal is administered by Caltrans and used by four public operators: Muni, Golden Gate, AC, and Samtrans. Caltrans indicated very few problems at the terminal. Issues of coordination are neither very numerous nor very serious: "Things usually work themselves out."[20]

The interconnection of bus routes with BART rail lines is an important area of interdependence. The most extensive connections are between BART and Muni and between BART and AC, while lesser connections obtain between BART and Samtrans and between BART and Santa Clara. Coordination problems hinge on bus access to stations, proper signing, availability of sufficient buspads, and the like. For the most part, coordination has been achieved by prior decision by BART, modified by negotiations with the other transit companies, because BART's stations were designed and constructed before bus routes were redirected to them. Both Santa Clara and Samtrans have bus lines that connect with stations also served by AC, but no problems of coordination have arisen there. However, Samtrans and Muni came into open conflict over use of buspads at BART's Daly City station. That problem was resolved when BART performed the role of informal mediator.[21]

Physical connection of BART and Muni Metro stations in San Francisco has prompted extensive negotiations on security, maintenance, day-to-day services, and the like. Many issues have been resolved, and some are still under negotiation.[22]

Issues arising from interdependence in the services area are more complex and difficult to resolve. Fares and transfers are primary concerns, along with routing of bus lines, timing of bus schedules, and physical locations for passenger transfers. Figure 8 indicates the pairs of operators with transfer arrangements in 1980. Figure 2 shows the number of interoperator trips made daily. Comparing the two figures, we find that transfer arrangements are in place where the frequency of interoperator transfers is high. Two notable exceptions are AC and Muni, and BART and Samtrans. Negotiations to arrange for transfers between these pairs of operators were under way as this study was being conducted.

As of April 1983, residents of San Francisco were able to purchase a joint BART-Muni Fastpass, which could be used on BART in San Francisco, Muni Metro, and Muni buses, and which provided for an unlimited number of trips. This improves existing fare-discount arrangements for transfer passengers and permits Muni to reduce some service overlaps with BART. Transit patronage should be encouraged by lower fares and greater ease of use. By comparison, no such joint "fastpass" exists for users of Washington Metrobus and Metrorail, even though they are part of the same organization. Fare discounts for transfer passengers between Metrobus and Metrorail are not as generous as they are between BART and AC or BART and Muni. AC and Muni are engaged in working out their own joint "fastpass." In another area, Muni and Golden Gate engaged in a demonstration project to ascertain the feasibility of ferry-bus transfers at San Francisco's Ferry Building. At this writing, no permanent arrangements had been made.

Another key concern in service interdependence is the routing of bus lines to facilitate transfers. When BART first commenced operations, AC rerouted over ninety of its District One bus lines so that they would connect with BART stations at one or more points. In San Francisco, Muni rerouted a large portion of its bus lines so that they would connect with BART trains. Samtrans went into operation after

To From	AC	Golden Gate	Muni	Sam-trans	Santa Clara	BART
AC	•	None	None	None	Free	None
Golden Gate	None	•	None	None	•	None
Muni	None	None	•	None	•	Half fare on Muni
Sam-trans	None	None	None	•	Free	None
Santa Clara	Free	•	•	Free	•	None
BART	Free	None	Half fare	None	Free	•

Figure 8   Transfer Arrangements in the Bay Area Public Transit System

As of 1 September 1980. Table adapted from Wolfgang S. Homburger and James A. Desveaux, *Joint Transit Fares in a Multi-Operator Region: A Conceptual Plan for the San Francisco Bay Area* (Berkeley: University of California, Institute of Transportation Studies, 1980), p. 14.

BART, and directed some of its lines to the BART Daly City station. AC connects with Muni at the Transbay Terminal, along with Golden Gate and Samtrans, but the level of transfers among those operators is low. Connections between AC and Golden Gate over the Richmond–San Rafael bridge would improve service, but the demand for it remains low.[23]

There has been no attempt to facilitate transfers by timing bus and BART train schedules, because the trains run on constant headways rather than at fixed times. However, coordination between bus and rail schedules is no better at Washington Metro. Furthermore, the complexity of timing buses to facilitate transfers within a single operator is so great that the schedulers can barely achieve that goal. The complications entailed in coordinating bus schedules with other operators render that feat nearly impossible. Costs would be high, benefits few.[24] In the cases of Samtrans, AC, and Golden Gate transfers with Muni, key Muni lines have such short headways that matching schedules becomes irrelevant; passengers never have to wait long for a bus. For the most part, just as within individual operators, coordination for interoperator transfers is left to the passengers themselves.

However, discussions between BART and AC, Samtrans, and Santa Clara have taken place concerning late night bus-train connections so that when service ends for the evening passengers will not be stranded at BART stations. AC's efforts to have BART install some sort of signaling devices at the stations to let bus drivers know when BART trains are approaching have not been successful. However, no signaling devices exist at Washington Metro either.

Peninsula service to and from San Francisco historically was provided by Southern Pacific. As financial difficulties from providing service mounted, Muni, Santa Clara, and Samtrans came together to administer and finance an innovative joint fare-discount program so that Southern Pacific's losses could be covered but fares would not go up, enabling service to be continued. Southern Pacific now provides the service under contract to Caltrans; Muni, Santa Clara, and Samtrans still contribute financially.

As noted, transit agencies also provide services for each other by contract, often on the basis of informal agreements. Contract services are provided because one agency has superior expertise in the relevant areas or has resources to provide services where the recipient does not. Such arrangements run the gamut from emergency agreements to long-term service provision with daily implementation. Even where contracts are formalized, the evidence indicates the importance of informal channels and conventions in the processes leading to the contracts or in their execution.

BART includes within its jurisdiction communities not yet served directly by rail service, but which still pay supporting property taxes as well as a special sales tax; consequently, it sought a way to serve them until rail service could be extended. The solution was to provide express bus service from these communities to nearby BART stations. However, BART had no buses, facilities for buses, or operational expertise. Besides, it had enough difficulty operating its rail service smoothly. The answer was to purchase buses and contract with AC to operate the service. It has been run in this fashion for a number of years now with little difficulty. As we have already seen, informal channels play a powerful role in the daily implementation of the service. Because rail extensions are unlikely in the near future, it is likely the arrangements will continue for some time. Existing capacity and expertise at AC for handling bus operations filled a need at BART.[25]

BART found itself in the opposite position in negotiations with Muni. BART had been in operation for several years, developing expertise on and a capacity for maintenance of rails and tunnels. As BART tracks and stations were constructed, Muni added Metro stations and its own underground rail lines. BART owns both sets of stations. In 1976 they signed a preliminary agreement covering their respective responsibilities for station operation and maintenance. In 1978 Muni asked BART to perform the Muni Metro station and track maintenance. Muni wished to avoid additional administrative overhead and to take advantage of BART's expertise, while BART could retain greater control over its own stations and the Muni Metro stations. As this research was being conducted, they were negotiating a long-term agreement.[26]

In 1978, at current headways, BART was running its Concord–Daly City line at full capacity during peak hours. Greyhound operated approximately parallel service, but at a loss and wished to abandon the service. The California Public Utilities Commission (PUC) would not let Greyhound do so until BART could absorb the additional passengers. BART could not do this until the PUC let it shorten headways, which in turn was predicated on long-term safety improvements. The solution was an interim agreement between MTC, BART, and Greyhound: Greyhound would continue operating the service, but would have its deficit covered by monies allocated by MTC through BART. Greyhound would officially run commuter service for BART until such time as BART could absorb the additional passengers. Use of grant monies to facilitate coordination is discussed in detail in Chapter 7.[27]

There are several other instances of coordination by contract in Bay Area transit. Golden Gate provided local bus service under contract to the MCTD, which was a "paper" organization with a tiny staff and no operating capability, but could raise revenues and receive grant monies. MCTD paid Golden Gate to provide service for Marin

County localities, as opposed to long-haul service Golden Gate operates on its own behalf. Until the recent formation of Contra Costa County Transit District and its venture into bus operations, AC provided local bus service under contract to several Contra Costa County communities and to some small transit districts.

To provide much of its commuter service, Samtrans contracts with Greyhound, which operates the service on a cost-per-mile basis. Samtrans benefits because Greyhound provides the service less expensively than Samtrans can. Contract service also means that Samtrans's service is covered by two different union locals—a conscious strategy by Samtrans management. The first contract for this service went into effect in 1977. Informal channels figured in the development of the contract: a key Samtrans manager had worked at Greyhound for twenty years.[28]

In one case, interagency coordination failed, principally because of differences in operating paradigms. When BART opened its Coliseum station, it asked AC to run special shuttle buses between that station and Oakland Airport. AC responded by extending existing lines. When BART asked for closer headways, AC asked them to show a need. Instead BART purchased two small buses to be operated as "AirBART" shuttles between the Coliseum station and Oakland Airport by the Port Authority of Oakland.[29] A similar situation obtained when BART asked Samtrans to run special buses between its Daly City station and San Francisco Airport.[30] In both cases, the bus agencies were reluctant to initiate service before a need had been demonstrated, while BART contended that initiating service would stimulate patronage. BART's response was simply to find another agency to provide the service.

There are other mutual-assistance pacts in Bay Area transit besides that between BART and AC. An analogous agreement exists between BART and Muni, but has been invoked much less often than that between BART and AC. Even when no informal agreement exists, wherever there are informal channels the potential for emergency assistance is high. For example, one Saturday BART had a temporary transbay tube closure, but AC had insufficient resources to cover. An AC manager called his Golden Gate informal contact at home and requested assistance. Golden Gate responded by sending sufficient drivers and buses to fill in the gap.[31] Golden Gate has also provided emergency backup service for the private operator of the Tiburon–San Francisco ferry service when weather conditions or other problems have prevented those ferries from running.[32]

Golden Gate rented shortened buses from AC on weekends. When the agreement's details were worked out, it remained informal. Charges for the buses were easily agreed to and procedures worked out for transporting the buses back and forth between AC and Golden Gate. Agreement was promoted by the high level of mutual trust between the personnel at the two operators. At the time of this study no formal contract covered the rental arrangements.

Despite the absence of a formally integrated and coordinated organizational structure, the Bay Area transit system displays a remarkably well-coordinated set of planning and operating arrangements that address the interdependence described in Chapter 3. Most of those arrangements were worked out through informal channels, and founded on informal norms. Many of them have been intentionally kept as strictly informal agreements. Note too that these agreements are largely bilateral, as befits the character of the interdependence in the system.

Such informal agreements have not only provided effective coordination in the areas they were intended to address, but have proved flexible and adaptive as unanticipated problems have arisen. Even where two organizations might have conflicts over issues of interdependence, they have been able to separate those conflicts from other problems of interdependence in order to work out solutions to the latter. Problem solving by decomposition of the larger, more complex system into smaller, less complex, more manageable components is a reality in Bay Area transit, made possible by the extensive informal networks of channels, informal behavioral norms, and informal agreements.

6

Factors Facilitating Informal Organization

> Trust is an important lubricant of a social system. It is extremely efficient; it saves a lot of trouble to have a fair degree of reliance on other peoples' word. Unfortunately this is not a commodity which can be bought very easily. . . . Trust and similar values, loyalty or truth telling, are examples of what the economist would call "externalities." . . . They are not commodities for which trade on the open market is technically possible or even meaningful.
>
> —Kenneth Arrow, *The Limits of Organization*

To this point, the development and persistence of informal mechanisms have been explained solely as a function of the presence of interorganizational interdependence and the resulting motivation to reduce the attendant uncertainty and to control or alleviate its effects. Although as a causal factor, interdependence may explain motivation, it is neither sufficiently precise nor powerful enough to explain differences in the actual development of informal organization under similar conditions of interdependence. How is the existence of an elaborate and well-differentiated informal system of coordination in one case and the lack of such a system in another explained, where each case is characterized by interdependence and the absence of a formal system of coordination?[1]

The answer is found by examining the conditions necessary for the development and maintenance of specific informal mechanisms along with the factors that promote those conditions. This chapter focuses on the development and maintenance of informal channels and informal norms. The former are examined in some detail, the latter in a more cursory manner as that task has been done elsewhere.[2]

Why are individuals inclined to develop informal channels in the first place, and once that behavior is initiated, why would they continue with it? The answer given so far hinges on the failure to reduce uncertainty resulting from interdependence (for example, to coordinate or to provide adequate mutual benefits or avoidance of mutual costs) or from the absence of formal mechanisms entirely. Here the motivations of the individual to engage in informal activities are more closely examined, in particular with respect to the exchange of benefits.

That the road to hell is paved with good intentions is a commonly accepted adage. Put more formally, motivation alone is insufficient to cause particular behaviors. Once the individual is motivated to act, what opportunities does he have to do so? If the individual has the motivation and opportunity to act informally, is he capable of doing so? All three factors must be present in order for behavior to occur: motivation, opportunity, and capability.

The opportunity and capability components of informal behavior are considered in light of three sets of factors that affect them: the characteristics of the organizational system (in this case, the properties of the system of transit operators in the Bay Area), relevant features of the particular organization in which the individual acts, and characteristics of the individual himself. Each set of factors affects the opportunity and capability of the members of the organization system to act informally. In addition to these factors, another principal underpinning of any informal system of coordination, deriving from values of the larger society, is the norm of reciprocity.[3] My interest in discussing those factors that appear to facilitate informal mechanisms stems both from a desire to develop the foundations for a broad theory of informal organization and to make some very practical recommendations about how managers might create conditions favorable for its development and exploitation for purposes of coordination.

The Norm of Reciprocity

It has been shown that a closed-system approach to the study of formal organizations is inappropriate for use in all but a handful of situations. Organizations are more accurately considered as open systems. In addition to the effects of the behavior of other organizations in their environment, organizations are subject to constraints imposed by the sociocultural setting in which they are found. For example, given recent political and cultural changes toward increased individual rights in the United States, the military has had to move away from the severe standards of discipline it once employed. Society no longer tolerates such methods, and contemporary recruits differ from their earlier counterparts in their attitudes toward authority, which makes these techniques less effective than before.

Of course, organizations are not only constrained by the values of the larger social system in which they are embedded; often they depend on such norms for their effective functioning. In the case of informal channels, the norm of reciprocity provides the foundation for their development and persistence as effective mechanisms for coordination. It is an informal value widely accepted throughout the larger society. In fact, the norm of reciprocity is a keystone of almost all societies, from the nearly prehistoric to the most modern and advanced:

> The suggestion is that the motivation for reciprocity stems not only from the sheer gratification that Alter receives from Ego, but also from Alter's internalization of a specific norm of reciprocity which morally obliges him to give benefits to those from whom he has received them. In this respect, the norm of reciprocity is a concrete and special mechanism involved in the maintenance of *any stable social system.*[4]

A norm of reciprocity in its universal form makes two interrelated, minimal demands: people should help those who have helped them, and people should not injure those who have helped them.[5] In general terms, the norm of reciprocity may be conceived as a dimension to be found in all value systems and, in particular, as one among a number of "principal components" universally present in moral codes.[6]

The entirety of the informal organization, especially informal channels, is predicated on the exchange of benefits. Benefits to be gained from any social relationship are of two types: intrinsic and extrinsic. Intrinsic benefits are those that derive not from what one does, but from the fact that one does it with someone. All associates benefit simultaneously from the social interaction, and the only cost incurred is the indirect one of giving up alternatives.[7]

Conversely, extrinsic benefits result when individuals derive specific gains from social relations because their associates go to some length to provide those gains for them.[8] The extrinsic benefits of social relationships are the most important for understanding the development and persistence of informal channels. The position taken here differs from the positions of those authors who contend that informal relationships perform primarily, if not exclusively, the function of providing intrinsic satisfactions of affiliation and personal integrity that are missing from formally prescribed roles or relationships.[9]

Despite the fact that the informal relationships considered in this study involve primarily the provision of extrinsic benefits such as expedited services and sensitive information to those involved, they tend to retain the external characteristics of social exchange, rather than the characteristics of economic exchange, which epitomize formal relationships.[10] Economic exchanges are typified by exact prices for goods stipulated in advance, explicit contracts, and remedial devices in case of failure to perform. On the other hand, social exchange is epitomized by a general, implicit contract and no exact prices for benefits, with future obligations and remedial devices left unspecified.[11] Put another way, the informal relationships observed here retain the appearances of what social network theorists call "sentiment relations," although their defining characteristics are in fact those of "instrumental relations" and "communications relations."[12]

Benefits exchanged in informal relationships are not prone to quantification, particularly in monetary terms. And no true coercive mechanisms exist to ensure conformity to informally bargained agreements. Why then should one party to the relationship be willing to make a commitment that involves a cost? Other than to terminate the relationship if the other party reneges, he has no mechanism to ensure repayment.[13] Gouldner provides one answer:

> Being indeterminate, the norm [of reciprocity] can be applied to
> countless ad hoc transactions, thus providing a flexible moral standard
> for transactions which might not otherwise be regulated by specific
> status obligations.[14]

The norm of reciprocity, recognized and accepted in a general
form, enables the parties to an informal relationship to break the impasse as to which one should take the initial risk and make the investment in providing benefits for the other: it reduces the hesitancy to be
the first to make a commitment. By creating an obligation for repayment, the norm makes it possible for informal relations to develop.
Still,

> Simmel took the extreme view that the first kindness of a person can
> never be fully repaid, because it alone is a spontaneous gesture of
> goodwill for another, whereas any future favor is prompted by the ob-
> ligation to reciprocate.[15]

The evidence in this study indicates that organizational actors do pay
attention to the norm of reciprocity. They recognize the importance
of obligations incurred, especially in regard to maintaining informal
relationships.

For example, the city planner in the Bay Area, whose duties include transportation planning, occasionally needs extensive information on bus routes and schedules and the financial impacts of transit
plans. To forestall the long turn-around times of formal communications, he has developed close informal channels at AC transit. He has
repaid his contacts for the instant information they provide by calling
to warn them of impending attempts by other operators to encroach
on AC territory.[16] The actors in the relationship consciously keep a
balance sheet of the exchanges.

No specific remedies are stated in case of failure to honor obligations incurred in the informal relationships; however, the norm of
reciprocity works:

> Failure to reciprocate engenders loss of credit and loss of trust, and it
> ultimately brings about an exclusion from further exchanges and a
> general decline in social status, particularly as a person's reputation as
> one who does not honor his obligations spreads in the community.[17]

Conformity to the norm of reciprocity in informal relationships thus
does not depend solely on a "good" attitude, because potential loss

of future benefits and social stigma serve as strong incentives to reciprocate. The consequences of failure to reciprocate reach far beyond the specific incident to hinder other informal relationships by planting seeds of distrust. Acceptance of benefits and failure to adhere to the norm of reciprocity may have negative long-term consequences. The more important are specific informal relationships for performing one's professional duties, the more disastrous will be the consequences.

The key to this phenomenon, as Axelrod has pointed out,[18] is the simple fact that these actors do not meet but once. Beyond any doubt they will meet again and again. Each participant has therefore a strong incentive to treat the other as he would wish to be treated in their next encounter; and there will always be a next encounter, at least in the foreseeable future, because "in more realistic settings, the players cannot be sure when the last interaction between them will take place."[19] Whereas Axelrod's formulation came about as he searched for solutions to the microeconomists' "prisoner's dilemma"-type situations—"Under what conditions will cooperation emerge in a world of egoists without central authority?"[20]—and found that "tit-for-tat" was the "best" solution, and Gouldner approached the problem from the perspective of social anthropology, they both came to very similar conclusions. Axelrod's formulation is attractive because it does not depend on the prior existence of any widely understood social norms in order to explain either the development of such norms or the emergence of cooperation in the absence of a central authority.[21]

Despite a generalized norm of reciprocity, no informal relationship is firmly established until a bond predicated on personal obligation develops. While mutual trust develops through a series of informal interactions, the norm of reciprocity and the consequences of failing to adhere to it carry the burden of holding the relationship together. Trust, that essential[22] ingredient to informal relationships, develops over the course of the relationship, which may be strictly formal at first and only gradually assume many informal properties. The development of this necessary trust occurs partly because the "establishment of exchange relations involves making investments that constitute commitments to the other party."[23]

Because informal exchanges by their very nature entail effort or exchange beyond that required by formal responsibilities, they inevitably create personal obligations. That additional amount of effort is what makes the informal channel valuable to the party involved and simultaneously provides the foundation for mutual obligation and trust. "Only social exchange tends to engender feelings of personal obligation, gratitude, and trust; purely economic exchange as such does not." [24] Trust makes possible coordinative arrangements through informal channels, whether these arrangements remain purely informal or are ultimately formalized, while continued contact promotes the development of the mutual consideration and respect that is so important to informal relationships: "the gradual expansion of exchange transactions promotes the trust necessary for them." [25]

When the norm of reciprocity is thoroughly internalized by members of an organizational system, it provides benefits beyond the actual exchanges in informal relationships by reducing the level of conflict in the system. Recall that the second aspect of the norm is that one should not hurt those who have helped: "it is morally improper, under the norm of reciprocity, to break off relations or to launch hostilities against those to whom you are still indebted." [26] The norm of reciprocity thus serves a stabilizing function. The more extensive the informal system, therefore, the more effective the norm of reciprocity should be in reducing conflict and promoting coordination, especially in an organizational system marked by differences in interest among its constituent parts, such as Bay Area transit.

Moreover, as Gouldner notes, "we should expect to find mechanisms which induce people to remain socially indebted to each other and which inhibit their complete repayment." [27] The difficulty in assigning specific values to the benefits exchanged in informal relationships makes the exchanges sufficiently ambiguous so as to preclude precise balancing of favors owed. Parties to informal relationships strive for balance, but neither can be sure of his exact position vis-à-vis the other. Debts are never fully repaid, and contribute thereby to the stability of the informal system, and concomitantly the larger organizational system. [28]

Concern about balance in informal relationships is sufficient to influence the choice of strategies for informal contact. A BART planner finds that "talking to a single person at a given operator allows me to develop a better long-term relationship and to keep track of the balance of favors owed more easily." [29]

However, while the primary function of such informal relationships may be the exchange of extrinsic benefits, some element of intrinsic benefit inevitably remains, creating tension between the desire for the achievement of instrumental goals and the desire for social approval. But people tend to specialize their relationships by obtaining extrinsic benefits from some associates and intrinsic benefits from others.[30]

In the context of interorganizational informal channels, specialization helps to resolve the apparent conflict between this study and findings in the literature. It is improbable that organization members will seek intrinsic benefits from interorganizational informal relationships when they can already obtain them through intraorganizational relationships. Therefore, an explanation of the development of interorganizational informal relationships must rest primarily on the extrinsic benefits they provide for those involved.

A principal difficulty for distinguishing between the two types of informal relationships is that those used for extrinsic gains are carried on under the guise of simple camaraderie. That is, the appearance of intrinsic attraction is maintained even though extrinsic benefits are the predominant reason for the development and persistence of the informal relationship.

In sum, the norm of reciprocity has several consequences for informal organization. It makes possible the exchange of benefits outside any formal contractual arrangements, an especially important factor because development of informal relationships requires a series of exchanges and involves exchanges on which no exact values can be placed. Acceptance of the norm of reciprocity makes it possible for one individual to make the first move with some reasonable expectation of being repaid in the future.

Over time, with multiple exchanges, willingness to provide extrinsic benefits becomes based on mutual trust specific to the particular relationship rather than a generalized norm of reciprocity. Nevertheless, the broader norm of reciprocity remains in the background. Parties to the informal relationship are aware that failure to reciprocate may result not only in the loss of that channel, but in the unwillingness of others to engage in future exchanges.

The norm of reciprocity also has consequences for the larger organizational system. By placing individuals under personal obligation to one other, they become less prone to do injury to one another when their interests conflict. This effect complements the development of "cosmopolitan" attitudes discussed in Chapter 4. And the more extensive the informal network for a multiorganizational system, the more likely it is that conflict will be attenuated.

System Properties

Contact must be established between personnel from different organizations for informal channels to develop. Formal coordination activities provide opportunities for such contact. The long-term effects of these contacts on informal mechanisms for coordination often overshadow any immediate results. The participants fully understand this. "During an important project there will be multiple contacts every day. Often these contacts become routinized and become very useful in the future," said one city official.[31]

In the Bay Area formal coordination efforts have produced many long-lasting informal relationships as by-products. In the BART-Muni coordination project, both staff and operations people were brought into close contact with each other, resulting in the development of informal channels.[32] The Northern California Demonstration Project, including AC, BART, and Muni, had similar effects.

The RTA was formed in 1975 as a response to the then ambiguous threat of the MTC to the independence of the transit companies. After initial difficulties in organizing, RTA began to provide a forum where top transit managers could get to know each other. As staff-level committees were created, they provided a similar set of opportunities for staff members from all sections of the transit agencies.[33] RTA's role in facilitating informal contact has not gone unnoticed by the actors themselves. Commented one MTC manager:

> The value of the RTA lies less in its actual accomplishment than it does in its initiation of contact between operators at both the general manager level and the lower staff levels; two years ago they were not even talking.[34]

In general, RTA provides the best opportunities for two types of personnel to make contact. The first set is composed of people who, by the nature of their professional roles, would normally have little occasion to interact with people from other organizations: purchasing, maintenance, and most operations staff. This sort of informal contact was discussed in Chapter 4 in terms of channels connecting technical cores of different organizations.

The other set is populated with persons who by virtue of their organization's operating area have little occasion to deal with personnel from other operators. BART personnel have relatively less advantage in this regard, whereas Golden Gate and Santa Clara personnel have the most. A Golden Gate planner found that, given Golden Gate's low level of operational interdependence with other agencies, he talks most often with their personnel at RTA meetings.[35] An AC planner was able to increase his otherwise limited exposure to other personnel through his participation in the RTA Services and Tariffs Committee.[36] Because it has developed and maintains these informal channels, the time and expense so far invested in RTA have been justified.

There are other formal arenas in Bay Area transit that have provided opportunities for informal contact. MTC, for example, has sponsored an increasing number of meetings and conferences over the past decade. The transit agencies also send representatives to county-level committees that allocate federal urban aid monies. These committees include city and county officials, transit operator staffs, and MTC personnel. Transit people make contact with local officials such as city managers and city engineers. At the Concord BART station, for example, there was an overflow from the parking lot onto residential streets. Local residents complained and the city of Concord publicly threatened to begin ticketing the cars. After BART's planning director called people he knew from the county committee to see what kind of bargain could be struck with the city, they made an informal arrangement.[37]

Various formal studies of transportation problems have also provided meeting grounds and reasons for continued contact. The San Francisco Northwest Corridor Study made it possible for one MTC manager to get to know the planning director at Golden Gate.[38] The Golden Gate Corridor Study provided the chance for a Muni planner to meet and develop ties with a Golden Gate planner (who was with MTC at the time) as well as with a current MTC manager (who was then a private consultant).[39]

The staff advisory committee for the proposed new Transbay Terminal (composed of staff from AC, Golden Gate, Muni, and

Samtrans) met monthly for more than a year and prepared joint reports and presentations for the Bay Area Transit Terminal Authority Board of Control. It did not generate new contacts, but provided opportunity for continued contact and common purpose.

At Washington Metro, there are activities intentionally designed to produce improved contact between individuals from different transit organizations. What is only an incidental consequence of the activities described in the Bay Area is raised to an explicit goal at Metro. For the past two decades, an annual conference lasting several days has been held at the Airlie House in Warrenton, Virginia. Conference members include top managers at Metro, Metro board members (who are also members of local transit and other local government bodies), staff from local governments, and officials from the local transit bodies that participate in Metro.

Formerly, the conference lasted for three days and the participants stayed at Airlie House for the duration, participating in conference activities and taking their meals together. Recently, however, financial exigencies have shortened the length of the conference. The conference includes formal addresses by board members and senior staff personnel, which cover such issues as bus and rail fare subsidies and the Metro rail construction schedule. However, the most important discussions occur outside of the formal arena. In between formal meetings, at meals, and in the evenings, informal caucusing of local boards and staffs, and meetings between different boards occur regularly. Officials get acquainted, exchange views, make informal bargains, and build informal coalitions. At Metro, these conferences are recognized as an important part of the process of political integration and coalition building. Officials realize that the formal meetings impart information but, more important, they provide the context for informal interactions. Their value is so great that such interactions are now built into the formal program.[40]

Formal arenas for coordination do not exhaust the system properties facilitating the development of informal mechanisms. Equally important is movement of personnel among organizations. Although usually turnover is considered bad for organizations, in moderate amounts it proves remarkably effective in promoting an informal system of relationships in a multiorganizational system. Unfortunately, empirical studies of this phenomenon are few in number, and most have focused on organizations in the private sector.[41] In Bay Area transit the movement has been continuous and extensive. And the reasons for that personnel movement do not need to be the promotion of informal mechanisms in order for such movement to have that effect.

In the Bay Area, most people appear to be lured away by better offers, not because they were forced out of their old positions. They leave behind at their old organizations friends and goodwill rather than animosity, which would render their professional activities more difficult. They carry with them an intimate knowledge of the formal structures and informal decision premises and processes of their former organizations. When situations arise that require communication or bargaining with their former organization, they know to whom they should talk and how to achieve successful coordination. For example, one agency's coordinator for the elderly and handicapped works through formal channels with his counterpart at another operator on routine matters, but when he wants "to know what's going on," he calls another person in a different section who used to work for him.[42] Furthermore, when people move from one transit company to another, they carry to their new organization their existing patterns of doing things, ranging from specific technical procedures to more general views of the world.[43]

Personnel movement in Bay Area transit is not large when compared with the total number of individuals employed at the agencies and MTC, but its significance becomes clear when the formal positions of those people who have moved are known. Personnel in key decision-making positions have moved from one organization to another, involving principally AC, BART, Golden Gate, and MTC. Samtrans, Muni, and Santa Clara have been less involved.

When Golden Gate started bus and ferry operations, it hired its bus manager from AC. He brought with him key AC operations and scheduling personnel. He hired one planner from MCTD and another from MTC. Later Golden Gate filled its auditor-controller position with someone from AC. This movement is especially noteworthy because Golden Gate bus operations had no history or existing operating procedures to constrain the new personnel. As a result its bus operation looks very much like that at AC. Even its maintenance program was designed by the (then) AC chief of maintenance. The only real constraint on the use of AC procedures was imposed because Golden Gate hired drivers from Greyhound (to meet UMTA regulations), making Golden Gate's labor contract an amalgam of AC and Greyhound provisions.[44] As was noted in Chapter 4, informal interaction between personnel at AC and Golden Gate far surpasses what would be anticipated from their low level of interdependence.

MTC's executive director came from BART, where he had been director of planning and research and, for a time, acting general manager. For one of his deputies he hired a man who had worked for him at BART. BART's current planning director and his senior assistant had been initially hired by the MTC deputy executive director when he was at BART. This history has made for strong informal ties. And BART's scheduling director came from the scheduling department at AC.

One MTC planner came from AC, where he had been a "rent-a-planner," financed by MTC. An AC assistant general manager came from MTC, where he had been a deputy executive director and had developed close ties with AC personnel. AC's director for elderly and handicapped issues moved to that position from Golden Gate. A Muni planner moved there from a similar position at Golden Gate. Several persons at Santa Clara came from AC. And there are others.

Even where personnel have come from outside Bay Area transit agencies, often they have come from organizations in closely allied areas with ready-made sets of informal contacts within the transit system. Of five section managers at MTC whose work has an external orientation, only one was hired through a formal hiring process. Of the other four, one had worked with a private consultant doing studies for MTC's BART Impact Program; one had worked with another private consultant on the Golden Gate National Recreation Area Study for MTC; another had been at Caltrans for some years and had worked on a joint project with MTC; and the last one had worked at the Washington, D.C., Council of Governments, but knew people at MTC. Other people have come to the transit system via the private-consultant/funded-study route or from local planning agencies, via mutual friends or previous associations with current transit employees. This extensive personnel movement has played a crucial role in the development of the informal system of communications in Bay Area transit, particularly where it has expanded opportunities for informal contact.

A similar, though less extensive, pattern of movement characterizes Washington Metro. For example, the general manager came directly from UMTA, as did his predecessor. He brought with him an administrative assistant and eventually hired an assistant general manager who had been a UMTA regional administrator. Given the extremely heavy reliance of the Metro on UMTA for rail construction funds, these connections are of great importance. The director of financial planning and Metro's public affairs coordinator came from the old National Capital Transit Agency (NCTA, the planning predecessor to Metro). The assistant to the general manager for legislative affairs worked first for the minority staff of the House District Committee (which influences federal spending for Metro). Just as many AC employees came from the old National City Lines Key System (which it supplanted), many Metro bus personnel came from the private operators that Metrobus replaced. There is one conspicuous difference between Bay Area transit and Washington Metro: no personnel movement has occurred between Metro and local jurisdictions (in either direction).

Typically, individuals who moved from one organization to another had favorable responses about the effects of their move (as were the responses of the people they left behind). For example, a BART planner who was hired by the MTC deputy executive director while he was at BART commented: "We have a great deal in common." When he is "hassled by MTC," he calls his former boss. And whenever he happens to be at MTC, he always stops and talks with his former boss for a half hour or so.[45] In a few instances, however, personnel movements complicated coordination as when people were forced to leave their old positions and responsibilities, and in their new organizations were put right in the middle of coordination problems with their former organization. This seems to be the exception rather than the rule, however.[46]

Although turnover resulting in movement among operators helps channel formation, when it results in personnel exiting the organizational system it is disruptive and injurious to informal channels. Because the informal system depends on people for its strength rather than formal positions, individuals are not easily substituted. Thus, whereas internal movement of personnel strengthens the informal system, departures of personnel can weaken the operator that loses personnel that way. Muni lost a valuable actor in the informal system, for example, when its planning director elected to take a job in Portland, Oregon.

Although I have discussed the effects of personnel movement from one agency to another under circumstances in which development and maintenance of informal channels did not appear to be the motivating factors (they have been merely fortuitous by-products of such movement), Edstrom and Galbraith have reported a multinational firm that intentionally moved its managers from one section of the corporation to another in order to promote the development of informal structures, particularly through socialization of its managers to common norms: "In this particular organization transfer of managers was a process for specialization and for creating a verbal information network." [47] In fact, Edstrom and Galbraith go so far as to suggest that "people movements" are the "primary determinants of organization structure and process rather than or in addition to size, technology, or task uncertainty." [48] Intentional transfers may be employed to improve coordination through standardization of decision premises. Interunit or interorganization coordination may be more effectively achieved by such techniques than by use of more typical organization-control strategies such as centralization and bureaucratization. [49]

> Similarly, Pfeffer and Leblebici have argued that the movement of executives between organizations is one form of interorganizational communication that can facilitate the development of interorganizational structures of behavior. [50]

Thus, personnel movements among organizations serve to facilitate the development of informal channels, knowledge of other organizations, and similarity of decision premises among comparable types of organizations, all of which serve to promote interorganization coordination directly or to lay a foundation for such coordination.

Organizational Properties

Properties of particular organizations affect the opportunity for and capability of their members to engage in informal relationships; policies of organization managers are particularly important. Are managers willing to allow their personnel to develop informal channels, or do they stand in the way of such contacts? Or do they actively encourage their staffs to establish informal lines of communications with members of other organizations? Attitudes about the nature of organizations appear to be linked with attitudes about the use of informal channels. For example, the manager who believes that "organizations are ten percent structure and ninety percent people" is far more willing to let his staff develop their own informal lines of communication than the manager with the opposite view.[51] Concern that his staff's development of informal channels will undermine his own authority also affects a manager's policies. Those who seemed the most secure in their positions were the most likely to view favorably the development of informal contacts by their subordinates.

There is little question that informal channels may be used for activities antithetical to the goals of management. Even where this does not hold true, those channels are often still found threatening. The cost of using informal channels may therefore be high. An AC staffer, on learning that AC's general manager had just died, called an informal contact at MTC to apprise him of the fact. A fellow staffer let slip to their mutual supervisor that the call had been made and the first staffer was fired.[52]

Willingness to permit informal channels also appears to be related to management style. Managers who want to make all decisions and put little discretion in the hands of subordinates may permit informal connections; but, as the subordinates cannot make commitments on their own, their effectiveness in the informal system is limited. However, if the informal channel is used simply to pass information from one organization to another, this may not be a problem. For example, one planner recognized that his counterparts at another agency had very little discretion. He simply tailored his suggestions, proposals, or demands to the expected response of the person he knew to be the key decision maker, using his informal contacts only as conduits.[53] An MTC manager worked a similar strategy. At one transit company, the staff was permitted virtually no discretion. When the MTC manager spoke with his informal contacts, he always knew to shape requests and communications to the peculiarities of the general manager, not the person to whom he was actually speaking.[54] The value of these informal contacts derives less from their intrinsic ability to accomplish tasks than from their role as conduits to those with the actual decision-making power.

Nonetheless, discretion affects desirability as an informal contact. Speaking of an AC staffer, the same MTC manager said: "I prefer to deal with 'P' because he wants to be helpful, but I am not sure how much clout he has within AC."[55] Sometimes there are heavy costs when strictures against the exercise of discretion in informal negotiations are violated. When one staffer at AC did try to express policy positions in informal meetings and discussions with other operators, he came perilously close to losing his job.[56]

Intentionally placing staff in situations where there is potential for making contacts promotes informal channels, yet managers may fail to do so. If not actively encouraging it, does the manager at least refrain from explicitly forbidding such activity? Banning informal contact does not eliminate the behavior, but it does raise its cost and therefore may have a chilling effect. It may also reduce the effectiveness of the informal channel as a coordination mechanism. Moreover, prohibition tends to drive informal communication underground, limiting its utility to the manager. Commented Moore: "Although the official (and in some cases the actual) policy of the management may be to seek out and eliminate every violation of company rules, the first-line supervisor can scarcely adopt such a policy and maintain his effectiveness."[57] It also raises the specter of sabotage.

But the value of informal channels can be maintained, and the manager can feel reasonably confident that the use of those channels remains consistent with his own policies. One BART planner has direct approval from his supervisor to make informal contacts with personnel at other operators, and to use (within limits) his own discretion in making policy statements or commitments on behalf of BART. Typically, when he sends information or proposals to other organizations, he writes a memorandum to his supervisor, summarizing that communication.

Managers also find it profitable to have subordinates with informal contacts because they themselves can benefit from them. When one MTC manager is working directly with the planning director at an operator and encounters some difficulty, he has his staff speak to one or more of their informal contacts in that agency's planning section.[58] In this case the staff's informal channels serve to back up the formal lines of the manager; they act as a redundancy.

Another section manager at MTC goes a step further. When he

visits the various operators to discuss problems, he takes his staff with him to introduce them to the operators' personnel. He wants members of his staff to "cultivate" people in order to ensure cooperation and access to information.[59] Yet another MTC manager said that he no longer deals directly with anyone at the operators now. He lets his staff do that. At first, he introduced his staff to potential informal contacts; now he lets them do the work on their own.[60]

Occasionally, prohibitions on informal contacts are communicated from managers to their counterparts at other organizations. For a time, MTC's official policy was that there was to be one person at each operator designated as the official contact for each section of the MTC. Like all such formal prohibitions, it worked only as well as the parties involved wanted it to work.[61]

A second organizational property involves personnel turnover. As already discussed, turnover of personnel in moderate amounts may be beneficial to the multiorganization system as a whole for developing informal contacts and can benefit individual organizations as well. But in several ways it can also hurt the maintenance of informal lines of communication for individual agencies. High turnover causes the organization to lose what might be called its "institutional memory"—knowledge of the informal norms and byways of the organization and of all of the facts that are never committed to paper or computer disk. The organization can be compensated when personnel move to other organizations in the same system, but not if they exit the system.

Too much of this sort of turnover cuts off the organization from informal communication. It takes time for informal contacts to develop, and during this lag the effectiveness of the organization is diminished. And such turnover makes it difficult for people outside the organization to develop stable informal relations with people inside, because informal attraction is more dependent on person than position. One manager at AC commented somewhat wistfully on the high level of turnover at BART during the tenure of one general manager: "I used to know many of the old guard, but they have gone elsewhere. I don't know many of the new people." [62] He had lost valuable resources.

Formal positions presumably can be filled by anyone who meets the job requirements. Little loss of efficiency is incurred. Such interchangeability is at the heart of the Weberian model of bureaucracy. But such a conception is at best a denial of the importance of informal aspects of organization and at worst a disavowal of their existence. Such an attitude is not limited to theorists of organizations. It finds expression among important and presumably astute managers. Listen to Alfred Krupp:

> What I shall attempt to bring about is that nothing shall be dependent on the life or existence of any particular person; that nothing of any importance shall happen or be caused to happen without the foreknowledge or approval of the management; that the past and the determinate future of the establishment can be learned in the files of the management without asking a question of any mortal.[63]

Krupp evidently believed that an organization could be run solely on the basis of formal structure, position, and routines. Were he correct, turnover in personnel would only inconsequentially affect the ability of the organization to conduct its business effectively. But informal structures do develop. They are important, and they depend on specific individuals.

Time and effort are required to develop and maintain informal channels. Ability to make such investments is closely related to a third organizational property, an adequate staff. From several sources I learned that the policy of MTC is not to alert local officials of new funding sources for transportation projects.[64] This means that the cities have had to develop and maintain informal contacts with MTC as best they can so that information on funding will reach them. The maintenance of a staff of adequate size to devote specialized attention to transportation issues appears to be essential to the development of these informal channels.

The cities of Hayward and Berkeley are an interesting study in contrasts in this regard. Berkeley had a transportation department until the late 1970s. For reasons of economy it was abolished and its functions were subsumed under the city planning department. Following the passage of Proposition 13 and the subsequent loss of revenue, the planning department lost six planners, including the sole transportation planner. "Since Berkeley does not have the staff, it cannot afford to cultivate regular contacts."[65] On the other hand, Hayward has managed to maintain a planner whose primary responsibility is to work on transportation-related issues.[66] This planner has established informal ties with a range of personnel at different operators and at MTC. He is "on top of funding sources" for transportation. Hayward devotes more staff resources to transportation issues and therefore seems to have a better-developed informal system of contacts than the city of Berkeley. The ultimate return on the investment has been in Hayward's success in obtaining funding for its transportation projects.

Larger or wealthier organizations clearly have an advantage, as they can afford larger staffs whose personnel may be dedicated to particular issue areas. "It is necessary to cultivate informal contacts. It takes time and one must have a purpose in mind. But 'full-time' contacts can be disadvantageous. Small cities cannot always afford such luxuries," was how one assistant city manager described the problem.[67]

The time and effort required for informal channels are graphically illustrated by the experiences of two section managers at MTC. Time is essential because the mutual trust on which informal relationships are predicated does not develop without a series of interactions. One MTC section manager, hired from outside the Bay Area, recognized that as a newcomer to MTC and an outsider to Bay Area transit he would be at an initial disadvantage. "People at the transit organizations originally thought I had no power at MTC—and many still do. I am trying to gain the confidence of individuals at the operators," but at the time I spoke with him he had not yet developed a network of informal contacts. People call him, but only with questions of a technical nature. He knows that he will have to pursue informal relationships actively and that it will be a matter of some time before he will be successful.[68]

Another section manager is well connected with the local transit companies, but he has acquired additional responsibilities that include dealing with local governments where he has no informal contacts. Currently he is "sort of shaking things out, finding out who is worth talking to in the public works departments," usually starting at the top and working his way down. "It is a learning process, as there are new actors and different constituencies to deal with." [69]

In sum, three properties of individual organizations affect the development and maintenance of an informal system. Managers' policies govern opportunities for contact with people from other organizations and the permissible use of informal channels by organization members. Turnover at a given organization can be beneficial in moderate amounts, but high turnover can be detrimental to the informal system. The maintenance of an adequate staff is essential to developing and maintaining informal contacts because of the time and effort they require.

Personal Attributes

Personal attributes affecting the development of informal channels fall into two categories: the individual's formal position within the organization, and one's personality and attitudes. Formal position has important ramifications for the opportunity and capability to make informal contact, and affects the individual's desirability as a contact for others. Also within this category is membership in professional organizations and social groups that increases the exposure of the individual to other professionals. The individual's job history, especially movement from one organization to another within the same system, also comes under this heading.

Formal position within the organization affects one's opportunity to make contact with people at other organizations. People occupying positions in the organization buffer are more likely to make contacts than people within the technical core, because of differences in the requirements of their positions.[70] One important consequence of the RTA is that it has narrowed differences between the buffer and the technical core in the opportunities available for informal interaction. Its staff committees on procurement, operations, and maintenance have made possible the development of informal ties among personnel who would likely never have met otherwise.

Formal position is also a source of information and discretion. Independent of the status formal position confers on one in the formal structure, it affects status in the informal organization. The more formal responsibility one has, the greater is one's potential for working effectively in the informal organization. Demotions or changes in position can dramatically reduce the value of an individual as an informal contact. An MTC staffer who went from an important position to a less responsible one (due to internal politics), referring to personnel at the operators, commented sadly:

I can't do much for people in my current position. In the old days people called me to see what fundings were available and how to get programs through MTC—questions of a political nature.[71]

Demotion reduced his value as an informal contact by decreasing his importance in the MTC policy-making process. He had fewer formal responsibilities and less access to restricted information—that is, fewer goods to exchange—making him less attractive as an informal contact to people outside his organization.

However, formal position does not guarantee importance in the informal organization. It merely provides the potential for exploitation by the person holding the position. Conversely, lack of an important position does not preclude effectiveness in the informal organization, but places more constraints on the individual. Sometimes people surmount these hindrances by becoming "operators" within their organizations, not unlike Luther Billis in James Michener's *Tales of the South Pacific.*

Position also permits access to perquisites to be used to establish obligations under norms of reciprocity. For example, a Golden Gate manager has access to the towers of the Golden Gate Bridge. He took a director of another transit property up in the south tower elevator of the bridge to show him the view, a treat outsiders are not privileged to enjoy. He does favors like this "with the expectation of some kind of return down the line." [72] BART personnel sometimes give honored guests a tour of the BART Central Control for similar reasons. The "small potatoes" that come with formal position are used as a way of creating a reservoir of goodwill to be tapped as needed in the future.

The ability of the individual to make binding commitments through informal channels is an important determinant of his attractiveness to others as an informal contact. This is a function of formal position as well as the policies of superiors.

Thus, formal position affects the number of resources the individual has to trade in informal exchanges—whether those resources are sensitive information, binding commitments, or "small potatoes"—and also affects the opportunity to make informal contacts.

In the second category are those personality traits and attitudes that affect the individual's capability for interacting informally. A person's attitudes about the sanctity of formally prescribed ways of doing things affect his ability to act informally. Some people take great sat-isfaction in circumventing formal procedures. Others treat formal rules as objects of worship:

> Discipline, readily interpreted as conformance with regulations, what-ever the situation, is seen not as a measure designed for specific purposes but becomes an immediate value in the life-organization of the bureaucrat. This emphasis, resulting from the displacement of the original goals, develops into rigidities and an inability to adjust read-ily. Formalism, even ritualism, ensues with an unchallenged insis-tence on punctilious adherence to formalized procedures.[73]

In this sense, personality plays a role in shaping attitudes about formal and informal organization, and thereby the ability to engage in informal behaviors. For example, one planning director was quite insistent that only people of the same rank attend RTA staff commit-tee meetings. He felt it a violation of formal etiquette that there be a variation in rank, even though those people might be very effective in handling problems of coordination.[74]

Ease in dealing with other people and good interpersonal skills fa-cilitate the development of informal relationships.[75] Their absence makes such development problematic. The same planning director found the development of informal ties a difficult task: "I am not a very sociable person. I don't mix well with other people and rarely see people I work with on a social basis."[76]

At some point, these personal attitudes will affect the importance of the person in the decision-making process of his organization: in-formal connections can render individuals more important than their superiors. A staff planner at one transit property is considered more important and useful to conduct business with than the director of planning.[77] The staff planner is more flexible and oriented toward pragmatic achievement of goals than his superior. Furthermore, the staff planner actively considers his informal activities to be key fac-tors enabling his section to function effectively in the face of the planning director's reliance on formal procedures and channels.[78]

One other personal characteristic affects informal contacts in much the same manner as formal position—membership in profes-sional associations and other social groups. Membership performs a dual function. It improves the probability that a person will meet others in the multiorganizational system. In several instances, transit personnel working only a few miles apart did not meet until they attended the same American Public Transit Association annual convention hundreds of miles away. A planner at Golden Gate met a BART planner in this way; over time they developed the contact into an informal working relationship.[79] Membership also increases the likelihood that two individuals will identify with each other through participation in common social activities, thereby developing values in common and paving the way for informal channels and, ultimately, coordination.

Other Factors: Serendipitous Propinquity

Not all of the factors contributing to the development and maintenance of informal systems of communication have systematic properties. Serendipity is important, especially with respect to propinquity.[80] Somewhat to my surprise, the number of informal channels in Bay Area transit with origins outside professional public transit was not small. This is less surprising when it is recognized that prior contact plays an important part in decisions on hiring.

Previous acquaintance in work situations outside public transit, education, and military service has helped to generate informal contacts used later in public transit activities. A BART manager met Muni's general manager through membership in the same veteran's association, and they became friends. They call each other on business now. If the BART manager needs to talk with someone at Muni about a particular problem and does not know the appropriate person, he calls the Muni general manager to find out who that person is.[81] A Muni planner met his Golden Gate counterpart and an MTC staffer through membership in the same San Francisco neighborhood association. When the Muni person wants inside information on activities at Golden Gate or on MTC projects, he has the appropriate contacts.[82] Such common experiences also presumably create a common bond among the individuals involved. More than one interviewee expressed the importance of the idea of a "transit brotherhood."

Chance meetings also play a part. A planner from one agency and the general manager of another frequent the same sandwich shops, sometimes meeting by accident as often as twice per week. The planner says that the general manager is a good source of information and almost always has something he wants to discuss.[83] The meetings are probably now no longer "accidental." A planner from AC transit is a close neighbor of a UMTA regional official. They talk regularly and exchange information on business.[84]

Conclusion

Individuals are motivated to develop informal mechanisms, particularly informal channels, by pressures for coordination in combination with the potential of those mechanisms for the exchange of extrinsic benefits. Development of these exchanges is facilitated and governed by the larger societal norm of reciprocity. Moreover, an entire complex of conditions governs the probability of that development by affecting the opportunity and capability of particular individuals for informal contact. Properties of the multiorganizational system (in addition to its interdependence), particular organizations, and the individual himself are important determinants of the extent and quality of the informal organization that ultimately develops in that system. Some of these properties are open to manipulation by managers so that probabilities of developing and maintaining effective informal organization (for purposes of coordination) is enhanced. That is, even though informal organization may be the cumulative result of many individual decisions, and it cannot be comprehensively planned and executed in the same manner as formal structures, conditions can be created that favor its development. Insofar as the manager recognizes the value of informal organization for the achievement of organizational goals, such as coordination, the creation and manipulation of the factors described in this chapter become important aspects of his job.

7

Informal Weaknesses and Formal Compensations

From decentralization we get responsibility, development of personnel, decisions close to the facts, flexibility—in short, all of the qualities necessary for an organization to adapt to new conditions. From coordination we get efficiencies and economies. It must be apparent that coordinated decentralization is not an easy concept to apply.

—Alfred P. Sloan, Jr., *My Years with General Motors*

No matter how well adapted to the usual operating conditions it faces, an organizational design inevitably contains weaknesses. Such weaknesses may apply across the board to all problems the organization is intended to confront, or only to some. The assumption made here is that there is no optimal organizational design, only designs that permit the attainment of some mix of goals, each at least at some satisfactory level.

Whereas Chapter 2 focused on the weaknesses of formal coordination schemes and the roles of those inadequacies in the development of informal mechanisms, this chapter considers the weaknesses of informal systems of coordination. In so doing I examine two distinct sets of problems intrinsic to such systems: those resulting from their informal character and those arising from multiorganizational structure and from the character of interdependence in the system. Then I explore the potential of a hybrid system of coordination to compensate for the failings of informal arrangements. To this end I examine the roles of the RTA and the MTC in the Bay Area transit system, before drawing more general conclusions about coordinating multiorganizational systems.

The Personal Nature of Informal Organization

Other things being equal, the personal nature of informal mechanisms means that favoritism will occur in communications and negotiations. One reason that political machines were attacked in the early part of the twentieth century was their unequal treatment of individuals, depending on their connection with the machine. The personal character of informal organization flies in the face of modern democratic beliefs that emphasize equality of treatment by official agents of government. Furthermore, it runs counter to the norm of impersonality, a principal foundation of modern bureaucracy.[1]

It is difficult to endorse officially a set of mechanisms based on relationships between persons (as opposed to positions) characterized by preferential treatment of parties involved in the relationships relative to those outside, and yet that is the principal value to those involved. In the context of modern bureaucracy, where individuals are to be considered by reference to professional competence and formal position, irrespective of personality, the intrinsically unequal treatment in the informal organization is problematic.[2]

This inequality is also offensive to democratic ideals, yet because informal organization is both inevitable and useful, the fiction of equal treatment is maintained through formal procedures and norms of behavior. If we seek to suppress informal organization because of this problem, we stand to lose valuable instruments insofar as we are successful. Apparently, however, we are never to be more than partially successful. The evidence indicates the omnipresence of informal organization.[3] It remains a question of tradeoffs between different values and goals. I believe that weaknesses of informal organization deriving from its personal character, when considered from a broader perspective, are largely offset by the important role it plays in the larger system.

For example, in situations where more complex systems are evolving from simpler systems, stable intermediate forms of organization make it possible for that evolution to proceed more rapidly than if they were absent.[4] If the multiorganizational system in Bay Area transit is evolving toward a higher level of interdependence, the system's capacity to deal with the increased interdependence, shy of formal consolidation, is improved by the existence of an informal organization during that process. When the adaptive capacity of the formal organization lags, informal mechanisms make it possible for the system to continue functioning effectively while the formal organization catches up.[5]

Some criticisms of informal organization stem from the perception that informalities serve personal ends first, and professional ends second, if at all.[6] Furthermore, personal ends of informal mechanisms are perceived to conflict with formal ends of the organization, through restriction of output, refusal to exercise discretion, resistance to authority, and so forth. Chapters 4 and 5 demonstrated how informal organization facilitates coordination. Here we examine its potential and actual impediments to coordination and other key goals of public organizations.

To be sure, personal ends of informal mechanisms are sometimes beneficial to the organization as a whole. For example, aspects of informal organization that enhance the self-esteem of individual members of the organization and their feeling of belonging improve morale, thereby indirectly contributing to the effectiveness of the formal organization.[7] Other personal ends are simply irrelevant to the formal organization. Only a subset of the personal uses of informalities actually conflict with the organization as a whole. Use of informal organization to protect or enhance personal position and power is a common phenomenon. The risk of such use is an everpresent weakness of informal organization.

Generally speaking, informal mechanisms are likely to be employed for personal ends that conflict with those of the formal organization when informal contacts and alliances give the individual an edge in organizational conflicts. These conditions are almost always present in organizations. In one case from the Bay Area, conflicts

over both substantive issues and the structure of power within an organization resulted in the use of informal ties to other organizations
and intraorganizational coalitions to bolster the position of one com-
batant. The result was interference with coordination and other goals
of the organization as a whole.

A high-level manager, "N," had acquired a great many more
duties than his formal job description contained, in part because of
the weakness of the organization's chief executive, "P," and the ag-
gressiveness of "N." It was clear to personnel at other organizations
that "N" was the person to see if you needed anything. "P" resigned
and an aggressive chief executive, "D," was recruited from outside
to take his place. On his arrival "D" began a reorganization to bring
"N" under control—to trim his power, in part by creating a new section that overlapped with his duties. "A," the section manager, was
overqualified for the position. "A" recognized that he was supposed
to do the best job possible but had been hired to "give 'N' an ulcer or
a heart attack, whichever came first." [8]

The new section's duties involved performance audits of the transit agencies, a task requiring field investigation. However, in an
effort to limit his effectiveness, "N" told "A" that his people could
perform their audits but were not to leave the office in doing so. After
several months of argument, "A" established the legitimacy of field
investigation for his section. When "A" did perform the audits,
however, personnel at the operators used their informal contacts with
"N" to complain. For his own purposes, "N" was quite willing to
attempt again to quash the efforts of the new section. But, given the
backing of "A" by "D," his efforts were unsuccessful.

In this case informal channels were used to obstruct rather than to
facilitate coordination. Because his personal power and position were
threatened by the new section, "N" used his informal contacts to
obstruct the execution of the formal duties of his organization. The
operators did not want the intrusion of performance audits, "N" did
not want the section to be effective; their interests coincided.

However, the question remains as to whether informalities usually
employed to achieve ends such as coordination are also alternatively
or simultaneously used for personal advantage. Informal mechanisms
promoting self-worth, for example, are specialized such that they do
not overlap with informal mechanisms used for interorganizational
coordination. The former involve intrinsic satisfactions whereas the

latter are characterized by the exchange of extrinsic benefits.[9] For strictly internal informalities, it is almost impossible to answer this question definitively. In this case, each channel has a mixture of intrinsic and extrinsic benefits. However, in the case of interorganizational informal ties, we are more confident in claiming professional motivations (extrinsic benefits) because personal needs have most likely been met in the intraorganizational informal features. Yet, as our example indicates, when personal power and position are threatened, interorganizational informal channels normally used for professional reasons may be called into service for personal ends.

One reason it is difficult to divine the motivations for the use of informal channels is that the goals of organizations are typically determined by informal processes of accommodation and coalition building.[10] For example, at one transit agency, plans were being made for a downtown "shoppers' shuttle" service. The general manager wished to retain the standard paint scheme for the shuttle buses so that they could be readily identified, while a planner argued for a distinctive color scheme so the shuttle would be attractive and stand out from the regular buses. The planner got nowhere. He began cultivating informal contacts in the downtown business community, quietly selling his plan for the distinctive color scheme, with the idea that his informal contacts would then exert pressure on the general manager to adopt his plan.[11] Certainly the planner thought his plan best, but was his motivation for using the informal network professional in nature and congruent with the formal goals of the organization, or was it for personal ends of power and position?

This is an endemic weakness of informalities but not one that negates their value for coordination. Moreover, it is no more realistic to seek to proscribe the personal uses of informal channels than to try to suppress informal organization in its entirety. As Simon, Smithburg, and Thompson note, "Not only is the formal plan always supplemented by informally-developed patterns, it is almost always contradicted in some respects by the actual patterns of behavior."[12]

A principal characteristic of informal organization is that value is accorded specific to the individual rather than attached to the position occupied. Although much of an individual's value may derive from the responsibility of his formal position, that is insufficient basis for value within the informal organization. Unlike the formal organization where individuals with presumably equivalent competence or formal training are essentially interchangeable, individuals in the informal system are valued for knowledge and skills that are rarely interchangeable. An individual's value within the informal system is based on human assets deriving from circumstance, personal skill, and motivation.

In the Bay Area transit system, one frequently sees disjunctures between formal position status and informal importance.[13] This is especially evident when an individual leaves an organization, taking with him his portion of organizational memory and his set of intra- and interorganizational informal contacts. The vacant position may be filled immediately, but the loss to the organization is not made up for some time, if at all. Take the case of the planner, who, by virtue of his informal contacts, skills, and willingness to engage in informal activities, is more important than his formal superior in determining some areas of policy. If he is replaced with another person whose formal training and background are comparable, the formal duties will still be performed, but the replacement's utility and importance will be far less until the time when he can establish his own informal status. The problem of nonsubstitutability derives from the time and investment it takes to learn the informal system; professional training does not appreciably decrease that time. The new individual may also lack the skills to work effectively within the informal system. Recall the planner at BART in this regard.[14]

Chapter 6 noted that the interorganizational informal system is benefited by a moderate degree of turnover because of the effects of cross-fertilization. However, an informal system is quite vulnerable to high rates of turnover, especially when they result in exits from the system instead of movements within the system. The more an organizational system (such as Bay Area transit) depends on informalities for coordination, the more it becomes vulnerable to these effects.

Enforceability, Time, and Accountability

Let us turn now to informal bargains. The apparent problem with informal agreements between organizations is that their enforceability as contracts is suspect and they are subject to potentially different interpretations. For example, many of BART's early plans and expectations were predicated on what it believed to be an agreement with AC under which AC would withdraw from transbay service once BART began its own transbay operations. AC did not do so. During the conflict over whether AC was obligated to withdraw, BART sent AC a copy of a 1958 report of an AC-BART liaison committee that contained statements to the effect that BART, on becoming operational, would take over transbay service. AC responded that "it was an informal conference whose recommendations its board never formally adopted."[15] Given AC's heavy dependence on its transbay revenues, it is easy to see why AC chose not to honor such an informal commitment.

On the other hand, there are informal agreements between the operators on smaller issues that involve relatively low costs and benefits to the parties involved. Agreements to match headways on BART trains and AC buses late at night to avoid stranding patrons exemplify this kind of informal agreement. However, there are also informal agreements that are activated regularly and involve large costs to the agencies involved. The AC-BART busbridge agreement is strong evidence against the argument that informal agreements are viable only when the stakes are low or when the agreement is rarely called upon. In theory, the legally binding nature of the agreement is open to question. AC does not *have* to provide buses in the event of a failure at BART, nor does BART *have* to compensate AC for services rendered. In practice, however, there have been few problems.

The AC-BART busbridge agreement works so well, in part, because no problems or real conflicts of interest have arisen where one party would be motivated to back out of its commitments. The level of trust between the relevant AC and BART personnel is sufficiently high to motivate them to avoid problems or work them out if they arise. This situation contrasts markedly with the early AC-BART agreement on transbay service.

However, given the dependence of informal agreements on the mutual trust developed through informal channels between persons, can they survive the departure of the original parties to the agreement? Is the agreement based only on a personal bond, which renders it meaningless when that bond is dissolved, or can it persist as a permanent fixture? The AC-BART busbridge agreement, at least, has persisted. It has been activated successfully many times, and its activation has involved many more personnel than the original parties to the agreement. It is recognized and accepted on both sides as a permanent operating procedure even though it has not acquired the status of a formal contract and one of the original parties to the agreement has since retired.

The time-consuming development of informal organization may also be considered a weakness. Whereas formal organizations spring almost fully formed into existence, informal organizations take time to evolve into effective mechanisms for coordination. Although it is undeniably true that no formal organization is ever designed completely,[16] formal organizations are superior to informal organizations when it comes to time of development. In the interorganizational case, extensive informal linkages must develop through a largely trial-and-error process of determining who at other agencies can expedite or treat favorably proposals from one's own organization. Once contact is made, it takes time for the requisite mutual trust to develop.[17]

In a similar fashion, informal decision processes and premises must be developed and agreed upon. They may either accompany or precede decisions on substantive issues of coordination. The import of development time was very evident in the RTA staff-level commitees. For example, in the Procurement Committee initial joint purchases took several months for completion, because procedural issues were being worked out concurrently with substantive issues. Once the informal procedures were worked out, joint purchases could be made in several weeks.

The speed of growth and the extent and stability of the interorganizational informal system depend on the presence of conditions that may or may not be possible to create. In this sense, an informal system of coordination may take more time to reach maturity than a formal system.[18] On the other hand, in the face of sufficiently complex problems, we may not at the outset be able to design completely a formal mechanism to deal with them effectively, and may have to depend on the development of informal devices, even knowing the time involved. We simply may not be able to do any better.

The relative obscurity of informal channels and norms makes them difficult to comprehend, even for insiders. Individuals interviewed for this research were as eager for me to tell them what I had discovered as I was for them to tell me about their informal connections. The informal organization is not written down on paper. Its power structure may bear little resemblance to the formal structure of an organization. Its participants, moreover, may seek to keep the profiles of the informal organization hidden from scrutiny. From the perspective of the general manager, an interorganizational informal system may threaten his control because it makes his organization more permeable by outsiders, and less subject to his immediate control.

The organization is more permeable because many more channels are opened into the organization than are designed into the formal structure. As long as informal channels are kept secret, the manager has little control over the inflow and outflow of information. Managers take this problem of permeability seriously: recall the AC planner who was fired for making a phone call to MTC. The effective manager will therefore give his qualified approval to the use of informal channels so that he can manipulate them for his own purposes, and at least will not be surprised by developments that take place through them.[19]

The relative obscurity of informal channels also creates a problem for accountability to the relevant constituencies. The essential importance of visibility to public accountability is clearly marked by various movements at local, state, and national levels in the 1970s (and earlier) for passage of so-called sunshine laws requiring public access to meetings of government bodies. The Freedom of Information Act was designed to shed more light on the decision-making processes of government.

Informal decision-making processes are often so important that formal decisions are simply ratifications of decisions reached earlier through informal means. Because accountability requires access to decision-making centers before, during, and after the actual decision making occurs, such access may be difficult to obtain if the actual decisions are being made informally.

Even if secrecy is not actively pursued, the costs of obtaining information about the contours of the informal organization remain high and may prove prohibitive to all but the most skillful and motivated citizens, preventing discovery of who made decisions, how they were made, or where the locus of responsibility is to be placed.

Thus, a wide range of problems stems from the character of informal mechanisms: their personal character, lengthy time of development, nonsubstitutability, and the relative obscurity of informal organization more generally. There are no apparent solutions to these problems, although with informal agreements at least, problems do not appear to occur frequently. Given the demonstrated utility of informal mechanisms for coordination and their apparent inevitability in any case, it may be sensible to consider these problems as costs attendant on the use of informal organization for coordination. The question remains as to whether these costs are greater than the costs of using formal hierarchies for coordination. It is a question of tradeoffs. We have to decide on the basis of particular conditions and problems found in specific situations which tradeoffs seem warranted.

Interdependence and the Multiorganizational System

An entirely different set of problems stems from the fact of a multiorganizational system, the nature of the interdependence in that system, and interaction between the two. A given organizational design, considered as an instrument, can be considered to have strengths and weaknesses only in relation to the specific set of problems it is intended to solve, or to the goals it is intended to achieve. The set of problems must be understood in order to comprehend the capacity of the design created to deal with it. Informal mechanisms are quite effective for coordination in a wide range of interdependencies. We need also consider the problems of interdependence, which are especially difficult for an informal system of coordination to resolve. To a certain extent, the problems most difficult to solve informally are no different from those that are difficult to solve in any system of coordination, formal or otherwise.

Each problem of interdependence may be conceived to have a range of alternative coordination solutions, each characterized by a particular distribution of costs and benefits to the parties involved. Where joint action is necessary for coordination, the problem is to find an alternative solution perceived by those involved to be preferable to the existing state of affairs. This is one of the key problems considered by contemporary theories of public choice.

The approach taken here is to categorize cases of interdependence by the distribution of costs and benefits (to the parties involved), characterizing their several alternative coordination solutions. Some distributions are more likely to result in coordination than others.

Much of the process of coordination involves altering or manipulating costs and benefits (either by the parties involved or by an outside party) so that the distribution becomes one that is acceptable.[20]

Table 6 shows possible distributions of costs and benefits between two interdependent organizations for alternative coordination solutions. For simplicity, costs and benefits are each treated as a single dichotomous variable. In reality, we know them to be both continuous and multidimensional. The analysis is also restricted to bilateral interdependence.

For each problem, there will likely be several alternative solutions, each with its own peculiar distribution of costs and benefits. The motivation to coordinate depends largely on the costs and benefits of alternatives. Two decisions are relevant. What is the distribution of costs and benefits of *any* solution when compared with the status quo: Is there an incentive to coordinate? If there is an incentive to coordinate, what are the distributions of alternative solutions that will be most attractive to the actors involved? At a minimum, some sort of rough symmetry between costs and benefits is required.

Distributions 1, 9, and 10 have symmetrical properties and ought therefore to be more attractive than those solutions that do not. Distribution 1 is the classic "distributive" case where both actors incur costs and receive commensurate benefits. That one might both incur more costs and receive more benefits than the other is not important. However, distributions 4, 5, 7, and 8 describe situations where at least one organization pays but receives no benefits. These are problematic distributions, having in Schelling's terminology aspects of "efficiency."[21] Insofar as coordination requires joint action, solutions with efficiency distributions are likely to be unattractive. If coordination can be achieved only through one of these distributions it is unlikely that an informal system will deal with it effectively, because informalities depend on voluntary action. As Scharpf notes, there is an important distinction

> between interactions which are intrinsically of mutual benefit to both interacting units, and those which are not. While mutually beneficial interactions (even though they may have to compete for attention within given capacity constraints) are more likely to be realized when the opportunity presents itself (Schmidt and Kochan, 1977), interactions which appear to be disadvantageous or indifferent to at least one necessary participant are unlikely to occur spontaneously.[22]

Table 6   Possible Distributions of the Costs and Benefits of Alternative Coordination Solutions to Problems of Interdependence

Distribution	Organization	Costs	Benefits
1			
	A	×	×
	B	×	×
2			
	A	×	×
	B		×
3			
	A		×
	B	×	×
4			
	A	×	×
	B	×	
5			
	A	×	
	B	×	×
6			
	A		×
	B		×
7			
	A	×	
	B		×
8			
	A		×
	B	×	
9			
	A	×	×
	B		
10			
	A		
	B	×	×

Distributions 2, 3, and 6 show another type of asymmetry, where at least one organization receives benefits out of proportion to what it pays. This type of distribution is not problematic, keeping in mind the referent of the balance of costs and benefits.

If we assume that not all interdependence will have coordination solutions conducive to voluntary action, it is important to find some way to achieve closure. One approach would be for a superior authority simply to dictate a solution to its subordinates. This is effective within hierarchies (although not without cost), but what can be done in a flat multiorganizational system? After all, a principal virtue of such systems is the absence of hierarchy.

The formal autonomy of organizations in an informal system of coordination underlies these difficulties. For coordination to occur, each organization must perceive a solution that is preferable to the existing state of affairs and to which the other can agree. Because they are formally autonomous, they cannot be compelled to accept a solution. The actors involved might themselves artificially alter costs and benefits through trading and side payments, such alteration being a typical feature of negotiated or bargained settlements, in order to move from problematic asymmetrical distributions to symmetrical ones.

Though useful, this typology suffers from oversimplification. Only relative costs and benefits were included in the scheme. That effort can be improved upon by considering the absolute sizes of costs and benefits of alternative coordination solutions. Furthermore, one problem of interdependence and its alternative coordination solutions is rarely considered in complete isolation from other such problems. Although decomposing larger problems can promote coordination, sometimes a problem of asymmetry in one area of interdependence can be corrected by including other areas of interdependence. Two organizations might seek to tie the solution of one problem of interdependence to another; if combined, the two would create the cost-benefit symmetry required. However, by doing so, they risk spillover and increasing the threshold of value agreement necessary for coordination. This can be done in time series or sequentially over time. No problem is ever really solved in complete isolation from other problems; every relationship of two actors has a history of interaction that conditions their behavior toward each other in any specific circumstance.[23]

Further complications occur when the questions of who directly benefits from coordination and who directly bears the costs are considered. Unlike the simple problems usually posed in "prisoner's dilemma" games, organizations directly involved in interdependence are rarely the only parties who bear costs and receive benefits from coordination. For example, suppose bus operators get together and develop standard formats for printing bus schedules and for delineating bus routes, standardize fares, and put together an all-inclusive schedule book for the San Francisco Bay Area. Although their riders would be the direct beneficiaries, the transit agencies would bear all the direct costs, including financial resources and loss of organizational autonomy (through conformity to common standards). The agencies might indirectly benefit through increased patronage and an improved public image; their clientele might suffer indirectly if fares or taxes were raised to cover the cost of coordination. Nonetheless, there remains a disjuncture between who pays the costs and who receives the benefits—not between the organizations involved, but between the organizations and their clientele. It could be argued that whatever benefits the clientele also benefits the operator, but when the motivation to coordinate is evaluated, clientele and operator as separate interests must be considered. The two cannot be assumed to be an identity.

When, for the alternative coordination solutions to a particular problem of interdependence the principal beneficiary is neither organization nor clientele, the problem is exacerbated. For example, in pursuing its own purposes MTC has used its resources to cajole or coerce Bay Area transit agencies into adopting standardized auditing-accounting procedures. Standardization reduces information collection and evaluation costs for MTC without providing any direct benefits to the operators. MTC bears no real costs but derives significant benefits. The operators have borne the costs of converting to a standardized format and the less tangible costs of using a system that may not be especially well adapted to their particular operating conditions. Coordination solutions with these characteristics are unlikely to be pursued by the operators on their own initiatives. In this particular case, they agreed to coordinate because of the implicit threat that funds (on which they depend) administered by MTC might be withdrawn.

A Hybrid System of Coordination: The Role of RTA

While little can be done to eliminate the weaknesses deriving from the essentially personal character of informalities, and they are perhaps best considered as costs attendant on coordination through informal systems, much can be done to alleviate the weaknesses that stem from the fact of a flat multiorganizational system. Multiorganization becomes a problem, even when informalities are well developed, when coordination solutions to the prevailing interdependence have certain asymmetries of costs and benefits, or when they require the cooperation of several agencies. In such cases outside organizations can play carefully circumscribed roles that compensate for the weaknesses of informal coordination in multiorganizational systems.

RTA and MTC play roles that permit Bay Area transit to retain an informal system of coordination while also acquiring some of the positive features of a more formal and centralized system. RTA addresses areas of multilateral interdependence that invite coordination, whereas MTC performs a multifaceted role including the representation of values that might otherwise be excluded (including regional orientations). MTC also affects coordination by altering costs and benefits of alternative coordination solutions. Said one Bay Area mayor: "Organizations such as MTC facilitate (informal) modes of coordination rather than supplant them with centrally planned and executed techniques of coordination." [24]

RTA furnishes a forum where informal processes of coordination can flourish. In Board of Control (composed of the general managers) and staff-level committees, processes of negotiation, reciprocity, and partisan discussion have been the rule. Voluntary membership of each operator has ensured that these processes dominate, because any decision agreed to by a majority can be cancelled by the withdrawal of an unhappy transit property. Concern about central domination was so strong that it took several years after formation of RTA before a joint-powers agreement was signed by all of its members. Furthermore, there has been great resistance to an independent RTA budget, or anything else that might make the RTA more than the sum of its members (even down to an unwillingness to have RTA stationery printed). This resistance has prevented RTA from developing into any sort of central coordinating entity in its own right.

Processes of mutual adjustment have remained the dominant mode of coordination. Although discussions over problems of coordination have been wide-ranging, particular emphasis has been placed on the identification of interdependence among the operators, and attempts made at coordination in areas of multilateral interdependence. RTA has also served to protect its members from perceived threats of MTC to their independence. Every staff-level RTA committee has had some tangible gains from its efforts to coordinate.

The Services and Tariffs Committee, composed of planning personnel, developed an inventory of existing system interfaces and existing transfer arrangements between the operators. It worked to distinguish regional trunkline service from strictly local service. In addition to identification tasks, the committee also developed procedures for jointly reporting patronage figures, a function that previously had been performed in different ways, if at all. It produced a report on the potential for a regional fare structure. The most concrete results of its efforts have been the development and implementation of a joint discount card for the elderly and handicapped, accepted by all Bay Area transit agencies and used successfully now for several years.

The Joint Procurement Committee has facilitated exchange of information on procurement procedures used at different operators, and, more important, it has made a number of joint purchases. It has sought to develop common equipment specifications, where feasible, to make joint procurement efforts more successful. Joint bids have been let for automotive air filters, automotive lamps, fluorescent office lamps, bus oil seals, bus batteries, brake blocks, brake drums, and other similar items. Joint purchasing has resulted in savings from economies of scale, especially for the smaller operators. It is remarkable that without prior precedent the members of RTA have been able to coordinate their activities, benefiting the public through reduced costs.

By providing a common forum, the Maintenance Committee has promoted the exchange of information among its members. The committee has visited each property to observe physical layouts and maintenance procedures. Members have exchanged information on shop safety procedures related to meeting occupational health and safety standards. They developed shared programs for training maintenance managers and mechanics. Such programs are especially valuable because the quality of maintenance at the member operators varies from excellent to poor; a great deal of learning has occurred. As with the Joint Procurement Committee, coordination has come from a recognition of mutual benefits available through joint action rather than pressures from interdependence.

The Operations Committee has considered issues similar to those at Procurement and Maintenance. Members have exchanged information on problems associated with wheelchair-equipped buses and rest-room arrangements on buslines for their drivers. They have worked on developing a common bomb-threat procedure, considered the potential for an areawide security network, and made efforts to develop common bookkeeping procedures for employee absences. The committee has also worked on a joint mid-management training program and has considered how to implement a supervisory interface between properties in areas of operational interdependence, although it has run into difficulties with their respective unions on this last issue. The most visible result of the Operations Committee's efforts has been a regional "bus roadeo," a competition among bus drivers that raises morale and encourages improvement of driving skills.

The Public Information Committee has been at least as active, producing RTA press releases and information signs for the Transbay Terminal, while planning jointly run information centers for the San Francisco Airport. Larger projects included development of a joint research and marketing program involving survey research and joint advertising. There are also plans for an integrated regional public transit telephone information center.

The Management Systems Committee began by conducting an inventory of computer hardware and software resources at each operator. It then developed a joint index of computer consultants and began exploring a consortium approach to software purchases. The members also exchanged information on the first performance audits then being conducted at their respective properties by MTC, focusing on joint measures useful for the audits.

There are other RTA activities, but these examples represent a fair sample of its coordination efforts. In certain instances RTA has picked up issues of multilateral interdependence that were not effectively addressed by the operators informally. In other areas, RTA has provided a mechanism for working out bilateral coordination problems.

RTA's greatest successes have come where all participants stand to gain and none stands to lose, such as financial savings through joint procurement, and where members have not had to spend resources above routine operating costs. Other successes have come where central operating procedures of individual members were not affected, where no procedures of any sort had been developed prior to RTA involvement, or where there was no need to surrender organizational autonomy. There has been success where significant benefits were expected with few costs, but often this has been in areas where no action had occurred before RTA's existence. Furthermore, monthly meetings of RTA's Board of Control permit MTC to keep abreast of the activities and views of top Bay Area transit officials and to communicate its views to them. Given RTA's voluntary character and the carefully guarded independence of its members, it is remarkable that it has achieved so much coordination, compensating for weaknesses of the informal system.

A Hybrid System of Coordination: The Role of MTC

Sometimes when there are no coordination solutions with a distribution of costs and benefits satisfactory to the parties involved—the status quo is preferred to change—the parties involved can alter costs and benefits to make the distribution a favorable one. In cases where they cannot, it is unlikely that coordination will occur without action by an outside party—for example, in the form of altering costs and benefits through incentives, disincentives, or some combination of the two.

MTC has used monies administered at its discretion to promote coordination among the transit agencies, occasionally making the continued flow of funds dependent on some aspect of coordination, as when MTC withheld funds until Muni established a planning function. But MTC also has used its discretionary funds positively to aid coordination between operators, by alleviating the costs of coordination for one or both agencies when it was apparent that those costs would prevent coordination from being realized. For example, MTC monies were made available to BART and AC to cover the cost of transfers between BART trains and AC buses, so that neither one would incur unreasonable costs. In another case, BART was operating at peak capacity on its Concord–Daly City line, and Greyhound wished to abandon a roughly parallel service because of the losses it sustained. Although it was in BART's interest for Greyhound to continue its service so that no patrons would be lost to the automobile, it did not have the funds to subsidize Greyhound. MTC subsidized

BART payments to Greyhound to cover its losses until BART could absorb Greyhound's passenger load. The contract between BART and Greyhound was dependent on MTC's involvement as a third party. Not until MTC altered the cost distribution could coordination occur. This moved the coordination solution (referring to Table 6) from distribution 8 to distribution 9, making adoption almost guaranteed.

This approach to resolving difficult problems of coordination creates a certain role specialization. Within the organizational system, the third party, MTC, becomes involved *only* when there is an impasse between two operators. This essentially facilitating role permits continued use of a flat informal system of coordination while compensating for some of its weaknesses. This approach is not unknown to public administration. The Model Cities program of the 1960s operated on the principle of inducement:

> If local organizations themselves will not take the measures necessary to reap the presumed benefits of coordination, then give them an inducement—in this case in the form of supplemental funds.[25]

Given the heavy workload of operational personnel, internal organizational considerations frequently take priority over efforts at interagency coordination. "Coordination is well and good, but we have an operation to run here. That is our first responsibility."[26] If a conflict occurs, external coordination will most likely run second to internal problems when it comes to allocating personnel resources. The problem is not a failure to recognize the need for coordination; it simply is not as pressing as internal problems.

Of course the problem is exacerbated when organizations encounter internal crises such as BART's tube fire and closure or AC's financial troubles resulting from Proposition 13. By supplying the necessary staff assistance, MTC has provided significant compensation where coordination is important but operators have been unable or unwilling to provide necessary resources. Such allocation has occurred on numerous occasions, especially in the activities of the RTA (which has no staff of its own).

Beyond helping to ensure the successful development and implementation of coordination solutions for problems of interdependence, MTC has other motivations for providing this assistance. It allows MTC to participate, and increases its influence over the direction of areawide activities. In some cases MTC has been able to supply better staff personnel than the operators or has provided personnel whose skills more closely match the problem at hand. By providing personnel and participating actively, MTC has been able to improve its legitimacy in the eyes of the operators. The nature of MTC's motivations, however, is less important than the fact that its provision of personnel has compensated for weaknesses of the informal system of coordination.

Of few problems involving public organizations can it be said that decisions affect only the parties to the decisions or that all significant effects are given adequate consideration. In part this is due to the necessity for incomplete analysis because of various limitations on analytic skills and resources. In part it is because of self-interest. When conflicts occur, organizations tend to pursue their own interests. The record of American chemical companies and toxic waste disposal makes this point painfully clear.

In Bay Area transit, MTC can act as a watchdog for such neglected or excluded interests, or for the larger regional interest. In the early history of BART and AC relations, the Bay Area Transportation Study Commission (BATSC) noted the scanty products of the Northern California Transit Development Project: "Our present institutional arrangements are not sufficient for a resolution of the issues." [27] The BATSC doubted coordination could be accomplished "without intervention at an effective regional policy-making level" because there is "clear evidence that regional interests often do conflict with local or departmental interests." [28] MTC eases this tendency.

Related to this difficulty is the possibility that the informal system will fail to place important issues on the agenda, as opposed to being unable to solve issues already there. In situations where benefits of coordination accrue either not at all or only indirectly to the organizations directly responsible for the costs, those issues are not likely to make their agenda. Or a problem may have significant import when considered from a regional perspective, or across the organizational system, but for any given organization its importance may be nil. No single group may be affected very strongly, but a majority of individuals may still be affected at some significant level. In such situations, the issue is not likely to be placed on the agenda by any one agency. MTC plays a positive role in coordination by ensuring that these issues are placed on the agenda and given adequate attention. It fills in gaps between the organizations in the system, by providing another point of entry for interested parties. It allows for representation of interests that is not available either at the level of the transit operators or other government agencies and also provides an appeals channel or backup forum for those who may have been unsuccessful before transit organizations.[29]

In the grant process MTC also compensates for weaknesses deriving from the multiorganizational system:

> MTC also influences state transit legislation, particularly as it affects the nine Bay Area counties. It represents region-wide interests as compared with the interests of specific operators or groups. Conversely, through TOCC [Transit Operators Coordinating Council], MTC provides an information service about pending transit legislation and its probable impacts on the operators—timely information any single operator could not easily find on its own.[30]

It has also provided a more diffuse sort of compensation for weaknesses resulting from functionally interdependent but formally autonomous organizations. The RTA was, initially at least, in large measure a defensive reaction to the then unknown but potentially serious threat MTC posed to Bay Area transit agencies. MTC's presence was itself sufficient to provoke the operators into discussion and efforts at coordination in ways they had never done before.

MTC also promotes coordination by facilitating the development of coalitions and alliances. It provides forums and opportunities for mutual discussion through hearings, committee meetings, and the like.[31] In some cases it acts as a go-between. As an aide to a San Francisco supervisor commented: "Before any action can take place, a political alliance must be created. At best, the MTC helps facilitate such alliances and coalition-building." [32]

Finally, MTC has served to foster a sense of identity on the part of local transit personnel—that they are indeed part of a regional transit system. The transit personnel have developed attitudes that recognize their organization as a component of a larger organizational system. In part this change has occurred because of intentional efforts by MTC to foster such a regional identity. In part it has resulted from the existence of the formally prescribed boundaries of MTC, which include and circumscribe the major operators, thereby establishing an arena for decision making that has definite boundaries and a definite membership. MTC activities, such as the publication of a regional transit guide and the preparation of a regional transportation plan, serve to reinforce the regional identity and the sense of interconnectedness of the operators. This development has only a diffuse effect on an informal system of coordination, but I believe it to be a significant one.

I have described the role of MTC in Bay Area transit in terms of its compensatory functions for the weaknesses of an informal system of coordination. However, an organization such as MTC is no more immune to the usual pathologies than any other public organization. It is subject to the same processes of institutionalization and goal displacement, to the same problems of self-interest and concern for autonomy and power as any other organization. The more superordinate role MTC (or any similar agency) assumes or seeks to assume, the more serious for Bay Area transit (or any similar organizational system) are the consequences of these pathologies.

> Each year the amount of money that flows through MTC to the operators has increased both in absolute terms and as a proportion of the operators' budgets. As UMTA and state funds increase relative to fare box or local revenues, MTC's power to affect operating procedures in the transit organizations is strengthened. Every dollar that flows through MTC has conditions attached, directly and potentially. For the three counties served by BART, twenty-five percent of the special half-cent sales tax collected is given to MTC to be used as a discretionary fund. One such condition placed on the redistribution of these funds is that one-third of the operating costs of the operators must be met through the fare box. AC, BART, and Muni have met this requirement and have drawn on the fund. And this is but a small part of the overall picture. By offering monetary inducements, MTC can stimulate programs that would not otherwise be attempted, and can influence existing programs and operations. Operators now tend to modify their grant proposals to conform to MTC guidelines—a practice which strengthens MTC even as it moderates potential conflict.[33]

The role of the MTC is therefore one that requires self-imposed restraint, as the operators themselves may not be sufficiently powerful to maintain an effective counterbalance. MTC will have to exercise this restraint consistently if it is to maintain its role as a compensatory and facilitating organization for the informal system of coordination without moving into the areas that are best left to that system's mechanisms. To maintain this division of labor, particularly where regional and operator interests collide, is no easy task. But it is an essential one if the MTC is to remain an asset instead of a hindrance to system reliability. As I said in the 1980 UMTA report:

> The patterns of behavior for the individual operators, RTA, and MTC are well established now. They imply a division of labor in which issues of coordination which are most appropriately addressed bilaterally will continue to be worked out between pairs of operators, either on their own initiatives or at the urging of RTA or MTC. RTA addresses issues that are best dealt with multilaterally, while MTC acts as the representative of regional interests and the goals mandated by the state and federal governments. But if issues are not resolved through the efforts of individual operators, they are likely to be picked up by RTA or MTC. We believe this means that very few problems of coordination will remain unrecognized and unaddressed. What falls through the cracks at one level is likely to be picked up at another level.[34]

Conclusion

No organizational design is without its weaknesses. In the case of informal systems of coordination, just as for formal, centralized systems, there are various sorts of weaknesses. Some weaknesses are due to the personal character of informal organization, are essentially ineradicable, and are best considered as the costs of using such a system for coordination. Other weaknesses are due to difficulties of coordinating formally independent organizations under certain conditions of functional interdependence. It is possible, however, to compensate for this latter category of weaknesses without going all the way to a formal, centralized system that would lose the virtues of the informal system of coordination while acquiring the pathologies of formal systems. Introduction into the system of third-party organizations with carefully circumscribed functions can provide this compensation, so that the positive virtues of informal coordination may be retained. In the Bay Area public transit system, the RTA and the MTC perform these compensatory functions. Because they have proved effective at this task, other organizational systems with properties similar to Bay Area transit might also benefit from the creation and introduction of comparable organizations.

8

Coordination and Tradeoffs with Other Goals

It should work here because it's a rational idea, but it won't happen because the regions in this area are so parochial and selfish.

> —Richard Sklar, (then) general manager of the San Francisco Public Utilities Commission, referring to a plan to centralize decision making for Bay Area public transit, *Oakland Tribune*, 10 September 1982

But my biggest problem would be the loss of local control. We at BART in Contra Costa County are already victims of a regional kind of government.

> —BART Director Nello Bianco, referring to the same plan, *Oakland Tribune*, 10 September 1982

Any consideration of whether a formal system of central coordination is to be preferred to an informal system of mutual accommodation and adjustment must confront the type and extent of interdependence of the components to be coordinated. Other things being equal, the more extensive the interdependence and the more it takes a multilateral form, the more appropriate would be a formal, centralized scheme of coordination. Systems described by less complex patterns of interdependence might be just as well coordinated by informal mechanisms. But other things are rarely equal.

In some cases formal solutions to problems of coordination may provide better results than informal solutions when those results are evaluated solely in terms of coordination. It is difficult if not impossible, however, to find an organizational system whose solitary reason for existence is to provide for coordination.

If what constituted an acceptable level of coordination could be ascertained, and it could be shown that additional increments of coordination necessitated lower attainment of some other important goals, we might tend to think twice about seeking that higher level. Rather than trying to achieve "optimal" coordination, we might choose to look for an organizational design that could provide an acceptable mix of goals. Such tradeoffs in goals are inevitable features of the process of organizational design. They may be set in legal terms or may have to do with the capacity of an organization to work well under one set of conditions and poorly under another. Frequently tradeoffs are no more than implicit. Sometimes they are quite explicit.

Simon describes the process as follows:

> In the decision-making situations of real life, a course of action, to be acceptable, must satisfy a whole set of requirements, or constraints. Sometimes one of these requirements is singled out and referred to as the goal of the action. But the choice of one of the constraints, from many, is to a large extent arbitrary.[1]

The problem therefore becomes one of deciding which organizational design permits the attainment of some satisfactory mix of the set of goals involved, especially where the achievement of any one goal may mean less of the others.

When we consider tradeoffs among conflicting goals, it is essential to probe deeper than simply the allocation of resources by an organization to one or another combinations of these values. The problem has to do with the design of organizational structures themselves. Superficial appearances of rationality are less important than achieving the given mix of values, whatever specific form it might take. For, as Niskanen notes, we should judge social institutions pragmatically, not in terms of the perceived rationality of their structure and procedures, but in terms of their performance in creating those conditions [we] value.[2]

If a determination is to be made of the overall effectiveness of one type of organizational system as compared with another, it is essential to state explicitly the mix of goals the system is supposed to achieve as well as the environmental constraints faced in the pursuit of those goals. What is the mix of goals that one system can provide as opposed to the mix provided by another? What other goals are important?

This chapter explores some characteristics of organizational designs that promote differentiation of services (flexibility), representation, and reliability.[3] Obviously there are other important goals, but the discussion focuses on these three because of their immediate importance to the delivery of public services, and because they adequately illustrate the problems inherent in designing organizations to achieve conflicting goals. By characteristics, I refer both to the features of individual organizations, and to those of the organizational system as a whole, including such factors as organization size, extent of formal autonomy, extent of overlap and duplication, and number of organizations within the system.

Differences in Operating Environment

Although organizations dramatically improve on the ability of the individual to make rational decisions, they are themselves subject to limits on rationality. The more complex their operating environment, the more likely organizations will oversimplify their models of reality and be correspondingly less effective. The capacity of an organizational system to match its procedures to the environment it faces—differentiation and flexibility—is therefore an important consideration.

Given the perspective adopted in this study that organizations are instruments,

there is no such thing as a "good" organization in any absolute sense. Always it is relative; and an organization that is good in one context or criterion may be bad under another.[4]

Building into an organizational design a capability for differentiating approaches as contexts vary and a capacity for flexibility in the face of changing conditions over time should improve the probability of effective performance and the "fit" of the "form" to its "context."[5] Several factors make it difficult for organizations to provide differentiated services. I suggest here some approaches that help to mitigate the effects of these factors even if they do nothing to eliminate the factors themselves. Given that this is essentially the same approach the Founding Fathers took toward the problem of faction in the design of the U.S. Constitution, it seems that I am traveling in good company.

That individual decision makers are capable of achieving no more than bounded rationality is well established. Limitations of intellectual ability, time, and other scarce resources prevent the decision maker from comprehensively evaluating all or even most possible goals, or if goals are fixed, from evaluating all possible alternatives for achieving those goals. The decision maker is therefore constrained to make most decisions at the margin and to limit substantially the range of alternatives considered.[6] It follows that after a certain level of complexity in the environment is reached, a given organization's model of reality will not become any more complex because of cognitive limitations on analysis. Even where conditions vary significantly in ways affecting the appropriateness of particular alternatives, the organization will tend to stick to the set of alternatives that it has already selected, in part because of the expense and difficulty of analysis. This can lead to forcing solutions onto areas where they are inappropriate and perhaps pathological. Asking a single organization to deliver services across several areas whose characteristics differ widely may be asking it to do too much. Rather than deliver services more effectively, it will be prone to deliver services poorly matched to the conditions of the areas it serves.

This in fact was one of the arguments made by the Antifederalists in their efforts to defeat the new Constitution proposed at the Philadelphia Convention:

> Within a large territory the various regions would strive against one another; different climates, products, interests, manners, habits, laws, would lead to discord. *How to legislate uniformly for a land so diverse?* A law which suited one part might oppress another.[7]

The Antifederalists contended therefore that the answer was a series of small republics, each of which could deal effectively with what would amount to a homogeneous population living under conditions of little diversity. The activities of government could be best carried out at the local and state levels, not at the national level.

The Bay Area transit system is marked by wide variation in the conditions facing the several operators. These conditions include technical issues to be resolved in providing service and special problems that confront each operator. Constraints deriving from formal political arrangements and clientele groups are dealt with later in this chapter, in the section on representation.

The size and shape of a jurisdiction, in concert with the existence of geographic barriers, affects the routes that can be established. These factors also influence development patterns, which in turn affect travel patterns. Among the operators, travel patterns vary a great deal in terms of off-peak travel, local versus trunkline service, number of major destinations, and length of trips. Differences between bus and rail are also significant. The latter remains fixed, the former can be modified as conditions indicate.

AC Transit operates in territory that is large in size and long and narrow in shape. There is one principal metropolitan area within its jurisdiction, Oakland, and it provides commuter service to San Francisco. On average, the population is of medium density in District One and low density in District Two. The only other operator with which AC is highly interdependent is BART. AC runs only buses, encompasses two counties, and is governed by an elected board.

Samtrans also has a geographically long and narrow jurisdiction, but has a smaller overall population, with density running from medium to low. In addition to local service, Samtrans provides trunkline service to San Francisco and the Daly City BART station, which are both at the northern end of its jurisdiction. AC and Samtrans both encompass hilly terrain. Samtrans is interdependent with BART, Muni, and Santa Clara and runs only buses. It is coterminous with San Mateo County and is governed by the county supervisors sitting as a transit board.

Santa Clara has a larger, generally flat territory. It also has the lowest population density in the Bay Area. County residents depend heavily on the automobile for transportation: only about 5 percent of the trips in Santa Clara County are made on public transit. There is a weak focus on San Jose as a destination. Santa Clara has only Samtrans (and BART at one station) to consider in problems of interdependence. It is the most functionally independent of the six operators. Santa Clara operates only buses, run as part of the county transportation agency (which is also responsible for county roads and airports).[8]

Golden Gate has the longest, narrowest territory of the six. It is bounded by hills that serve as geographic barriers. Beyond U.S. 101, it has few highways to serve. Almost all its commuters go to San Francisco, with little drop-off before that destination. There is far less indigenous employment in Marin and Sonoma counties than in San Mateo or Alameda counties. The major streets run north-south with few east-west lines of communication. Relative to the trunklines, local service demands are not very great. Neither is there much of a reverse commute. Golden Gate runs both ferry and bus service and operates the Golden Gate Bridge and its approaches. It is governed by a composite board of local Bay Area government officials, and its principal revenue is derived from tolls on the Golden Gate Bridge.

Muni contrasts with the other bus operators more than they differ from each other. It operates in a compact, almost square, geographic area, with a higher population density than any other agency. Travel destinations are widely dispersed. Furthermore, there is considerable off-peak travel by residents. Muni operates buses, trolleys, light-rail trains, and cable cars. Unlike other operators, it carries many tourists on all of its modes, not just on the famous cable cars. Muni's jurisdiction is also a focal point for other operators—BART, AC, Golden Gate, and Samtrans. Muni lies entirely within the city and county of San Francisco and is operated as a city agency (which means it must compete with other city agencies for funds), responsible to the San Francisco Public Utilities Commission and Board of Supervisors.

BART is different. It employs a heavy-rail mode and was "superimposed" on existing agencies. By the very nature of its design, it is entirely a trunkline service. It depends greatly on other operators for feeder service to its trunklines. Superimposition means that BART competes more with others than any of the other operators. It also has the largest jurisdiction of any operator, encompassing three counties. It is run by an elected board.

Consider for a moment the ramifications of these differences. High-density, compact areas are best served by grid systems of bus routes, especially where there are a number of general destination areas. Conversely, low-density areas characterized by elongated shapes are better served by looping bus routes. The former depend on close headways with frequent transfers, the latter on fewer transfers and correspondingly longer headways.[9] Travel patterns typified by long commutes along narrow corridors (such as Sonoma County to San Francisco) preclude buses from making more than one trip per peak period, necessitating split shifts for the drivers. On shorter routes straight shifts are possible. Technical requirements for equipment differ between long-haul and short-haul runs, differences ranging from seating configurations to transmission gearing and air conditioning. Maintenance requirements are also different.

Population density affects the kind and quality of service that can be offered, particularly frequency of buses. Routing and scheduling are also affected by the distribution of destinations. If destinations are dispersed, it matters whether they are along a corridor or radially distributed. The need for cooperation from other operators—high levels of interdependence—to operate one's own system effectively alters the need to consider outside factors. Organizations competing for passengers face a similar problem, as does the operator that is a focal point for the passengers of other operators. In this respect, Santa Clara can operate much more freely of other agencies than can BART or Muni. The institutional environments of the operators affect their funding and independence. AC can operate with greater independence than Muni, for example. Similarly, the number of local jurisdictions that the operator encompasses affects the complexity of its institutional environment. Complexity of this type, for example, is more characteristic of BART than of Samtrans.

General differences in operating environments cannot be analyzed apart from the major problems peculiar to individual agencies,[10] because "each operator faces uniquely different operating problems. These individual operating problems and the management regimes which have emerged to cope with them also tend to limit the areas of mutually beneficial coordination and cooperation."[11] These unique problems combine with different operating conditions to defy attention by a single management regime either simultaneously or in series. No transit agency in the Bay Area has its own problems sufficiently under control to permit it to acquire the additional burdens that would result from any formal consolidations.

At Muni, improving service standards, including operator competence and courtesy, was essential. Muni was plagued by a series of accidents. Its physical plant was badly rundown. The cable cars were in the process of a multimillion dollar restoration. Maintenance quality at Muni was also below par. And Muni had to devote time to constructing and debugging its new Metro light-rail system. Because Muni is a department within the city and county of San Francisco, it must compete for budget attention with other departments; it has no dedicated source of subsidy.

On the other hand, BART has a relatively new physical plant. Its resources have been devoted to debugging its highly complex rail system in order to improve service reliability and safety. It has also expanded its operating hours and direct service to San Francisco. Each change has required adjustments in train schedules and maintenance operations. BART management has also had two major labor strikes and a host of all-consuming technical and political problems created by the 1979 tube fire with which to contend. Their aftereffects are still being felt. BART has also had to spend resources to rebuild public confidence in the wake of its failure to deliver on the many promises made during its design and construction phase. It has had difficulties with Contra Costa County, which pays for rail service, but receives very little, and Daly City, which receives rail service but lies outside the BART district. And some effort is being made toward expanding service in BART's southern area.

Golden Gate has two thorny political problems to confront. Its widely anticipated ferry service has been plagued by problems of reliability. The gas-turbine-powered ferries are both expensive and difficult to maintain.[12] Because they have never approached the passenger load that was forecast for them, they require large subsidies. To make matters worse, the subsidies pay for service provided to relatively affluent Marin County commuters. Tied into the issue of the ferries is the levy of tolls for the Golden Gate Bridge. Once the bridge debt was paid off, toll revenues were diverted to subsidies for the buses and ferries. The ferries consume a disproportionate amount of these subsidies.

Santa Clara has had to devise an entire bus system to replace the dying private operators it supplanted. One of its major problems is to provide adequate service for transit captives in a county that has low population density and heavy reliance on automobile travel. Santa Clara is probably the antithesis of Muni in this respect. It has also had to remedy a bad management decision, made early in its history, to purchase propane-powered buses that proved unreliable.

AC, as one of the oldest operators, has its routes and clientele well ordered and deals with a stable population in most of its service area. Its primary efforts are directed to fine-tuning and day-to-day operations. For some years its maintenance program has been considered to be among the best in the country. However, in the wake of Proposition 13, AC had to devote attention to managing cutbacks, including both layoffs and service cuts. Both are highly charged political issues. It is also facing declining patronage on its transbay runs (and some other runs in the East Bay) that compete with BART service. Its declining passenger load has become its single largest problem.

In general, Samtrans has had no special problems analogous to those described for the other operators.

The interaction of operating conditions with the problems peculiar to each operator heightens the differences between agencies and the approaches they must employ to be effective. Nowhere is this more evident than in the problem of fare evasion. Muni is faced with a loss of fare revenues estimated to be 11 percent of fares collected. On the other hand, BART lost only about $1 million during a two-year period in which it collected some $90 million in fares, a little more than 1 percent. Muni uses cash fares, passes, transfers, and magnetically encoded farecards. BART uses only magnetically encoded farecards. Differences in techniques are a function of different transit modes. Each system is therefore open to unique kinds of fare evasion and fraud. Furthermore, Muni must rely on its operators alone for enforcement of its fare policies, whereas BART has its own police force, including both uniformed and undercover officers. The high usage of Muni's services precludes a self-service fare system combined with roving inspectors, such as San Diego Transit uses on its "Tijuana Trolley." Different passenger loads, types of vehicles, and fare devices make for different solutions to fare evasion. No one system can work for all.

It is simply unreasonable to expect any one set of managers to contend with so many different operating conditions and so many different urgent problems. By themselves they are complex and difficult; combined they are no less than overwhelming. The results of a consolidated transit agency for the Bay Area would be standardization, oversimplification, and de facto decentralization to an extent that would defeat the intent of such a consolidation. Even lesser plans for consolidation of pairs of operators would increase the complexity of problems to impossible levels. Where it might make sense to consolidate operators on the basis of similar operating conditions, such as Samtrans and Golden Gate, there are great differences among clientele and urgent problems. Where there is geographic contiguity (if not overlap), such as between AC and BART, differences in technology and operating conditions would make consolidation equally complex.

Consistency, Goal Displacement, and Institutionalization

So far only cognitive limitations on the ability of organizations to contend individually and effectively with variations in operating conditions have been discussed. There are also important social and psychological processes that tend to suppress differences in organizational approaches and simultaneously to produce drives for homogeneity: pursuit of consistency as an intrinsically valuable goal, displacement of goals, and institutionalization.

For some years boarding charges for bus service at Washington Metro differed among the three local jurisdictions. However, there was persistent and strong pressure on the District of Columbia to bring its fares in line with the fares in Virginia and Maryland, both by those two jurisdictions and by Metro's management. The District was pressured to raise its fares to give the three jurisdictions a consistent fare policy. The District of Columbia, however, resisted these pressures because it felt an obligation to subsidize transit services for its extensive poor population. In January 1981 the District finally came into line with the other jurisdictions, not because of a change in philosophy, but because financial constraints compelled it to do so. At last the fares were consistent.

Now, why should fares be consistent? In this case, consistency for its own sake appears to be the answer. The drive for consistency became more powerful because it occurred within the context of a single operating entity. The problem is that "the pursuit of consistency from one coordinating decision to another in central coordination often degenerates into the pursuit of some kind of superficial uniformity." [13] At Metro it was argued that different fare structures were too confusing for patrons, but it seems more likely that "limited competence and weak motivation both tempt[ed] coordination to substitute a routine yea- and nay-saying for a more creative approach to consistency and coordination." [14]

At the Metro one finds a much stronger (and more effective) drive to produce consistent fare policies than in the Bay Area transit system. This occurs even though differences in philosophy and wealth among Metro's members indicate that a differentiated fare structure would probably serve their constituencies better. In the Bay Area, MTC may push for consistency of fares, but it can only indirectly influence the adoption of such a policy by the operators. Because of its multiple independent agencies, the Bay Area exhibits less pressure for consistency in the first place, and greater ability to resist such pressure in the second, than does Washington's unified organizational structure.

Displacement of goals has to do with both Veblen's notion of "trained incapacity" and Dewey's concept of "occupational psychosis." "In general, one adopts measures in keeping with one's past training, and under new conditions which are not recognized as *significantly* different, the very soundness of this training may lead to the adoption of the wrong procedures." [15] Processes inherent in bureaucratic forms of organization tend to reinforce this propensity:

1. An effective bureaucracy demands reliability of response and strict devotion to regulations.

2. Such devotion to regulations leads to their transformation into absolutes; they are no longer conceived as relative to a set of purposes.

3. This interferes with ready adaptation under special conditions not clearly envisaged by those who drew up the general rules.

4. Thus, the very elements which conduce toward efficiency in general practice produce inefficiencies in specific circumstances. . . . These rules in time become symbolic in cast, rather than strictly utilitarian. [16]

Although Merton aimed his discussion of goal displacement at the problems of changing conditions facing one organization over a period of time and of anomaly in the face of generally applicable rules, it is not difficult to see the role that displacement of goals plays in a situation characterized by great diversity. The same problem of trained incapacity arises as does the absolutism of rules. Like a push for superficial consistency, displacement of goals weakens the ability of an organization to deliver different kinds of services where it is appropriate to do so. If several organizations are employed, each matched to a specific set of conditions, the effects of goal displacement in this sense will be minimized even though the base causes remain untouched.

If one consequence of goal displacement is the conversion of procedures and rules from utilitarian to symbolic in character, institutionalization refers to sociopsychological processes that move ultimately toward the same end:

> To institutionalize is to infuse with value beyond the technical requirements of the task at hand. The prizing of social machinery beyond its technical role is largely a reflection of the unique way in which it fulfills personal or group needs. . . . The test of infusion of value is *expendability*. If an organization is merely an instrument, it will be readily altered or cast aside where a more efficient tool becomes available. . . . The transformation of expendable technical organizations into institutions is marked by a concern for self-maintenance. . . . Various elements in the association have a stake in its continued existence.[17]

Thus Muni personnel infuse the use of a grid system for bus routing with intrinsic value; they personally identify with that particular technique. Their criticism of agencies, such as Samtrans, that do not use such a system neglects the importance of differences in operating conditions for determining the appropriate techniques.[18] The same process may also be seen in the controversy over whether to use a light-rail system or buses for public transit. Attachment to light-rail by its proponents exceeds its instrumental value for providing effective public transit.

As techniques or operating paradigms undergo a transformation from extrinsic (or instrumental) to intrinsic valuation, it becomes increasingly difficult to adapt them to different demands and different conditions. How can the effects of this process be mitigated? One approach is to minimize the variation in operating conditions faced by any one organization, so that institutionalization would have the least possible effect. Instead of consolidating organizations, organizational designers might elect to create new ones in order to match them as closely as possible to homogeneous sets of operating conditions. Attachment to particular techniques or operating paradigms will be less likely to cause serious disturbance under this arrangement. Muni's grid system is appropriate to its operating conditions, so institutionalization of that technique is not important, as long as relevant conditions do not change significantly. Even though Muni and Samtrans are interdependent, we might be slow to consolidate them, as they face such different operating conditions that differentiation of services is an important goal.

However, understanding the processes of goal displacement and institutionalization only helps explain motivations for individual or group behavior. It does not explain how they are translated into organizational behavior. Organizational goals and procedures are established by individuals who collectively have sufficient control of organizational resources to commit them in certain directions and withhold them from others.[19] This collectivity within the organization is referred to as the "dominant coalition." How is the dominant coalition linked to goal displacement and institutionalization? "So long as the organization presents favorable spheres of action to individuals in highly discretionary jobs, we have strong motivation for them to avoid decisions which would end those spheres of action."[20]

Techniques or operating paradigms with which those who comprise the dominant coalition identify will be employed by the organization. Inasmuch as the fate of the members of the dominant coalition depends on those particular techniques or operating paradigms, the more will they resist their modification or deletion. The stronger the dominant coalition within the organization the more likely it is that operating paradigms that are no longer instrumentally useful (or would be misapplied) will be retained. Retention of particular techniques serves personal or group ends; the dominant coalition provides the mechanism for their achievement. As the survival of the horse cavalry in the U.S. Army up to World War II (even after German armor and mechanized infantry had decimated the renowned Polish cavalry) attests, institutionalization and the dominant coalition combine to make even obviously obsolete operating paradigms highly resistant to change.[21]

Furthermore, by setting the goals of the organization, the dominant coalition focuses the organization's attention (which is limited by intellectual abilities and organizational resources) on particular sets of problems. It cannot deal with all problems and therefore is likely to resist the intrusion of new problems. It therefore tends to deemphasize those that do not fit its own ideas of what the organization is about, thus making differentiation more difficult.

For example, at Washington Metro the dominant coalition was composed of rail design and construction personnel at a time when private bus companies were collapsing around them amid public clamor for a public bus agency. Although its full energies were focused on the design and construction of the rail system, Metro was forced to absorb bus operations because it was the only public transit agency available.

Metro's dominant coalition regarded the buses as an intrusion and a distraction from its real goal—building a railroad. Rail was the preferred mode of transit in any case. There was real rail-bus conflict. Had Metro acquired bus operations under different conditions or at a later date, conflict likely would have been less severe, but the bus people would still have had to fight their way into the decision-making processes of the organization. As it was, bus operations were relegated to stepchild status and received little attention from Metro management. Buses are still not run as effectively as they are at AC Transit, which was established at the same time as BART, permitting it to focus all of its attention on bus operations while BART specialized in rail design and construction.

Representation

Public transit is subject to more political conflict at the local level than virtually any service, excluding police services and education. The issue is characterized by intense feelings, diversity of opinion, and substantial subsidy of capital outlays and operating costs by local taxpayers. Political differences and problems of representation are inescapable facts of transit organization, and any design that emphasizes efficiency and coordination to the exclusion of these other goals is doomed to failure, as an Oakland city councilman noted:

> Academicians seem to forget at times that we cannot begin with a clean slate. There are all sorts of problems of equity, conflicts of organizational character and methods, and diverse actors and interests involved which would mitigate against any merger or consolidation proposal. These problems and differences must be worked out.[22]

Given differences among various interests in the Bay Area transit community, representativeness is another important goal.

Public organizations "draw their support, in the coinage of taxes and political legitimacy, from the coffers of the general public,"[23] yet these organizations do not (for the most part) operate under market conditions. So consumers have only indirect influence on their activities. Moreover, because such entities operate on the basis of subsidies, those bearing the cost of subsidies and those benefiting from them may be different. Representation of these different groups is therefore especially important in the provision of public transit and other similar public services.

Because the daily operation of a modern government is impossible by direct democracy, and some delegation of authority is therefore required, a key problem becomes linking the views of those governed with the behavior of their representatives. Although several factors affect the quality of representation in any organizational system—for example, characteristics of groups, the position of groups within the social structure, and the quality of the groups' organizations[24]—in the context of a discussion of organizational design, access to decision-making points is a more important consideration:

> Power of any kind cannot be reached by a political interest group, or its leaders, without access to one or more key points of decision in the government. . . . The key decision points may be explicitly established by the formal legal framework or they may lie in the gaps and interstices of the formal structure, protected by custom or semi-obscurity.[25]

Group characteristics are outside the scope of this study. As my concern is with the impact of organizational design on representation, I focus on the problems of access and accountability: What features of an organizational system are particularly effective for promoting access and accountability? What changes can be wrought in the configuration of the organizational system to improve existing access and accountability?

Another argument made by the Antifederalists in support of small republics was their capacity for ensuring "a strict responsibility of the government to the people." [26] The problem of a republic is to make the representatives responsible to their constituents. Toward that end, short terms of office, frequent rotation, and numerous representatives contribute, but are insufficient to ensure it: "Effective and thoroughgoing responsibility is to be found only in a likeness between the representative body and the citizens at large." [27] According to Melancton Smith, representatives "should be a true picture of the people; possess the knowledge of their circumstances and their wants, and be disposed to seek their true interests." [28] It was important to minimize the diversity of interest contained within a particular jurisdiction for it was possible for governmental actors to know clearly the interests of their constituents only under those conditions. This point continues to be relevant. Smaller jurisdictions not only promote greater access to governmental actors but the greater ability of those actors to comprehend the interests of their constituents as well.

A defining feature of the federal and state governmental systems in the United States is that they contain a multiplicity of points of access. This is no less true for local government and public transit agencies as they exist in the San Francisco Bay Area and in the Washington, D.C., metropolitan area, where one finds not only multiple independent agencies, but significant overlap among those agencies as well. In systems characterized by mutual adjustment processes "almost any value that even relatively small numbers of citizens moderately or strongly wish to see weighed into the policy-making process will be weighed in at some value significantly above zero," [29] because processes of mutual adjustment (characterized by multiple independent organizations) permit multiple points of access.

Clearly, a principal advantage of multiple points of access to decision making is the increased probability that one will find someone congenial to one's point of view who also happens to be in a position to make decisions. This is one of the underlying features of Lindblom's disjointed incremental decision-making system. "Multiplicity copes with the inevitability of omission and other errors in complex problem solving." [30] Multiple access points are of course simply a form of organizational redundancy, which is most effective when domains of the access points overlap. However, multiplicity can be effective, even when there is no overlap, through the informal application of pressure from one organization to another. As Lindblom notes: "multiple decision makers . . . will compellingly call to each others' attention aspects of the problem they themselves cannot (or will not) analyze." [31]

Although, over time, the fact of multiple independent organizations may tend to promote parochial interests at the expense of more broadly defined "public" interests,[32] it is not the case that where differences in interest exist consolidating those organizations will decrease or eliminate them (or, for that matter, the conflict resulting from them).[33]

Formally, AC is supposed to provide transit service for a specific geographic area. But within the larger Bay Area transit system, it represents the views of its patrons as opposed to the patrons of BART. The *Oakland Tribune* reported the comments of AC's (then) general manager, a long-time participant in Bay Area transit politics:

> "If we become an adjunct of BART or part of a consolidated system, we might be put on a back burner," Nisbet said. "We worry that the needs of people who depend on AC might be overshadowed by a glamorous rail system that serves a different clientele. White, middle-class people going to San Francisco might benefit, but it would be at the expense of service we provide to lower income people who may ride a bus for only a few blocks or who may have no need to ride BART." [34]

Or take MTC. While formally playing the role of a Management and Planning Organization for the nine Bay Area counties transit systems, MTC also acts informally as a lobbyist on behalf of the Bay Area in the state and federal capitals, and within the Bay Area represents regional interests.[35]

Although some in the public administration are prone to dismiss conflict between organizations as an artifact of their independence, conflict often reflects basic underlying differences among the clientele they serve. However,

> even single organizations will often not pursue logically consistent policies because there is no way to aggregate the preferences of a few

individuals—say members of a city council, school board, or legislature—so that the resulting outcomes of decision-making processes
are logically consistent with each other.[16]

In such cases merger does not eliminate conflict; it often elevates
it beyond its original level by predicating successful coordination on
agreement across a wider range of values, and by creating a zero-sum
game. It reduces the potential for successfully decomposing complex
sets of problems, and makes their solution more difficult. Certainly
conflict among local jurisdictions in Washington Metro has not been
eliminated by the fact of a single operating organization.

When interests are represented by separate organizations, it is
relatively simple to ascertain the agendas of those organizations.
Conflicts between organizations tend to be out in the open and are
therefore more easily comprehended than when they occur within
single organizations where different interests may be represented by
informal factions. Conflict within organizations may also result in internal sabotage. Therefore, in situations where very real differences in
interest exist it may be better to retain multiple independent organizations in order to contain and manage conflict more effectively.

For example, at Golden Gate there are conflicts at the board level
that frequently revolve around differences in interest between the
northern counties (Sonoma, Marin, Mendocino) and San Francisco.
Where San Francisco, in order to alleviate traffic congestion and
parking problems, seeks to stem the tide of automobiles into the city
by charging higher tolls on the Golden Gate Bridge, the northern
counties (especially Marin and Sonoma) seek to maintain lower tolls
to facilitate that access for their constituents. This conflict over-
shadows and colors other issues at Golden Gate.

Informal organization facilitates representation in two ways. It
plays an indirect role by coordinating multiple independent organizations, thereby making possible the coexistence of effective coordination and multiple points of access. It also directly affects representation by providing access to decision making through informal
channels that complement formal channels. This role is performed in
two ways: when individuals or groups develop informal ties to decision makers, and when other organizations (such as city governments) make informal connections with transit organizations and are
thereby better able to represent their own clienteles.

Sometimes elected governing boards of organizations are less important than their general managers and staffs as points of access to the decision-making process. Administrators frequently control their boards to such an extent that they become little more than rubber stamps for staff policies.[37] Certainly this was the case during one general manager's tenure at AC, and for one at Metro as well. In fact, it is a common drive for general managers to seek to control their governing boards. To the extent they are successful, they eliminate a great deal of uncertainty from their immediate environment. However, simultaneously, they reduce the board's representative function and increase the importance of public access to the staff.

Control of governing boards appears to be enhanced by several factors, including nonpartisan elections, lay board members, and highly complex technical issues. Established informal norms against serious questioning of management also play an important role. In the case of AC transit, board members who tried to play activist roles were sanctioned informally by other members. The ability of the board to perform its representative function is also limited by the general manager's ability to monopolize expertise and information. Recognizing that monopoly, people from outside the organization, say from MTC, who have difficulty working on programs with the general manager and staff will go directly to board members with information on these programs, apprising the general manager of their action, but simultaneously weakening his hold on the board.[38] The problem of monopoly of information is especially important, because, unlike legislative bodies such as the U.S. House of Representatives, these boards have no full-time professional staffs to provide them with independent sources of information and advice.

Issues of representation were frequently raised in the early organizational planning and development of both BART and AC, issues that remain at the heart of the current organizational arrrangements. "Important people in Contra Costa County opposed AC district formation because they feared domination by downtown Oakland."[39] The proposed AC district was generally well received in Contra Costa County, but business interests were more ambivalent:

> The chairman of the County Board of Supervisors, H. L. Cummings, opposed the ACTD [Alameda-Contra Costa Transit District]. This development-oriented activist thought the East Bay district benefited only downtown Oakland; he also objected to the structure of representation on the board of directors, which, Cummings felt, favored Ala-

meda County. . . . The East Bay district plan was geared to taking over the Key System which did not serve central Contra Costa. His county's prospects for service in an East Bay district were very uncertain.[40]

Business groups favored BART and opposed the formation of AC fearing that it would be dominated by Alameda County. "Moreover, these opponents feared the unlimited taxing power granted to the district."[41] In fact, in 1959, after the formation of AC, Contra Costa seceded from AC, but in 1960 some of the cities that had received Key System service rejoined the district. Cummings "stood for BARTC's [BART Commission's] plan because it offered the promise of service for Contra Costa."[42] Perhaps ironically, as implemented, BART provides rail service only to Richmond, which was already well served by the Key System and then AC. And it was not until 1980 that Richmond began receiving any direct service to San Francisco. But, at the time, "BARTC's plan offered a more attractive political and transit vehicle for Contra Costa's development aspirations."[43]

Officials in San Francisco were concerned that enabling legislation for BART was so structured that the city would not receive services commensurate with its financial contributions.[44] Peninsula speakers insisted that peninsula communities should not be forced to accept a regional rapid transit system without their explicit consent.[45] "A councilman from the peninsula city of San Carlos told the hearings that his people questioned the benefits regional transit would bring to them," given the economic and demographic changes occurring in San Mateo County. They were no longer simply a bedroom community for San Francisco.[46] Now, of course, the residents of San Mateo County have no voice on the BART board because the county withdrew from BART in 1962. And although they pay no taxes to subsidize BART's operations, they benefit from the presence of the BART Daly City station.

The disjuncture between those receiving services and those paying for them is evident in a report released in 1957 by the Commonwealth Club of San Francisco. It questioned the construction of a rail line from San Francisco to Marin that would make up some 16 percent of the overall construction costs, yet would serve only an estimated 4 percent of the population, and furthermore would make up only about 3 percent of the assessed valuation of the BART district.[47]

Conversely, the southern section of BART's East Bay line was added to the original plan in order to make Alameda County's share of the construction proportional to its financial contribution.[48] A similar circumstance has obtained in the scheduling and implementation of construction for the Washington Metro Rail system. In these examples, the independence of the local jurisdictions permitted them to exercise a kind of veto over plans that went against their interests, whereas in the case of Contra Costa County the fact of overlapping transit organizations gave the county interests a choice of plans to support.

The existence of multiple independent organizations in the same system not only provides more points of access to decision making by interested parties but also means that those organizations may themselves act as representatives of affected interests. The transit operators provide a focus for the organization of interests. The relations of the MCTD and Golden Gate are instructive on this point. MCTD was a paper organization that generated tax revenues and was eligible for MTC-administered funds. MCTD contracted with Golden Gate for local service in Marin County. An annual battle occurred between MCTD and Golden Gate for Transit Development Act funds allocated for use in Marin County. If MCTD got the money, it went into local service. If Golden Gate got the money, it went into commuter service. Without the existence of both organizations with overlapping interests, it seems probable that one or the other sets of interests would have been dealt out of the game. Each championed the interests of the groups it perceived to be its clientele. But MCTD went out of existence in 1984.

This contrasts sharply with the situation at Metro, at least within the District of Columbia, with a single planning entity: "Blacks in southeast Washington, for example, probably considered the rearrangement of their transit system unreasonable—and so it was, from their perspective and for their interests. Yet it made good sense for long distance commuters."[49] The existence of MCTD in overlap with Golden Gate helped to ensure that local clientele were not ignored in favor of long-haul patrons: "A monopoly bureau is likely to tailor programs for a specific interest group, while overlooking other groups' interests." In terms of representation,

> Whatever the cause of selective orientation, the political costs of monopoly bureaus in heterogenous task environments can be substantial.

To those not in the chosen clientele group, bureaucratic behavior may appear arbitrary and capricious. . . . Multiple bureaus, using personnel with different expertise, with different equipment, and with diverse programs will satisfy a broader range of persons.[50]

Overlap of organizational jurisdictions promotes representation of diverse interests in two ways. As in the case of the BART-AC overlap, patrons are offered a choice, and through competition the quality of service is maintained or improved. As in the case of MCTD and Golden Gate, overlap resulted in the provision of services to competing interests. In the first instance one set of interests is better served by organizational service competition, whereas in the second divergent interests are served better by competition at the planning stage.

Organization size also enters into issues of representation and problems of access. The larger the organization, the more difficult it is to reach those individuals with sufficient discretion to make a decision. There is a basic tension between limiting the span of control within an organization and the number of levels through which a matter must pass before it can be acted upon.[51] It stands to reason, therefore, that if the span of control is held roughly constant while the size of the organization increases, the number of layers in the organization hierarchy will have to increase. Simultaneously, in a single large organization, the number of individuals responsible for particular areas will be fewer than in several smaller organizations. After all, a principal reason for consolidation is to eliminate redundant administrative positions, thereby reducing the number of accessible decision points while increasing the number of layers.

Local control of government functions *is* decreased by larger organizations: "I have learned that the larger the government entity, the more difficult it is to communicate your needs and solve your problems. Integration of transit operators would make them more remote than they already are."[52] From the standpoint of representation it is more useful to have six organizations with six boards of directors and six staffs to serve the Bay Area than a single consolidated entity or a consolidation of any subset of those six.

Ostrom, Tiebout, and Warren have referred to large organizations designed to deal with metropolitanwide problems as "gargantua." They contend that

gargantua, with its single dominant center of decision-making, is apt to become a victim of the complexity of its own hierarchical or bu-

reaucratic structure. Its complex channels of communication make its
administration unresponsive to many of the more localized public interests in the community.[53]

The existence of multiple independent organizations or multiple independent, overlapping organizations makes possible more points of
access to the decision-making process. It increases the probability
that through sheer numbers different interests will find someone congenial to their points of view. It increases the probability that these
differing points of view will be forcefully represented and makes
more probable that minority sectors will have some say over activities that affect their lives. However, multiorganization is no guarantee of responsiveness. The likelihood of response is simply improved. "The multiorganizational system [is] not behaviorally more
responsive to clientele, but it provide[s] a richer set of options and
more resistance to reducing that set."[54]

Reliability

In the public administration an emphasis on efficiency is
often closely allied with a focus on coordination. Although concern
for efficiency is largely directed toward private organizations, public
organizations have never escaped this orientation, especially in the
post–Proposition 13 era. I understand that any given decision can be
described as efficient

> if it achieved the greatest possible results with given opportunity
> costs, or if it achieved a given level of results at the lowest possible
> opportunity cost.[55]

By no means is concern for economic efficiency misplaced, but a sin-
gular worry about efficiency to the exclusion of other goals is at best
problematic. In part, economic efficiency has gained a certain pre-
eminence because of all possible values used to evaluate organizational performance, it is probably the most easily understood and
measured.[56]

Concern for economic efficiency is often closely related to movements to consolidate apparently messy organizational systems that
possess varying degrees of competition and duplication and overlap.

However, autonomous organizations in the same organizational system, especially when they are characterized by overlap, provide benefits that would be absent from a system without those characteristics. It is not even clear that such a system is any less efficient than a consolidated arrangement.[57] Obviously it is important to look beyond economic efficiency.

Landau has argued persuasively that the pursuit of reliability by organizations may well prove more beneficial in the long run than concern for efficiency. Instead of managing for success, Landau asserts that we are better off managing to protect against failure.[58] Although failure may come from many sources, concern for reliability recognizes the essential fallibility of human organization, whatever its source. Where the provision of services is essential to the public welfare, concern for reliability is not a luxury but a necessity. Inexpensive operation of public transit or any other public services is of little utility if it is prone to unmitigated failures.[59]

It is no less an error to assume that reliability can be obtained through the perfection of the parts of a system:

> In public administration the standard policy for improving the performance characteristics of an agency has rested upon the classical axiom that the reliability and efficiency of an operating system, man or machine, is dependent on the reliability and efficiency of each of its parts, including linkages.[60]

The theory of redundancy sets aside the "doctrine that ties the reliability of a system to the perfectibility of its parts and thereby approaches the pragmatics of a system in action more realistically."[61] With the development of certain redundancies, it is possible to construct a highly reliable system from basically unreliable parts. The probability of system failure decreases exponentially with simple increases of redundancy. Redundancy becomes increasingly important as the interdependence of system components increases, because the failure of any one component will send shocks rippling through the system. The 1983 strike at Chrysler's Ohio door subassembly plant shut down six other assembly plants at an estimated loss of $75 million, all because there was no reserve inventory of doors, a tactic intentionally pursued by Chrysler management in an effort to improve efficiency. The organization had voluntarily stripped itself of its own redundancy.

In the detection of errors, overlapping competing organizations generate far more information than in situations characterized by monopoly organization, a fact duly taken into account in the unorthodox administrative style of Franklin Roosevelt. Once an error does occur, insofar as the organizations are independent but duplicate each other, one can provide emergency backup for the other.

In public transit, duplication of services by two agencies does not necessarily mean that they are ill-coordinated nor does it mean that waste is involved. It makes sense, however, to specify the failures redundancy is intended to protect against. In the Bay Area transit system there is the potential for both technical and organizational failures. Technical problems have to do with failures of equipment, including train breakdowns and tunnel emergencies for BART and Muni; problems with the Golden Gate and Oakland Bay bridges that would prevent traffic from crossing them, along with closures of other major arterials such as Highway 101; and weather or mechanical problems that would prevent Golden Gate's ferries from operating. Organizational failures include shutdowns due to labor slowdowns and strikes.

BART and AC transbay services are both organizationally and physically independent. BART's trains cross the bay in a tube resting on the bottom, while AC buses use the regular traffic lanes of the Bay Bridge. If both used the bridge, and the bridge was obstructed, the fact of two different modes with overlapping service would be useless. However, both AC and BART have been able to backup each other on numerous occasions.[62] BART and Muni are able to provide backup for each other in a similar manner in San Francisco, although the fact of shared stations diminishes their physical independence. If the Golden Gate Bridge is forced to close, its ferries can transport a portion of the transit load, and vice versa.

Organizational failures have resulted from labor slowdowns and strikes. The Bay Area is characterized by multiple operators with different unions. Washington Metro, a unified operating authority, has a single union for both rail and bus modes. A comparison of the effectiveness of each system during labor strikes indicates the value of redundancy.

In 1979 and 1980, transit strikes in Los Angeles and New York crippled public transit. Despite strikes at BART in 1979 and AC in 1974 and 1977, for the most part people dependent on public transit were still able to get around. The organizations are separate. No union local represents workers at more than one operator. In fact, workers at some operators are represented by more than one union. The Bay Area has several different unions, not simply locals of the same union. The contracts negotiated have different provisions and different renewal dates. Even if one union strikes a given operator, other unions at that operator have not been likely to go on strike, let alone unions at the other operators. For example, at Golden Gate bus drivers and ferry personnel are represented by different unions. When ferry workers struck in 1979, the buses continued to roll, providing necessary backup services.

Although Metro may have a capacity similar to the Bay Area for providing backup to protect against technical failures, it does not have the ability to deal with organizational failures caused by labor problems. Apparently the development of a single union occurred with the blessing of the Metro management, perhaps because of the greater simplicity of dealing with only one labor union. "Of course when a strike does occur, we can confidently predict that it will be more disruptive than those in the Bay Area because of the combined effect of nonredundant service and unified union."[63] And so has been the case.

As we have seen, informal organization compensates for the weaknesses of an organizational system characterized by multiple, formally independent organizations, by providing a coordination mechanism to deal with the system's interdependence. Informal organization also compensates for the problems created by multiple overlapping organizations through personal trust and reciprocal relationships, thus helping to stabilize a redundant system. Other factors also tend to improve the stability of redundant systems:

a. Legal complications that make merger difficult and expensive—for example, when jurisdictions overlap only partially.

b. Strong support of individual organization clientele.

c. Sound financial condition of the organizations involved.[64]

Bendor also concluded:

Redundancy is more stable, and therefore more practical if overlapping bureaus do not have a powerful superior authority close at

hand. . . . Though a few higher-ups may promote redundancy, I believe superiors more often reorganize duplication out of existence than
they promote it. For this reason redundancy is probably more feasible
among special districts than among regular departments, because districts are less frequently embedded in hierarchies.[65]

Redundancy presents managers with a more demanding arrangement
to manage. Conflicts and confusions over channels and lines of authority occur frequently. Also justifying a redundant system to a pe-
nurious public is increasingly difficult. Therefore, whatever assists a
system of independent organizations to persist will also help to maintain the stability of redundancy, thereby promoting system reliability.
By providing coordination mechanisms, informal organization indirectly helps to maintain redundancy by maintaining the conditions
that facilitate it. Although a centralized system may support some
redundancies, a decentralized system is far more likely to provide the
conditions necessary for long-term support. One cannot imagine a
single organization having the excess capacities of AC and BART for
transbay service for very long. In fact, the elimination of that redundancy has been a primary argument made in favor of consolidation of
the two organizations.

Conclusion

The argument made in this chapter differs significantly from
those made in previous chapters. Earlier chapters examined the capacity of flat informal systems to provide effective coordination
under certain conditions of interdependence. This chapter's concern
turned to goals other than coordination. I suggested that where a mix
of goals is sought, it is not unusual to achieve higher levels of some
values at the expense of lesser amounts of other values. If we assume
that under some conditions formal centralized systems provide better
coordination than an informal system, is that additional increment of
coordination achieved only at the cost of other goals, such as differentiation, representation, or reliability? An informal system of coordination, by permitting multiple independent organizations, under
the conditions I have identified—complex operating environments,
diverse interests, and potential technical and organizational fail-

ures—tends to promote these three goals more effectively than a formal centralized system, while simultaneously providing at least a satisfactory level of coordination. Ultimately, however, the question remains as to which tradeoffs among goals one wishes to make in any particular organizational design. As Simon has noted, such tradeoffs are a function of individual motives that lead people to select some goals rather than others as premises for their decisions.[66]

9

Conclusion

Those who were best at planning and coordination at MAP were those who felt that complete overall planning and coordination by a central directorate was quite impossible.

—Ely Devons, *Planning In Practice*

In cases in which coordination can in fact be reasoned (where there are agreed and workable criteria), then it need not after all be central. . . . Thus when the situation is most conducive to successful centrality, centrality is dispensable.

—Charles E. Lindblom, *The Intelligence of Democracy*

Unnecessary Surgery

Physicians are censured for performing unnecessary surgery. Attorneys are discouraged from frivolous litigation. Should those who pursue unnecessary reorganization be looked upon any differently? Reorganization has no intrinsic value; it is used simply to fix something that is diseased. It follows that before any modification of an organizational system is attempted, the ailment to be relieved should be carefully diagnosed. Then specific cures for specific problems may be proposed, selected, and implemented. Careless tampering with a healthy organizational system may destroy its vitality and bring into being new and unexpected problems.

Successfully maintaining a loosely coupled organizational system is very different from decentralizing an existing system that has been organized as a formal hierarchy. It is more difficult to flatten a system that has been peaked than to maintain an existing loosely coupled system. This fact alone should make us think very carefully about consolidating loosely coupled systems; should we decide eventually that we have erred, we may not be able to retrace our steps.

Despite surface appearances of fragmentation and ill-coordination of services and resources, given the extent of its interdependence, the Bay Area transit system is highly coordinated and appears to be becoming more so. Integration is made possible by an extensive series of informal relationships between key actors in the system, founded on and buttressed by informal conventions, and supplemented by informal agreements.

These informalities develop because individual actors in the system seek ways to reduce uncertainty resulting from interorganizational interdependence. Uncertainty is produced because organizations, as open systems, depend on each other, but cannot control the behavior of others that affects them. Organizations, as problem-solving entities, operating under norms of rationality, seek to reduce uncertainty. In such circumstances, because absorption or annihilation of other organizations is not an option often available in the public domain, the principal avenue for reducing uncertainty is coordination.

In the absence of formal coordinative arrangements, informalities make coordination possible. Because of these informalities, fragmentation of formal organizational arrangements in Bay Area transit does not present a serious problem for coordination. In fact it is more accurate to refer to Bay Area transit as a loosely coupled organizational system, whose coordinative arrangements match its relatively low level of interdependence. Attempts to integrate formally the currently independent actors would surely disrupt the existing informalities that currently make coordination possible, without any guarantee of improvement.

The findings of this study, although preliminary and suggestive rather than conclusive, have a series of ramifications for organizational systems outside of public transit. Although by organizations I am referring to administrative organizations in the public domain, with careful attention to the differences between them, these findings should also be applicable to other kinds of organizations. To make a definitive statement regarding the relative effectiveness of one organizational design versus another, some sort of census of the problems that the system faces, and a track record of efforts to deal with those problems, would be useful. This study did not develop such a census, nor did it have a set of experimental conditions in which two (or more) different organizational designs confronted precisely the same set of problems under the same conditions. The occasional rough comparison between the more centralized Washington Metro and the decentralized Bay Area transit system, however, was possible.

Most areas of interdependence that could be identified in the Bay Area transit system required only unilateral or bilateral action; relatively few demanded attention on a multilateral basis. The Bay Area transit system could be decomposed into its several components; intracomponent linkages were indeed much stronger than intercomponent linkages. In fact, the overall level of interdependence was lower than appearances indicated: organizations in the system could behave independently, for the most part, with little effect on each other. Where interdependence in the system was relatively higher, the corresponding density of informal channels was greater than where interdependence was lower, consistent with the hypotheses initially posed in this study.

It would be helpful to develop some way to ascertain more precisely the interdependence between any two (or more) organizations. What percentage of decisions made in any given organization must consider the behavior of other organizations in order to approach some minimal level of rationality? Those percentages could then be distributed into bilateral and multilateral categories. In theory, at least, thresholds at which it would be sensible to consolidate formally could be established, based on analysis of a number of cases with different such percentages and organizational designs.

It also would be useful to develop a distribution of all problems of interdependence requiring coordination solutions by their state of resolution, such as that shown in Figure 9. Which organizational design permits approaching the theoretical limits of coordination most closely? If it was found, for example, that a large proportion of the problems faced by an organizational system fell into the right side of

		Resolved	Unresolved
Action Required	Unilateral		
	Bilateral		
	Multilateral		

Figure 9   Distribution of Problems Requiring Coordinated Solutions

the figure, it might be appropriate to revamp the system. But by what criteria would the success of the system be evaluated? And what allowances should be made for variation in importance of the problems? Moreover, if it were possible to devise such a census, then there would already be sufficient knowledge to program decision making for the system, making choice among alternative designs a moot point: a programmed structure would be optimal.

More generally, I suggest that coordinative arrangements be adjusted to the interdependence characterizing any particular system, using the general rule that no more machinery be used than is absolutely necessary to provide a satisfactory level of coordination. On this basis alone, other things being equal, informal mechanisms are to be preferred to formal coordinative arrangements for any given set of interdependence problems. The demands they place on the participants, both cognitively and politically, are less than those imposed by formal systems of coordination. They are also less prone than formal mechanisms to increase artificially the interdependence in the system.

However, informal mechanisms are proposed neither as a panacea for all the ills of formal organizational arrangements nor as appropriate devices for coordination in all cases. Certainly, they are not the pathological developments that they were once thought to be, nor are their beneficial effects merely incidental. Informal channels, conventions, and agreements are capable of performing many of the functions of formal mechanisms, as well as some functions formal devices cannot. They do persist apart from formal structures, and they are far more effective coordinative devices than previously supposed, even where organizations actively compete or where significant resources are involved.

Although informal coordinative systems surely appear "messy," with inconsistency, conflict, competition, and duplication and overlap as major characteristics, coordination occurs where needed. And, as Simon has demonstrated, much problem solving that ultimately leads to superior results is very messy in the process.[1] Coordination as an end product should not be confused with coordination as a process. There is, indeed, more than one way to skin a cat. Coordination takes place through many processes, some of which are not usually identified with it. The lesson is clear: bearing in mind always their peculiar operating conditions, *organizational arrangements should be judged by their results, and not by their apparent rationality.* Substance is to be preferred to procedure: in considerations of coordination, concerns about superficial consistency, neatness, and the elimination of redundancy are badly misplaced.

Limits to Informal Coordination

Aside from their considerable instrumental value, informalities do have limits, but ironically those limits have not been as systematically explored as those of formal mechanisms. In this study I explored those limits of informalities that are related to asymmetries of costs and benefits in coordination solutions. Because no organizational design is without costs or tradeoffs, that informal mechanisms have costs attached to them is no more an indictment than it would be of formal mechanisms. The coordinative capacity of informal systems can be enhanced by an organization that plays the role of facilitator in situations where asymmetries of costs and benefits render coordination improbable among formally independent organizations. This organization could also represent systemwide interests. Such a hybrid system compensates for the weaknesses of informalities without exhibiting the pathologies of formal, centralized systems of coordination. Certain conditions that increase both the capability and opportunity of actors to interact informally were identified and suggestions as to how to create and manipulate those conditions were made.

The central focus was on a multiorganizational system whose component organizations were characterized by similar technologies, common professional backgrounds, and generally similar goals, all of which facilitate the development and maintenance of informal mechanisms. In multiorganizational systems composed of organizations employing different technologies, whose members have divergent backgrounds and whose goals are dissimilar, can a similar quality of informal coordinative arrangements be expected? Can sanitation districts interdependent with highway departments reach informal accommodations as effectively as interdependent transit agencies? Can police departments informally cooperate with recreation agencies as well as BART and Muni work together? Will the same sorts of informal mechanisms develop, and if so, will informal coordination result? I believe they will, wherever there is interorganizational interdependence and some common interest can be established between the organizations involved.

I hypothesized that problems of interdependence involving only two organizations could be more easily resolved than those involving more organizations, irrespective of the type of coordination process. Informal mechanisms, for various reasons, were seen to be particularly well suited to coordinating bilateral interdependence. Their record in areas of multilateral interdependence is less clear, but there appears to be reason for optimism. Even though Bay Area transit is a multiorganizational system, it is characterized primarily by a series of bilateral interdependencies, which existing informalities handle effectively. The system's ability to coordinate the multilateral interdependence that does exist is improved by a voluntary association that easily permits needed action. For multiorganizational systems characterized primarily by multilateral interdependence, informal mechanisms may be less effective. However, Seidman has documented the relative impotence of formal interagency coordinating bodies for handling multilateral problems, and the importance of informal mechanisms for the same.[2]

As Landau and Stout have pointed out,[3] many problems endemic to large-scale organizations are mistakenly attributed to faulty or inefficient implementation of "good policy," when they actually result from levels of value disagreement or lack of knowledge that would be very difficult for any organizational design to contend with. That is, it is the end product of coordination that is difficult to achieve under the particular circumstances and the character of the problem confronted, regardless of what coordination process might be employed. However, instead of taking these difficulties into account, organizations are frequently redesigned to increase "rationality," to the point of overdetermination. Ironically, this lowers capacities to manage and results in less effective coordination. This action rests on two mistaken assumptions: better coordination is always possible, and it is possible only through centralized formal arrangements.

In a similar manner, it is a mistake to assume that problems afflicting individual organizations will be solved once those organizations are merged. In fact, the probability of solution may be diminished because the attention of top managers will be stretched further than before, or because of problems of institutionalization and dominant coalitions. Yet it is precisely this assumption that is currently being made with respect to the woes of individual transit operators in the Bay Area.[4] Poor decisions may be made in any form of organizational arrangement.

Only some coordination can take place by central directive, or indeed need take place by centrality. In fact, Arrow has argued that (formal) organizations are only a means of "achieving the benefits of collective action in situations where the price system fails."[5] And even a price system cannot realize the benefits of coordination without "a well-designed system of rights and liabilities"[6]—for example, informal norms and conventions. The failure Arrow finds absolutely central to understanding organizations is uncertainty about cause-effect relationships. In part, uncertainty derives from the inadequacy of information resulting from the absence of reliable channels of communication.[7] Informal channels help to redress this problem.

Where centralized coordinative arrangements are in place, their effectiveness often depends on largely informal processes. Lindblom has even suggested that where the conditions essential for successful central coordination exist, no central coordination is necessary.[8] Where agreed and workable criteria exist, central coordination is at its best. "At the same time, under these circumstances, any competent mind will be brought by application of the criteria to the same decision as would be reached by any other competent mind employing the same criteria."[9] In principle, at least, multiple actors (or organizations) should be as satisfactory as one for the problem of coordination.

While the coordinative capacity of systems of mutual adjustment has been made clear by Lindblom and others, for the most part only the processes have been specified, not the mechanisms through which they take place. This study's findings lead me to conclude that informalities provide the foundation that makes possible those processes of mutual adjustment described by Lindblom. Their influence is pervasive in such systems, just as it is in centralized structures. Informal channels facilitate the exchange and acquisition of information essential to coordination through mutual adjustment. Personal trust developed through informal relationships acts as a lubricant for mutual adjustment. Informal conventions preclude some behaviors, establish commonly understood coordination procedures, legitimate the use of sanctions if those boundaries are crossed, and frequently define appropriate sanctions.

It is equally important to note that much, perhaps most, coordination of human behavior occurs through mechanisms other than formal hierarchies. Human behavior regularly is coordinated without conscious thought, through habit. Conscious or unconscious obedience to rules or laws has a similar effect. As Tocqueville noted more than one hundred fifty years ago:

> Nothing is more striking to a European traveler in the United States than the absence of what we call the government, or the administration. Written laws exist in America, and one sees the daily execution of them; but although everything moves regularly, the mover can nowhere be discovered.[10]

Sometimes general rules and specific understandings can be combined to promote coordination in several ways. They reduce problems of trust, fraud, and extortion. They reduce the costs of selecting from among a set of several preferred outcomes of coordination—in part, through various informal devices that share the normative insistence on certain patterns of behavior. Rules and laws also reduce the costs of communication and identification.[11] In multiorganizational systems, informal mechanisms, including conformity to group pressures and the norm of reciprocity, contribute significantly to the development of such agreed upon rules of behavior.

In a similar way, the findings of this study complement the work of public choice theorists on problems of coordination. I do not believe the approach taken here competes with that of public choice theory. Complex problems are rarely adequately explained by single-variable theories; coordination is no exception. Where public choice theorists have focused principally on issues of motivation and interest, and alternative coordination solutions that address the differences and commonalities of interest among interdependent actors, this study has centered on the informal processes and mechanisms that make possible those solutions, paying particular attention to the opportunities and abilities to develop informal relationships afforded the actors involved. With Axelrod, I have emphasized that meeting more than once has special effects that tend to make formally independent but functionally interdependent actors more prone to develop stable norms of behavior and to find coordination solutions that satisfy all of the relevant actors.

Ultimately, choosing a centralized, formally integrated organizational system over a "messy," decentralized, informally coordinated multiorganizational system depends less on careful, pragmatic evaluation of relevant conditions and actual results than it does on a world view that emphasizes order, consistency, and apparent certainty and cannot tolerate overt disagreement and ambiguity. Such a world view also apparently values command and coercion over negotiation and voluntary agreement as mechanisms for bringing about coordinated action.

Alternatively, selection of a hierarchical coordinative structure may be a function of a desire to impose one's own values on the rest of an organizational system, a difficult feat in a system composed of multiple, independent organizations. In this case, (proposed) organizational arrangements have less to do with achieving coordination in the face of interdependence than they do with enforcing behavioral conformity to a given set of values or decision premises to be imposed from the top down. Related to concern about imposing values is a devaluation of the importance of individual autonomy and pluralistic pursuit of divergent values.

Another component of this world view is an infallible belief in the human capacity to devise institutions artificially. As Simon describes it: "One kind of optimism, or supposed optimism, argues that if we think hard enough, are rational enough, we can solve all our problems." [12] Hayek, among others, also sounds a cautionary note about this capacity:

> The fact, however, that in spite of all the advance of our knowledge, the results of our endeavours remain dependent on circumstances about which we know little or nothing, and on ordering forces we cannot control, is precisely what so many people find intolerable. [13]

Referring to the economic system, he says:

> The delusion that advancing theoretical knowledge places us everywhere increasingly in a position to reduce complex interconnections to ascertainable particular facts often leads to new scientific errors. . . . Such errors are largely due to an arrogation of pretended knowledge, which in fact no one possesses and which even the advance of science is not likely to give us. [14]

To be sure, reliance on informal mechanisms and processes of coordination in lieu of formal mechanisms (particularly hierarchical ones) requires trusting that they will develop in the relevant areas. We know that formal devices can be there when needed; we have constructed them before after all and usually they have some form of legal charter. The issue is whether they will be effective for coordination. Informal mechanisms depend, however, on voluntary actions of many actors, and have no legal recognition, making their ultimate trustworthiness suspect. However, the evidence in this study indicates the regular self-conscious development of stable, enduring, and reliable informal mechanisms for instrumental reasons, particularly for coordination.

Problems, Expectations, and Satisfactory Coordination

Sciences, such as physics, are equipped to understand recurrences of similar problems. Physicists and mathematicians have developed powerful techniques of probability theory and statistics to contend with problems of "disorganized complexity," [15] in which the number of variables is very large, and one in which each of the many variables has a behavior which is individually erratic, or perhaps totally unknown. However, in spite of this helter-skelter, or unknown, behavior of all the individual variables, the system as a whole possesses certain orderly and analyzable average properties.[16]

However, a whole range of problems does not exhibit these properties,

problems which involve dealing simultaneously with a sizable number of factors which are interrelated into an organic whole. They are all . . . problems of "organized complexity."[17]

The variables are interrelated in a complicated, but not random, fashion. These problems cannot be handled with the statistical techniques effective in describing average behavior in problems of disorganized complexity.[18] Most problems confronted by social, economic, and political systems possess characteristics of "organized complexity." There are many factors involved, related in systematic, nonrandom ways, and whose first-order effects on each other are not easily ascertained, let alone their second- and third-order effects. Certainly most multiorganizational systems exhibit the characteristics of organized complexity.

Frequently, problems of organized complexity facing organizational systems are only "ill structured," as opposed to "well structured," where structure is understood to be a function of knowledge and understanding of the patterns of interrelationships among the components. Problems only become well structured when we are able to impose a structure on them. Most problem-solving effort is directed at structuring problems. Only a fraction of it is devoted to solving problems once they are structured.[19]

Problems begin to acquire structure when they are decomposed into various problems of component design—that is, into a series of smaller problems that can be well structured because they are sufficiently simple to be comprehended. This results in a problem "well structured in the small, but ill structured in the large."[20] The problem is solved by confronting each component individually, with the result that interrelationships among the various well-structured subproblems may be neglected or underemphasized. "However, there are ways of dividing the whole problem into parts that do less violence to those interactions than other ways of dividing it."[21] And the interrelationships among the smaller well-structured problems can then be treated as separate problems.

If organizations are conceptualized as extensions of our problem-solving capacities, then an analogy is drawn between problem-solving method and organizational structure, and problem structure becomes extremely important. Such an analogy suggests that coordinative mechanisms that permit the decomposition of problems into manageable components be employed. Centralized, programmed structures are poorly adapted to contend with ill-structured problems, in part because they are not suited to assimilating new information and integrating it with long-term memory. This approach is consistent with Thompson's and Tuden's (and Lindblom's too, for that matter) contentions that different organizational structures should be linked with different decision strategies. Well-structured problems involve computational decision strategies.[22] Similarly, centralized, programmed structures rest on assumptions of near-complete knowledge of cause-effect relationships and value agreement.

Conversely, a decentralized, flat organizational structure permits the handling of smaller, well-understood, well-structured problems by programmed structures, and the ill-structured interrelationships among those problems to be dealt with by flexible, adaptive informal mechanisms, which place minimal cognitive demands on the actors involved. Thus, AC and BART can each be operated by formal, centralized arrangements because the problems each faces are well structured, whereas their less well-structured interdependence can be addressed by informal devices. This approach corresponds with my earlier arguments concerning "localizing interdependence." It is also consistent with Lindblom's arguments about simplifying problems by excluding some factors, the difficulties arising from that exclusion to be solved as separate problems.

Little reason exists to employ coordinative arrangements that obstruct the decomposition of problems or that create linkages among problems where none previously existed. Tighter interdependence increases the cognitive difficulty of the problem. It also requires that more actors be involved in the solution to each problem. Involving more actors magnifies the political complexity of the problem, makes coordination more costly, and reduces the probability of an expeditious solution. Using smaller formal hierarchies to handle those problems sufficiently simple and known to be categorized as well structured, and informal mechanisms to coordinate where interdependence arises among them—ill-structured problems—seems to me an appropriate if radical proposal, given prevailing trends in the public administration. The use of informal mechanisms, constructed by many different actors at different times, follows Dewey's notion of problem solving—that issues be dealt with as they arise in the course of doing one's work, not comprehensively or ahead of time according to some overall master plan.[23]

Even in the unlikely event that we should possess complete cause-effect knowledge, and face only well-structured problems, we might still choose an organizational design that provides less coordination than a competing alternative. Few organizational systems are characterized by a unitary value or a unitary ordering of values: in theory we can devise a welfare function; in practice, rarely. In such cases, issues of accountability and representation assume vital importance. Although frequently the argument is made that only a unitary centralized organizational structure can provide accountability, I contend quite the opposite: multiorganization is more likely to promote accountability and representation, directly and indirectly.

Profound consequences would follow from the elimination of the fragmentation of authority that is so frequently proposed by reorganizers of the public administration. It would "imply the creation of a sovereign authority as the locus of an ultimate authority in society that can coerce others to obey its decisions but cannot itself be coerced by others."[24] Limits on authority, as specified in the U.S. Constitution, are only practicable in a system where shared powers permit veto by one organization of another organization's actions.[25] "The device of popular election may not be sufficient to hold governments accountable,"[26] and so the different components of government must be set against each other. This was the wisdom of James Madison and the Founding Fathers. They sought to institutionalize—not reduce—conflict among the branches of government, recognizing that it certainly would promote accountability in ways no other institutional arrangements could.

The costs of coordination may be cast in terms of tradeoffs with other important values. If improved coordination can only be achieved

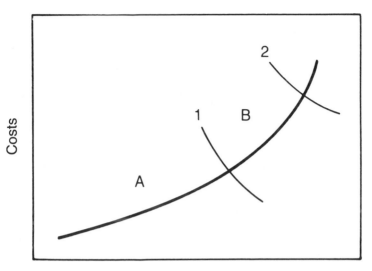

Figure 10   Costs of Coordination

by eliminating multiorganization, accountability will suffer, along with flexibility and reliability. The Constitution itself, with its separation of powers, "testifies to the willingness of even bold men to sacrifice efficiency in the interests of avoiding risks and to accept instead the price of tedious processes of persuasive coordination." [27]

And while I have no direct evidence, it seems to me that the cost-coordination relationship is probably not merely linear; it quite possibly takes the form shown in Figure 10. In Section B of the curve, each additional increment of coordination costs substantially more than each additional increment in Section A. Where Line 1 intersects the curve is the theoretically satisfactory level of coordination, defined by an acceptable marginal cost. Line 2's intersection with the curve marks the theoretical limit to coordination, which may also be considered the optimal level of coordination. It simply costs too much to move from Line 1 to Line 2 on the curve: additional increments of coordination may not be desirable in light of the required tradeoffs with other important values, and with the cost of search.

Similar satisfactory levels of coordination can be produced by rather different organizational designs; thus, reaching for optimal levels of coordination may not be particularly desirable: "If the general magnitude of the available search effort is known in advance, then following an optimizing procedure until the cost of additional search exceeds the expected gain is *not* equivalent to employing the best satisficing procedure." [28] It may be quite reasonable, therefore, to aim simply for a satisfactory level of coordination. If it is true that "for the satisficer, the unique solution is the exception rather than the rule," [29] in a situation of multiple satisfactory solutions, other than by tossing a coin, how can a decision be made among organization designs? Inclusion of other values permits choice among nonunique satisfactory coordination solutions to a problem—the expression of preferences in style. More generally, as relevant conditions vary, it may be appropriate to adjust our expectations of what can be achieved and the sorts of mechanisms that should be used.

Simple faith in our ability to devise formal, artificial structures that will efficiently solve all problems of interdependence simultaneously leads us to expect too much of our public organizations, to reorganize frequently with little real gain but with substantial cost, and to neglect other powerful tools at our disposal—informal mechanisms.

10

An Afterword

Dealing with Bay Area transit politics is like
dealing with Beirut.
                        —Ralph Stanley, Urban Mass
                        Transportation Administrator

   The terror of any social scientist engaged in research concerned with a continuing process is that between the time the research
was conducted and the time at which it is reported, the process (or its
outcomes) will have changed in ways that significantly alter the va-
lidity of the findings. The temptation remains strong, therefore, to
keep adding new data in order to obviate that problem. Of course,
that solution in turn creates a new problem: closure is never reached
and the research fails to see the light of day. I have tried to tread the
fine line between the two problems: without redoing entirely the
original research I have sought to update my findings by documenting the significant changes that have occurred in interorganizational
interdependence and coordination in the San Francisco Bay Area
public transit system.
   The research reported here was conducted during 1978–80, a
time of great volatility and change in the public transit system of the
Bay Area. In reporting that research I attempted to provide a snap-
shot of a single point in an ongoing process. A vast amount of water
has passed under the bridge since then. Although I believed very few
(if any) changes since then would appreciably affect the contours of
the theories of informal organization developed herein, alterations in
the particulars of the coordinative arrangements would lend more or

less credence to the arguments I have made about the relative efficacy of informal mechanisms for providing coordination in multiorganizational systems. It therefore was with some trepidation and concern that I returned to the Bay Area to see what had transpired in the interim. I was pleasantly surprised to find that interorganizational coordination had proceeded apace in operations, services, and planning, that considerable stability characterized the cast of central actors in the informal network, and that the roles, as I had described them, of the RTA and the MTC had not changed significantly.

What follows, then, is a general update of my original findings on the extent and quality of interorganizational coordination in the San Francisco Bay Area public transit system.[1]

Changes

The six major public transit operators in the Bay Area have been joined by two more: Caltrain, which is the Caltrans entity operating the Peninsula Commuter Service formerly provided by Southern Pacific, and the Central Contra Costa County Transit Authority (CCCTA). Southern Pacific still actually operates the Peninsula Commuter trains under contract to Caltrans. The rolling stock is owned by Caltrain. The trains carry about 16,000 passengers daily. Santa Clara, San Mateo, and San Francisco counties share the operating costs with the state of California. San Francisco supervisors are now pushing for an extension of the rails and a new San Francisco terminus to be built in the downtown area.[2] There are also a number of smaller operators: Eastern Contra Costa County Transit Authority (Tri-delta), Fairfield Transit, Livermore Transit, Napa City Transit, Santa Rosa Transit, Sonoma County Transit, Union City Transit (the Flea), Vallejo Transit, and Western Contra Costa County Transit (WestCAT).

The RTA still operates under a joint Exercise of Powers Agreement, and remains composed of the same six major operators that were members at its initiation. Caltrain and CCCTA participate in the activities of the RTA on an informal basis. RTA continues to operate under a Board of Control with various staff-level committees performing the actual work in service coordination, joint procurement, marketing, transit crime and vandalism programs, involvement of women- and minority-owned businesses, and information sharing.

The 1987–88 total operating deficit (the difference between costs and farebox revenues) for BART, AC, and Muni is expected to top $350 million. The three are expected to collect fares totaling $177 million while spending $527 million to operate. And the pot of federal, state, and local subsidies to make up that gap is shrinking.

Meanwhile, Golden Gate has lost about 40 percent of its bus ridership since 1982. The projected Golden Gate budget deficit for 1987–88 is $6.4 million. Bridge tolls were last raised in 1981, transit fares in 1984. The district general manager, Carney Champion, prefers to avoid a transit fare increase: "We have to protect the transit system because the bridge and San Francisco can't sustain any more traffic."[3]

Raising bridge tolls would increase revenue more quickly as morning automobile traffic is steadily increasing—over 10 percent in the past five years—and might have the secondary effect of encouraging motorists to return to the transit system. The district had not decided how best to address the problem at the time this was being written.

BART has lost nearly 20,000 riders per day from its peak daily loads of about 216,000 in 1984–85. BART directors have approved extension of its rail service in southern Alameda County from San Leandro thirteen miles to Dublin, with construction scheduled to commence in 1995. An extension in San Mateo County to Colma is also being planned. This extension should increase ridership by at least 12,000 passengers per day, and annual revenues by $6.2 million. San Mateo County has agreed to cover the entire operating deficit for the new line, estimated at $2.9 million. BART is also working on plans for an extension to San Francisco airport, which would add approximately 40,000 riders per day. Meanwhile, Contra Costa County officials are seeking a BART extension from Concord to Pittsburg and Antioch.

AC has maintained its daily passenger load of 250,000 but is not growing. It has been forced to cut a number of routes from its schedules, beginning with some that compete with service provided by BART. Before those service cuts, the projected deficit for AC for 1987–88 was about $6 million (that figure is the shortfall *after* all sources of revenue, including property and sales taxes, are taken into account).[4] Muni carries over 815,000 passengers per day and appears to be gradually gaining riders.

Some of the passenger load decreases appear to be related to increased fares;[5] some seem to have resulted from movement out of San Francisco by large private firms; and the price of gasoline has fallen significantly, making private transportation more attractive again.

Since 1980, the eastern sections of Alameda County and the northern sections of Contra Costa County have experienced dramatic population growth, creating another major problem for decision making in public transit. In addition, housing prices in counties outside the core Bay Area counties (Alameda, San Mateo, Santa Clara, Contra Costa, and San Francisco) such as Napa, Sonoma, and Solano counties are as much as $100,000 lower. About the problem, Brigitte LeBlanc of the Bay Area Council, a regional business-sponsored public affairs organization, had this to say:

> Historically, all roads led to San Francisco, Oakland, and San Jose, but that scheme is changing as the locations for jobs have become decentralized.
>
> Neither the public transit systems nor the highways were equipped to handle this shift. Now you find more people driving because public transit won't go where they work.[6]

The long-term problem is for the various transit properties to make adjustments to the new demographics. Whether the system will be able to respond effectively is not yet clear. The immediate effect, however, is to increase pressures both from within the Bay Area and from without for increased economic efficiency, and the reflexive response of consolidation is being made again.[7]

Coordination Activities

In concert with MTC, RTA has developed a five-year plan for marketing Bay Area transit services, aimed at coordinating public information and marketing among the operators, in order to provide transit patrons with "adequate information regarding the regional transit network, its services, schedules, and fares."[8] The plan includes specific project proposals, a financial summary, and an overall work program, including staffing requirements, agency responsibilities and a schedule for implementation.[9] Objectives included identifying opportunities for enhancing efficiency and effectiveness through regional activities, increasing patron awareness of services, promoting sales of tickets and passes through a regional network, providing accurate information at all regional transfer points, and developing a coordinated outreach program with local schools to promote transit awareness.

RTA marketing programs already underway encompassed a Regional Transit Guide (originally published in 1981, updated in 1983, and now out of date), now supplanted with a streamlined version entitled "Best of the Bay Area by Public Transit"; a Regional Discount Card Program, revised extensively in 1984; Regional Transit Ticket Offices, the first of which was opened by CCCTA in March 1986, while AC opened one in the Transbay Terminal in July 1986, with plans to open several more; a Regional Transit Information Centers Project, providing improved regional transit information at all major regional transfer points (see Table 7); and an UMTA-funded demonstration project for a regional distribution network for transit tickets and passes called the Regional Transit Connection. RTA has also played significant roles in providing special transit services during special events, such as the 1984 Superbowl, the All-Star Baseball game, and the Democratic National Convention. It is developing an annual calendar of events requiring special transit information and coordination.

Other coordination activities concern service and fares.[10] In early 1986 the Interoperator Schedule Coordination Improvement Plan project was launched. MTC manages the project with technical assistance provided by transit operator staff. The aim is to resolve technical problems of interoperator transfers. It has the following basic objectives:

   a. To establish baseline data on interoperator transfer volumes for regional transfer points as a means of identifying locations most in need of improvement.

   b. To create a list of regional transfer points in priority for future improvement in regional schedule coordination.

   c. To develop a regional plan for implementing schedule coordination improvements.[11]

*Table 7   Priority List for Installation of Regional Transit Informa-
tion Centers*

Priority	Site	Service Available
1	BART/12th Street	AC, BART
2	Santa Rosa downtown	Golden Gate, Sonoma, Mendocino, Santa Rosa
3	BART/Hayward	AC, BART, Samtrans
4	BART/Daly City	BART, Muni, Samtrans
5	Caltrain/San Jose	Amtrak, Caltrain, SCCTD
6	BART/Concord	BART, CCCTA, Tridelta
7	Caltrain/San Francisco	Caltrain, Muni, Samtrans
8	BART/Civic Center	BART, Golden Gate, Muni, Samtrans
9	BART/19th Street	AC, BART
10	BART/Berkeley	AC, BART
11	Caltrain/Palo Alto	Caltrain, Samtrans, SCCTD, AC
12	BART/Powell	BART, Muni
13	BART/Embarcadero	BART, Muni
14	BART/Montgomery	BART, Muni
15	San Francisco Ferry Terminal	BART, Golden Gate, Muni
16	Oakland Airport	AC, BART
17	BART/Fremont	AC, BART, SCCTD
18	BART/del Norte	BART, WestCat
19	BART/Richmond	AC, Amtrak, BART
20	Caltrain/Sunnyvale	Caltrain, SCCTD, Greyhound
21	BART/Walnut Creek	BART, CCCTA
22	BART/Coliseum	AC, BART
23	BART/Bayfair	AC, BART
24	San Rafael	Golden Gate
25	Petaluma/Greyhound	Golden Gate, Petaluma, Sonoma
26	Caltrain/Redwood City	Caltrain, Samtrans
27	Caltrain/Menlo Park	Caltrain, Samtrans, SCCTD
28	Palo Alto–Page Mill	Samtrans, SCCTD

Source: Metropolitan Transportation Commission, *Transit Coordination Evaluation,* 1984.

The project is intended to result in a schedule coordination improvement plan for the eight major operators by June 1987, and implementation of recommendations embodied in the plan in 1988.

Since 1980 there has been in progress a Multioperator Pass/Transfer Project, managed by MTC and directed by general managers from the major transit operators. By the close of 1986 it had resulted in an AC/Muni Transbay Pass and a BART/Muni Fastpass for travel within San Francisco. An AC/BART Fastpass was introduced in early 1987, which offered a discount off fares for both operators of 18 percent. The earlier AC/BART discount transfer program has been continued, albeit in a slightly altered form technically. There is a Muni/Samtrans Transfer agreement, in which Muni Fastpass holders can transfer free to designated Samtrans lines. Samtrans and Santa Clara County Transit accept each other's transfers for local rides free. An analogous program exists between AC and Santa Clara in Fremont, and between Santa Clara and BART. In 1984, Caltrain, Muni, Samtrans, and Santa Clara County Transit introduced a Peninsula Pass permitting unlimited rides on Caltrain and connecting bus operators. There is no program currently available to monitor its effects on bus and train ridership. There are several other transfer arrangements between the major operators and smaller ones. The one regression was the abandonment of the Golden Gate Ferry to Muni transfers, which were eliminated in July 1986.

At long last, beacons to signal buses to wait for passengers debarking BART trains at the Hayward, Bayfair, El Cerrito del Norte, Walnut Creek, and Concord stations were installed. AC expanded feeder bus service to BART stations and agreed to eliminate competing transbay services when BART is able to operate at designed capacity. BART agreed to subsidize some AC night service to and from BART stations.

The general picture that emerges is one of a continuing incremental advance toward a better coordinated multiorganizational system, where problems, as they are identified and given priority, are placed on an agenda for resolution. Some of the problems are technically difficult, some have considerable political factors attached, and some are characterized by both. As such they remain thorny and are likely to require substantial effort, compromise, and time to resolve. Even with a formally unified, centralized decision-making structure, it seems doubtful that these problems of interdependence would be resolved any more quickly or efficiently than the existing process permits.

The original busbridge agreements between BART and AC, and BART and Muni remain intact, and in their original forms as informal oral arrangements between the relevant operating personnel. Procedures to be followed in the event of a major problem were worked out by a joint emergency plan task force composed of personnel from the three operators. The procedures remain essentially the same as they were when this study was first conducted, with some refinements to make them work more smoothly.

At 9:10 A.M. on the third Sunday of May 1987 BART suffered an unexplained power failure in the transbay tube, when ten heavy-duty switches that feed power along the 5.4 miles of track from the BART Oakland West station to its Embarcadero station suddenly kicked out.[12] This created a difficult situation because this was the day of the annual Bay to Breakers race in San Francisco (which attracted some 100,000 participants). BART initiated a busbridge and AC provided transbay service between the Transbay Terminal on the San Francisco side and the BART MacArthur station in the Eastbay, putting some thirty-five buses into service overall, with twenty-five operating at any one time. AC then billed BART for its costs incurred in providing the service. The arrangement worked very smoothly, just as it had in the past.

Because Muni runs surface lines more or less parallel to BART rail lines in San Francisco, BART has had less occasion to ask for a busbridge from Muni. BART usually simply advises Muni of any problems it might have, and Muni may or may not add buses to those lines. In October 1985, however, BART suffered a power substation failure in Daly City, and for several days Muni provided a busbridge, using some thirty buses between BART's Daly City station and its Balboa Park station. The arrangement, as before, was executed smoothly.

BART also from time to time calls on private transit operators for busbridges, especially if problems arise at peak commuting hours when the capacities of the public operators are strained. Since the 1979 transbay tube fire, BART has compiled a list of some thirty-five private operators and the appropriate contacts at each one, making such requests more routine and simple to execute than before that time.

The only dark cloud currently looming over these arrangements is the drive by UMTA to "privatize" provision of BART's express bus services, which are currently provided under formal contract by AC. Privatization would likely have a twofold effect on the busbridge agreement between BART and AC. If it loses the contract, AC will be less favorably disposed toward providing busbridge service to BART. AC will also have a smaller reserve of buses should it lose the contract and move those buses formerly dedicated to the service into other areas, making a busbridge more difficult and less probable. More generally, anything that acts to decrease duplication in Bay Area transit will simultaneously reduce its reserve available for use during emergencies.

MTC as Coordinator and Regional Representative

Since 1981, under California State legislation (PUC Section 99282.5) regulating transfers between public transit operators, MTC has annually produced a *Transit Coordination Evaluation* (*TCE*). The point of the evaluation is to assess progress by the transit operators toward coordinating their services, and to establish evaluation and implementation processes for the coming year. The overall goal is to "improve travel for patrons who require more than one operator to complete a transit trip." [13] The 1986 report noted that the "most effective efforts have been those which address a coordination problem on a region-wide basis rather than rely on the efforts of a single operator." [14]

However, it also commented that the *TCE* process retained some deficiencies, and the 1985 *TCE* recommended that the *TCE* process become a "regional implementation plan for improvements in selected focus areas." [15] In other words, it would become more than simply an annual evaluation of activities carried on by the operators themselves; it would become a program for planning on a more centralized basis, in particular by linking these evaluations and recommendations with the Productivity Improvement Program. Whether this will actually come to pass remains unclear. Equally important, the 1986 *TCE* specifically recognized that "most regional coordination projects will be multi-year efforts" and therefore the evaluations should be modified accordingly. The direction in which this process seems to be moving is what I would expect from an MTC program: toward greater central decision making and control for Bay Area public transit.

MTC has also continued to conduct or sponsor other studies evaluating existing transit arrangements and establishing priorities for future funding and development. In 1981, for example, MTC conducted a regionwide travel survey of some 7,200 households, gathering information on socioeconomic characteristics and the travel habits of some 20,000 residents for one day. Along with the Association of Bay Area Governments, MTC completed in 1979 an analysis of land use and transportation policies for rapidly growing Santa Clara County, and in particular the so-called Guadalupe corridor, which led to a light-rail project intended to move some 40,000 people per day along a sixteen mile corridor, with the initial stretch of nine miles opening in late 1987. Other corridor studies have focused on acquiring and using abandoned rail rights of way for modern rapid transit systems in Fremont, the Peninsula, and the Marin-Sonoma Highway 101 corridor.

Finally, MTC has been in the process of conducting a study to determine

> whether costs can be reduced by consolidating segments of the public transit network or by centralizing selected functions such as marketing, purchasing, maintenance, financial planning, and scheduling.[16]

The study was expected to be completed by spring 1987, but as of this writing had not been finished. MTC was put in the curious position of being criticized by State Senator Quentin Kopp for "digging in its heels" and stalling this study because of an alleged interest in maintaining the system as it is currently configured.[17] Kopp believes that now (spring 1987) is an opportune time for consolidation, given the passage of similar legislation concerning the Los Angeles metropolitan area and because federal transportation officials say they are bewildered by the number of Bay Area systems and the "lack of coordination among them."[18]

MTC has continued its role of representing the larger interests of the Bay Area transit community in Washington and Sacramento, putting its expertise to use on behalf of the operators and their clientele.

MTC has spent considerable time and effort in searching for additional funding for the region's transit operators, this function becoming especially important as the Reagan administration began to cut federal subsidies for public transit. In particular, MTC joined other transit leaders across the country in lobbying against proposed budget cuts and in favor of renewing the Surface Transportation Assistance Act of 1982, which earmarked a portion of the federal gasoline tax for public transit. Where the Reagan budget called for a two-thirds cut in federal transit spending, the 1987 budget reduced it only slightly. MTC also joined other transit agencies in arguing for greater flexibility in federal highway funding programs.

In Sacramento, where state transit revenues had decreased (due to the fall in gasoline prices), at the behest of MTC the Legislature passed Senate Bill 878 giving Bay Area residents the opportunity to vote by county on a sales tax increase for transportation projects. Other legislation backed by MTC included an appropriation of $35 million for statewide transit capital projects.

MTC has thus continued to work effectively as an umbrella lobbying organization for the Bay Area's transit operators, providing staff functions and expertise in an area that could not be readily duplicated by the operators themselves.[19]

A Final Note

Overall, it appears that MTC and the major transit operators of the Bay Area have formed better working relationships than ever before, particularly in the face of funding cuts from the federal and state levels. To be sure, the operators retain their own individual agendas, and come into conflict with the MTC frequently, but for now there appears to be a mutual recognition of the value of the MTC and the existing institutional arrangements for the operators.

MTC has not become a dominating central influence in transit planning and operations in the Bay Area. It has continued to play the multiple roles of representing the regional interest both internally and externally to the system, and to promote interoperator coordination through a variety of incentives and threats. It has continued to play a key role in setting agendas, and establishing priorities for planning and funding for the region as a whole. For the 1985–86 fiscal year MTC approved or distributed federal, state, and local monies amounting to $592 million to Bay Area transit operators, thus guaranteeing that it will continue to be a very important actor.

Whether the operators will manage to maintain their independence in the face of steady inroads from MTC and external pressures for consolidation remains to be seen. Whether the Bay Area public transit system will be able to plan effectively to adjust to population growth and shifting transportation needs is not clear. It is a difficult set of problems whose resolution probably depends less on specific organizational designs than upon intelligence and some minimal capacity to develop compromises among competing values and points of view. And whether the various operators and MTC will be able to resolve satisfactorily the problem of increasing operating deficits in the face of decreasing federal and state subsidies, and an insufficient local tax base is another question that as yet has no answer. Certainly, however, there is no clear evidence linking operating deficits with existing organizational arrangements and no reason to believe that consolidation would reduce such deficits. More probably operating deficits are a structural feature in the provision of public transit services in the United States. The significant threat remains that the still loosely coupled Bay Area public transit system will become more tightly coupled, not through increased natural interdependence but through artificially induced interdependence; that problems that were once permitted to be decomposed in order to be solved will no longer be treated that way; and that as the complexity of the system is thereby increased, the capacity to solve the problems generated by it will correspondingly decrease.

Nothing I found on reinvestigation suggested even remotely that informal mechanisms operated any differently than when I first observed them or that they had diminished in importance as coordinative devices. For now, at least, the Bay Area public transit system's informal mechanisms continue to provide the basic foundation for processes of coordination, and its hybrid organizational arrangements appear stable.

Appendix A: Abbreviations

ABAG	Association of Bay Area Governments
AC	Alameda–Contra Costa County Transit District
BARTC	Bay Area Rapid Transit Commission
BARTD	Bay Area Rapid Transit District
BATSC	Bay Area Transportation Study Commission
Caltrans	California State Department of Transportation
CCCTA	Central Contra Costa County Transit Authority
Golden Gate	Golden Gate Bridge, Highway, and Transportation District
MCTD	Marin County Transit District
Metro	Washington Metropolitan Transit Authority
MTC	Metropolitan Transportation Commission
Muni	San Francisco Municipal Railway
NVTC	Northern Virginia Transportation Commission
PUC	California State Public Utilities Commission
RTA	Regional Transit Association
Samtrans	San Mateo County Transit District
Santa Clara	Santa Clara County Transportation District
SM	San Mateo County Transportation District
SP	Southern Pacific Railroad
TDA	Transportation Development Act
TOCC	Transit Operators Coordinating Council
Tri-Delta	Eastern Contra Costa County Transit Authority

UMTA	Urban Mass Transportation Administration
WASHCOG	Washington Area Council of Governments
WestCAT	Western Contra Costa County Transit Authority
WMATA	Washington Metropolitan Area Transit Authority
WSTC	Washington Suburban Transportation Commission

Appendix B: Formal Structures and Responsibilities of the Major Bay Area Public Transit Operators

Alameda Contra Costa County Transit District

AC Transit was formed by California State legislation in 1955 providing for the creation of a special transit district in portions of Alameda and Contra Costa counties. A subsequent vote by citizens in those areas established AC.

AC is governed by a seven-member elected Board of Directors, with five members representing wards and two members elected at-large. Terms for the directors are four years in length with staggered expiration dates. The general manager, attorney for the district, and secretary to the board report directly to the board. Three assistant general managers report to the general manager.

AC's service area is bounded by San Pablo Bay on the north and the City of Fremont in the south. It provides service in Alameda and western Contra Costa Counties, including both local routes and trans-bay service to San Francisco. AC also serves areas of suburban Alameda and Contra Costa counties under contract, and BART contracts with AC to provide BART express bus service.

Bay Area Rapid Transit District

BART was created by California State legislation in 1957, following studies by a predecessor planning organization, the Bay Area Rapid Transit Study Commission. Its creation was not subject to voter ratification. BART's jurisdiction now includes only Alameda and Contra Costa counties and the City and County of San Francisco. Initially, it also included San Mateo and Marin counties, but these two withdrew before rail construction began.

BART is governed by a nine-member Board of Directors, whose members are elected by district, although originally they had been appointed by conferences of city mayors and county supervisors. It is headed by a general manager who reports to the board. It employs about 2,300 people, and operates about 550 rail cars over 71 miles of track in its three-county jurisdiction.

Golden Gate Bridge, Highway, and Transportation District

The district was incorporated in 1928 under provisions of the California State Legislature Golden Gate Bridge and Highway District Act of 1923. Its jurisdiction then (and now) included the City and County of San Francisco, the counties of Marin, Sonoma, and Del Norte, and most of Napa and part of Mendocino counties. Golden Gate is governed by a Board of Directors, appointed by the elected representatives of its member counties. For the City and County of San Francisco, the Board of Supervisors appoint eight directors, and the mayor, one. The Board of Supervisors of Marin appoints four, Sonoma three, and one each is appointed by Napa, Mendocino, and Del Norte counties, for a total of nineteen directors. Each director has one vote. A general manager, who is responsible for district operations, reports directly to the board, along with an attorney, district secretary, chief engineer, and auditor-controller.

Originally formed to build, maintain, and operate the Golden Gate Bridge and its approaches, Golden Gate commenced transbay ferry operations between Marin and the San Francisco Ferry Terminal in 1970, and bus service at about the same time. It employs about 900 persons, operating four ferries and nearly 300 buses, as well as the Golden Gate Bridge.

San Francisco Municipal Railway

The Muni is one of three operating divisions of the Public Utilities Commission of the City and County of San Francisco. It is headed by a general manager who reports to the general manager of the PUC of San Franscisco, who in turn is responsible to that body, which is then responsible to the mayor. Three deputy general managers report directly to the general manager, along with the departments of Planning, Scheduling, and Community Affairs at Muni.

Its jurisdiction encompasses the City and County of San Francisco. It also provides service to the BART Daly City station. Muni operates buses, trolleys, light-rail vehicles, and, of course, the cable cars. It has about 3,800 employees, of whom some 2,500 are employed in the operations division, and operates in excess of 1,000 vehicles over nearly 100 lines.

San Mateo County Transit District

Samtrans, a special-purpose district created by California State legislation, is governed by a Board of Directors, with members appointed by the San Mateo County Board of Supervisors (two) and local city councils (three), with four citizen members appointed at-large. Samtrans also has a formal Citizens Advisory Committee, consisting of fifteen residents, intended to represent a broad spectrum of the community served, including senior citizens, members of minorities, the handicapped, students, and regular bus and rail commuters, along with business, industry, and labor interests.

Samtrans operates buses throughout San Mateo County and commuter lines into San Francisco, including the Transbay Terminal, and into Santa Clara County. It employs about 450 persons, and operates about 350 buses.

Santa Clara County Transit District

The district was authorized in 1969 by California State legislation, and was activated by Santa Clara County voters in 1972. It serves all of Santa Clara County, an area of some 250 square miles and 1.3 million residents. It is administratively responsible to the Santa Clara County Transportation Agency, an umbrella organization created by the county board of supervisors in 1974, which is also responsible for county road operations and county-operated general aviation airports. The Board of Supervisors also serves as the policy board of the transit district. Additionally, the Santa Clara County Transportation Commission serves as an advisory body on transportation matters to the board. It consists of 29 members, 15 elected officials representing the cities of the area, and 14 appointed citizen members. There are two other transit advisory groups: the Paratransit Coordinating Council Executive Committee, and the Ad Hoc Committee on Service to the Handicapped. The district operates about 550 buses over nearly 80 routes.

Appendix C: The Metropolitan Transportation Commission

The MTC was created by Assembly Bill 363 in the California State Legislature in 1970

to prepare a regional Transportation Plan for the San Francisco Bay Area. Under State law, all applications for State and Federal transportation assistance must be approved by the Commission.

Policy direction is provided by 18 commissioners. Fourteen members are appointed directly by locally elected officials, two members represent other regional agencies (the Association of Bay Area Governments and the Bay Conservation & Development Commission), and two non-voting members represent State and Federal transportation agencies. (Information prepared by the Metropolitan Transportation Commission for Neil Goldschmidt, U.S. Secretary of Transportation, 1979)

Alameda, Contra Costa, Marin, Napa, San Francisco, San Mateo, Santa Clara, Solano, and Sonoma counties comprise the jurisdiction of the Commission. Within those nine counties are ninety-three cities. The population exceeds five million people with a land area of some 7,000 square miles.

The commissioners are supported by a professional and clerical staff of about one hundred, headed by an executive director.

In 1972 MTC became responsible for administering funds for the state-authorized Transportation Development Act. It completed the first Regional Transportation Plan in June 1973. In 1975 it acquired responsibility for administering Section 5 operating grants provided for in the Federal Urban Mass Transportation Administration's Act (Metropolitan Transportation Commission, *Annual Report, 1979/80*). In September 1977, Assembly Bill 1107 made MTC responsible for evaluating the annual budgets of the region's transit operators and to disburse a special three-county (Alameda, Contra Costa, and San Francisco) half-cent sales tax. In July 1979 Assembly Bill 842 incorporated an MTC plan for easing fiscal woes of the transit properties, related to Proposition 13, and authorized it to work with the operators on the development of a long-range financial plan. In 1980 it completed "the first round of performance audits outlining programs for improving transit operators' efficiency and effectiveness," and in December of that year it issued a study detailing the capital funding needs of the transit operators over the next fifteen years (Metropolitan Transportation Commission, *Annual Report, 1980/81*, pp. 20–21).

By 1983 MTC was distributing or approving the spending of over $500 million in public transit funds each year. "MTC works with the operators to develop a yearly productivity improvement program, conducts performance audits every three years, reviews the operators' budgets and assists with financial planning. MTC also sets capital investment priorities for both transit and highways" (Metropolitan Transportation Commission, *Annual Report, 1982/83*, p. 3).

Appendix D:
The Regional Transit Association

The RTA was formed in 1977 as an organization of the six major public transit operators in the San Francisco Bay Area: AC, BART, Golden Gate, Muni, Samtrans, and Santa Clara. By 1979 all members had signed the Joint Exercise of Powers Agreement. Other transit systems, such as Caltrans (which operates Caltrain) and CCCTA, participate in RTA activities informally. RTA exists to "share information and to undertake cooperative projects of mutual benefit to the members and the transit riding public." (*1986 Regional Transit Association Handbook,* p. 1)

RTA, governed by a Board of Control composed of the general managers of the six member operators, meets monthly. The actual work of the RTA, which has no employees of its own, is carried out by employees of the member operators, involving some sixty individuals in the various staff-level committees, which include operations, planning, public information, marketing, maintenance, and procurement. Its annual budget for 1986 totaled $1,125,000, of which $675,000 came from California State funds, $362,500 from federal funds, and $87,500 from contributions by the member organizations.

Notes

Preface

1. On this point see Herbert A. Simon, "Human Nature and Politics: The Dialogue of Psychology with Political Science," *American Political Science Review* 79(1985): 293–304. Simon distinguishes between "two theories of human rationality that have found application in political science: procedural, bounded rationality from contemporary cognitive psychology, and global, substantive rationality from economics" (p. 293).

2. Wesley C. Mitchell, "Facts and Values in Economics," *Journal of Philosophy* 41(1944): 217.

3. See Richard Fenno, "Observation, Context, and Sequence in the Study of Politics," *American Political Science Review* 80(1986): 3–15.

4. See for example Herbert A. Simon, *Reason in Human Affairs* (Stanford, Calif.: Stanford University Press, 1984).

5. F. Darwin, *Life and Letters of Charles Darwin* (London: John Murray, 1888), as quoted by W. I. B. Beveridge, *The Art of Scientific Investigation* (New York: Vintage Books, 1957), p. 123.

6. My use of these terms follows Abraham Kaplan, *The Conduct of Inquiry: Methodology for Behavioral Science* (San Francisco: Chandler, 1964), pp. 3–12. W. I. B. Beveridge makes a similar distinction in *Art of Scientific Investigation*, p. 111. And see F. C. S. Schiller on the difference between the "order of discovery" and the "order of proof" in his "Scientific Discovery and Logical Proof," in *Studies in the History and Method of Science*, ed. Charles Singer (Oxford: Clarendon Press, 1917), pp. 235–89.

Chapter One: Multiorganizational Systems

1. *Oakland Tribune*, 10 September 1982, p. B-1.

2. David W. Jones, *The Politics of Metropolitan Transportation Planning and Programming* (Berkeley: University of California, Institute of Transportation Studies, 1976), pp. 27–33.

3. *San Francisco Chronicle*, 24 September 1985, p. A-1.

4. *San Francisco Chronicle*, 19 May 1987, p. A-6. The Metropolitan Transportation Commission began a consolidation study in 1986.

5. *Los Angeles Times,* 8 February 1987, p. II-1.
6. *Los Angeles Times,* 27 March 1987, p. II-1.
7. *Los Angeles Times,* 7 April 1987, p. I-18.
8. Douglas Yates, *The Ungovernable City: The Politics of Urban Problems and Policy-Making* (Cambridge, Mass.: M.I.T. Press, 1977), p. 34.
9. *Los Angeles Times,* 6 November 1985, p. II-1.
10. Along with Martin Landau and Melvin Webber.
11. Martin Landau, Donald Chisholm, and Melvin Webber, *Redundancy in Public Transit, Volume I: On the Idea of an Integrated Transit System* (Berkeley: University of California, Institute of Urban and Regional Development, 1980), p. i.
12. Ibid., p. 2.
13. Ibid., p. 5.
14. Ibid., p. 3.
15. Ibid., p. 4.
16. Ibid.
17. Ibid., p. 5. See also Martin Landau and Russell Stout, "To Manage Is Not to Control or the Folly of Type II Errors," *Public Administration Review* 39 (1979): 148–56.
18. See James G. March and Johan P. Olson, "Organizing Political Life: What Administrative Reorganization Tells Us About Government," *American Political Science Review* 77(1983): 281–96, for an analysis of the political history of the twelve twentieth-century efforts at comprehensive reorganization in the U.S. federal government.
19. As quoted by March and Olson, "Organizing Political Life," p. 283.
20. Landau, Chisholm, and Webber, *Redundancy,* p. 10.
21. March and Olsen, "Organizing Political Life," p. 289.
22. Wolfgang S. Homburger and Vukan R. Vuchic, "Federation of Transit Agencies as a Solution for Service Integration," *Traffic Quarterly* 24(1970): 373–91.
23. Harold Seidman, *Politics, Position, and Power,* 3rd ed. (New York: Oxford University Press, 1980), p. 204.
24. Bernard H. Baum, *Decentralization of Authority in a Bureaucracy* (Englewood Cliffs, N.J.: Prentice-Hall, 1961), p. 78.
25. Ibid., p. 142.
26. Landau, Chisholm, and Webber, *Redundancy,* p. 6.
27. Ibid., p. 12.
28. Robert Rider, "Decentralizing Land Use Decisions," *Public Administration Review* 40(1980): 594.
29. On this point see Charles T. Goodsell, *The Case for Bureaucracy: A Public Administration Polemic,* 2nd ed. (Chatham, N.J.: Chatham House, 1985).
30. Landau, Chisholm, and Webber, *Redundancy,* p. 7.
31. W. Ross Ashby, "Principles of the Self-Organizing System," in *Principles of Self-Organization,* ed. Heinz von Foerster and George W. Zopf, Jr. (New York: Pergamon Press, 1962), p. 265.
32. Ibid., p. 265.
33. Herbert A. Simon, *The Sciences of the Artificial* (Cambridge, Mass.: M.I.T. Press, 1969), p. 110.
34. Ibid., p. 106.
35. Burton Klein, "A Radical Proposal for R and D," *Fortune* (May 1958): 112.
36. Martin Wachs, "Fostering Technological Innovation in Urban Transportation Systems," *Traffic Quarterly* 25(1971): 49.
37. See Landau and Stout, "Type II Errors," for a full discussion of the mis-

application of programmed decision making to arenas characterized by uncertainty, conflict, and variability.

38. Seidman, *Politics*, p. 217.

39. Ibid., p. 206.

40. Some informal communications are considered illegal. Off-the-record contacts between administrative agencies and parties to agency proceedings, for example, are considered to be an important part of the administrative process, but they raise certain elemental questions about issues of fairness. Improper political access is considered one of the greatest problems. For a discussion of these issues, see "Due Process and Ex Parte Contact in Informal Rulemaking," *Yale Law Journal* 89(1979): 194–212. Chapter 7 of this study considers the problem of illegal access through informal channels.

41. Landau, Chisholm, and Webber, *Redundancy*, p. 13.

42. Jones, *Politics*, p. 23.

43. Landau, Chisholm, and Webber, *Redundancy*, p. 15.

44. Ibid.

45. Ibid., p. 16.

46. *Oxford English Dictionary.*

47. Kurt W. Bauer, "Regional Planning in Southeastern Wisconsin," *Traffic Quarterly* 28(1974): 551.

48. Peter L. Shaw and Renee B. Simon, "Changing Institutional Relationships— The Los Angeles County Transportation Commission Experience," *Traffic Quarterly* 35 (1981): 588. Note that this study precedes by six years the current efforts of the state assembly to consolidate Los Angeles County public transit agencies.

49. Landau, Chisholm, and Webber, *Redundancy*, p. 10.

50. Ibid., p. 11.

51. Ibid.

52. This discussion derives, in part, from W. Richard Scott, "Developments in Organization Theory, 1960–1980," *American Behavioral Scientist* 24(1981): 407–22.

53. Victor Thompson, *Bureaucracy and the Modern World* (Morristown, N.J.: General Learning Press, 1976), pp. 16–22.

54. See, for example, Peter M. Blau, *The Dynamics of Bureaucracy* (Chicago: University of Chicago Press, 1955); Michel Crozier, *The Bureaucratic Phenomenon* (Chicago: University of Chicago Press, 1964); and Herbert Kaufman, *The Forest Ranger: A Study in Administration* (Baltimore: Johns Hopkins University Press, 1963). Each of these works provides a description of the informal features of the organization(s) studied, even though the primary intent of the research may lie elsewhere.

55. For example, see Chester I. Barnard, *The Functions of the Executive* (Cambridge, Mass.: Harvard University Press, 1971).

56. See Robert K. Merton, *Social Theory and Social Structure* (New York: The Free Press, 1968), chap. 1; Alvin Gouldner, *Patterns of Industrial Bureaucracy* (New York: The Free Press, 1954); and Philip Selznick, *TVA and the Grassroots: A Study in the Sociology of Formal Organization* (Berkeley: University of California Press, 1949).

57. Alvin Gouldner, "Organizational Analysis," in *Sociology Today: Problems and Prospects*, ed. R. K. Merton, L. Broom, L. S. Cotrell, Jr. (New York: Basic Books, 1959), p. 410. Simon has noted that: "Residual categories are tenacious: it is extremely difficult, or even impossible, to prove that they are empty. The scope of a residual category can be narrowed progressively by explaining previously unexplained phenomena; it cannot be extinguished as long as a single phenomenon remains un-

explained." Herbert A. Simon, "The Structure of Ill Structured Problems," *Artificial Intelligence* 4(1973): 181.

58. Selznick, *TVA*, pp. 251–52.

59. F. J. Roethlisberger and William J. Dickson, *Management and the Worker* (Cambridge, Mass.: Harvard University Press, 1947), p. 525; emphasis added.

60. Martin Landau, *Political Theory and Political Science* (Atlantic Highlands, N.J.: Humanities Press, 1971), p. 177.

61. March and Olson, "Organizing Political Life," p. 282.

62. One notable exception is Robert Axelrod, *The Evolution of Cooperation* (New York: Basic Books, 1984).

Chapter Two: Formal Failures and Informal Compensations

1. The discussion that follows is intended neither as a comprehensive review of research on informal organization, nor as history of such research. Rather, it considers a number of works that I believe represent the range of perspectives to be found in research on informal organization. Social networks, a major component of informal organization, and various sociometric approaches to their study are considered in Chapter 4.

2. Wilbert E. Moore, *Industrial Relations and the Social Order* (New York: Macmillan, 1951), p. 289.

3. F. J. Roethlisberger and William J. Dickson, *Management and the Worker* (Cambridge, Mass.: Harvard University Press, 1947), p. 548.

4. Ibid., p. 524.

5. Ibid., p. 548.

6. George Washington Plunkitt, *Plunkitt of Tammany Hall*, recorded by William L. Riordan, with an introduction by Arthur Mann (New York: E. P. Dutton, 1963), p. 71.

7. Robert K. Merton, *Social Theory and Social Structure* (New York: The Free Press, 1968), p. 71.

8. Merton, *Social Theory*, p. 72.

9. Moore, *Industrial Relations*, pp. 282–89.

10. Ibid.

11. Ibid., p. 291.

12. Chester I. Barnard, *The Functions of the Executive* (Cambridge, Mass.: Harvard University Press, 1971), p. 122.

13. Ibid.

14. Victor A. Thompson, *Bureaucracy and the Modern World* (Morristown, N.J.: General Learning Press, 1976), p. 17.

15. Ibid.

16. Ibid.

17. Ibid., p. 16; emphasis added.

18. Roethlisberger and Dickson, *Management and the Worker*, p. 535.

19. Thompson, *Bureaucracy*, p. 17.

20. Barnard, *The Executive*, p. 115.

21. Ibid., p. 116.

22. Harvey M. Sapolsky, *The Polaris System Development: Bureaucratic and Programmatic Success in Government* (Cambridge, Mass.: Harvard University Press, 1972), p. 122.

23. Ely Devons, *Papers on Planning and Economic Management,* ed. Sir Alec Cairncross (Manchester: Manchester University Press, 1970), p. 53.

24. Harold Seidman, *Politics, Position, and Power,* 3rd ed. (New York: Oxford University Press, 1980), p. 205.

25. *Oxford English Dictionary.*

26. Ibid.

27. Herbert A. Simon, *Administrative Behavior,* 2nd ed. (New York: The Free Press, 1957), p. 140.

28. Seidman, *Politics,* p. 204.

29. Simon, *Administrative Behavior,* pp. 12, 116.

30. Ibid., p. 149.

31. Herbert A. Simon, Donald W. Smithburg, and Victor A. Thompson, *Public Administration* (New York: Alfred A. Knopf, 1964), p. 87.

32. Devons, *Planning and Economic Management,* p. 53; emphasis added.

33. See Joseph Berliner, "The Informal Organization of the Soviet Firm," *Quarterly Journal of Economics* 66(1952): 342–65; and *Factory and Manager in the USSR* (Cambridge, Mass.: Harvard University Press, 1957). See also Leon Lipson, "Testimony Before the U.S. House of Representatives Permanent Select Committee on Intelligence, Subcommittee on Program and Budget Authorization," Thursday, 24 January 1980.

34. Devons, *Planning and Economic Management,* p. 53.

35. Simon, Smithburg, and Thompson, *Public Administration,* p. 88.

36. Thomas B. Buell, *Master of Sea Power: A Biography of Fleet Admiral Ernest J. King* (Boston: Little, Brown, and Co., 1980), pp. 228–29.

37. On this point, see Martin Landau and Russell Stout, "To Manage Is Not to Control or the Folly of Type II Errors," *Public Administration Review* 39(1979): 148–56.

38. Merton, *Social Theory,* p. 195.

39. Martin Landau, Seminar Presentation, Fall 1978.

40. Barnard, *The Executive,* p. 117.

41. Allen Barton, "The Emergency Social System," in *Man and Society in Disaster,* ed. George W. Baker and Dwight W. Chapman, with a foreword by Carlyle F. Jacobsen (New York: Basic Books, 1962), p. 223. See also James D. Thompson and Robert Hawkes, "Disaster, Community Organization, and Administrative Process," in the same volume.

42. Barnard, *The Executive,* p. 117.

43. See Robert Axelrod, *The Evolution of Cooperation* (New York: Basic Books, 1984). The mesh of Axelrod's argument and that made in this essay is discussed more fully in Chapter 6.

Chapter Three: The Problem of Interdependence

1. James D. Thompson, *Organizations in Action: Social Science Bases of Administrative Theory* (New York: McGraw-Hill, 1967), chap. 1.

2. Martin Landau, *Political Theory and Political Science* (Atlantic Highlands, N.J.: Humanities Press, 1979), p. 218.

3. For a more extensive discussion of organization and environment, see Donald Chisholm, *Organizational Adaptation to Environmental Change,* IGS Studies in Public Organization, Working Paper no. 86-1 (Berkeley: University of California, Institute of Governmental Studies, 1986).

4. D. J. Hickson, C. R. Hinings, C. A. Lee, R. E. Schenck, and J. M. Pennings, "A Strategic Contingencies Theory of Intraorganizational Power," *Administrative Science Quarterly* 16(1971): 219.

5. *Oxford English Dictionary.*

6. Charles E. Lindblom, *The Intelligence of Democracy* (New York: The Free Press, 1965), pp. 21–22.

7. Thompson, *Organizations*, p. 13.

8. Ibid., p. 99.

9. See Chapter 1.

10. The approach to interdependence in this study follows Simon's use of "decision" as the focus of analysis. Presumably, for any given organization a census can be made of decisions covering a fixed period of time. The resulting population of decisions can then be analyzed as to whether each has an internal referent only, or whether to some degree significantly above zero each takes into account factors external to the organization, e.g., other organizations. Decisions can then be categorized on the basis of internal/external referents.

An overall ratio of internal to external decisions for any given organization can then be calculated that will give a measure of that organization's interdependence with the environment. It is not clear what the absolute meaning of any resulting ratio would be—that is, whether there exists some threshold value above which an organization can safely be considered to have a high degree of interdependence. However, ratios of different organizations could be compared to assess the relative interdependence of each with its respective environment.

The relative degree of interdependence of the focal organization with each of several other organizations could also be established. This would permit statements about the relative interdependence existing between pairs of organizations. A somewhat more accurate approach would entail devising a system for weighting decisions based on their importance before calculating the interdependence ratio, because not all decisions are created equal.

This approach should not be sensitive to the size of the organization, its personnel, or its budget, as would be measures based on expenditures or numbers of staff interactions between organizations.

11. There are eleven other agencies involved in the provision of public transit for the Bay Area. BART, AC, and Muni carry more than 1 million of the 1.6 million daily transit passengers in the Bay Area. To simplify an already difficult task, these other agencies are excluded from this study because of their relatively less important roles in the system during the time of the study (1978–80).

12. These arrangements are themselves examples of informal norms that are powerful determinants of behavior in the Bay Area transit system.

13. Thompson, *Organizations,* chap. 5, pp. 119, 140.

14. Herbert A. Simon, "The Architecture of Complexity," *Proceedings of the American Philosophical Society* 106(1962): 467–82.

15. Russell Hardin, *Collective Action* (Baltimore: Johns Hopkins University Press, 1982), p. 185.

16. Thomas C. Schelling, "An Essay on Bargaining," *American Economic Review* 48(1956): 281–306.

17. In an analogous situation, it is clear that treating different aspects of nuclear force reduction independently of one another has facilitated progress in the Strategic Arms Limitations Talks of the past seven years.

18. W. Richard Scott, "Developments in Organization Theory, 1960–1980," *American Behavioral Scientist* 24(1981): 407–22.

19. I return to this point in Chapter 7.

20. I return to the problem of decomposition in the concluding chapter.

Chapter Four: Informal Coordinative Mechanisms

1. The difference is analogous to that between students of international relations, such as Robert Jervis, who explore problems of perception and communication between nations, and those who take into account only differences in national interest in their attempts to predict and explain behavior of nations. See Robert Jervis, *Perception and Misperception in International Politics* (Princeton, N.J.: Princeton University Press, 1976).

2. Robert Axelrod, *The Evolution of Cooperation* (New York: Basic Books, 1984); and Russell Hardin, *Collective Action* (Baltimore: Johns Hopkins University Press, 1982).

3. As anonymity was promised to all those who participated in this study, interviews are identified only by geographic location and number. In addition to the interviews I conducted in the San Francisco Bay Area and in the Washington Metropolitan Area, I relied on interviews conducted by Thomas Cordi in 1979 in the San Francisco Bay Area. Chisholm Bay Area Interview #42.

4. Chisholm Bay Area Interview #8.

5. See Chapter 6 for a more extended discussion on this point.

6. Martin Landau, Donald Chisholm, and Melvin Webber, *Redundancy in Public Transit, Volume I: On the Idea of an Integrated Transit System* (Berkeley: University of California, Institute of Urban and Regional Development, 1980), p. 19.

7. Chisholm Bay Area Interviews #11, #13.

8. Chisholm Bay Area Interview #23.

9. Chisholm Bay Area Interview #4.

10. Chisholm Bay Area Interview #24.

11. Pondy suggests, however, following Schelling, that "perfect knowledge about each other's options may make coordination more difficult." See Louis R. Pondy, "Varieties of Organizational Conflict," *Administrative Science Quarterly* 14(1969): 500.

12. Chisholm Bay Area Interview #7.

13. Chisholm Bay Area Interview #7.

14. See Susan Crawford, "Informal Communication among Scientists in Sleep and Dream Research" (Ph.D. diss., University of Chicago, 1970); and Noah E. Friedkin, "University Social Structure and Social Networks Among Scientists," *American Journal of Sociology* 83(1978): 1444-65.

15. See below for a discussion of the term "network."

16. See Joseph Fiksel, "Dynamic Evolution in Social Networks," *Journal of Mathematical Sociology* 7(1980): 27-46, for a discussion of evolutionary patterns of social networks.

17. See François Lorrain and Harrison C. White, "Structural Equivalence of Individuals in Social Networks," *Journal of Mathematical Sociology* 1(1971): 49-80, on the problem of "role." The importance of individual traits in the development of informal channels is discussed in Chapter 6.

18. See Chapter 6.

19. "Network" has been a metaphor often used to describe social structure at least since the work of Simmel. See Georg Simmel, *The Sociology of Georg Simmel,* trans. and ed. Kurt H. Wolff (New York: The Free Press, 1950) (originally published in 1908).

20. For an excellent summary of network analysis, see David Knoke and James H. Kuklinski, *Network Analysis* (London: Sage Publications, 1982). For exemplars of mathematical approaches to the study of social networks, see Lorrain and White, "Structural Equivalence," pp. 49–80; Harrison C. White, Scott A. Boorman, and Ronald L. Brieger, "Social Structure from Multiple Networks. I. Blockmodels of Roles and Positions," *American Journal of Sociology* 81(1976): 730–80; Paul Holland and Samuel Leinhardt, "A Dynamic Model for Social Networks," *Journal of Mathematical Sociology* 5(1977): 5–20; Ross P. Kindermann and J. Laurie Snell, "On the Relation Between Markov Random Fields and Social Networks," *Journal of Mathematical Sociology* 7 (1980): 1–13; and Martin Everett and Juhani Nieminen, "Partitions and Homomorphisms in Directed and Undirected Graphs," *Journal of Mathematical Sociology* 7(1980): 91–111.

21. Knoke and Kuklinski identify seven relational types: transaction, communication, boundary penetration, instrumental, sentiment, authority/power and kinship/descent. See *Network Analysis*, pp. 15–16.

22. Knoke and Kuklinski, *Network Analysis*, p. 16.

23. In network analysis, the term "cluster" is used to denote informal channels characterized by greater density, compactness, and mesh than is found in the larger universe—where density is understood to mean the ratio of observed to possible direct relations between pairs of individuals (e.g., each member is directly linked with every other member); compactness describes the shortness of paths needed to connect all pairs; and mesh indicates multiple, short paths connecting pairs. See Noah E. Friedkin, "University Social Structure and Social Networks among Scientists," *American Journal of Sociology* 83(1978): 1447–49. This approach was inappropriate for the present study. My interest was solely in direct informal relationships. Because I was concerned solely with the instrumental use of informal channels, ratios of observed to possible channels were not relevant. Thus, although my use of "subset" is analogous to "cluster" as used in network analysis, it has a different specific meaning and for that reason I have chosen to employ a different name.

24. This was the technique employed by Berelson and his colleagues as they attempted to identify social influences on voting behavior. Bernard R. Berelson, Paul R. Lazarsfeld, and William N. McPhee, *Voting: A Study of Opinion Formation in a Presidential Campaign* (Chicago: University of Chicago Press, 1954).

25. My approach here, though simpler, is consistent with contemporary mathematical models of social networks. For example, see Joseph Fiksel, "Dynamic Evolution in Social Networks," *Journal of Mathematical Sociology* 7(1980): 27–46, for his treatment of "societal network."

26. Differences in the type of business conducted in each informal network are analogous to differences in "relational types" commonly found in research on social networks.

27. Chisholm Bay Area Interview #13.

28. Chisholm Bay Area Interview #45.

29. Chisholm Bay Area Interview #46.

30. See Chapter 6.

31. Chisholm Bay Area Interview #11.

32. This is analogous to the concept of "status homophily" advanced by Lazarsfeld and Merton in a discussion of the development of friendships, where status is understood to mean "observed tendencies for similarities between the group-affiliation of friends or between their positions in a group." See Paul F. Lazarsfeld and Robert K. Merton, "Friendship as Social Process: A Substantive and Methodological Analysis," in *Freedom and Control in Modern Society,* ed. Morroe Berger, Theodore Abel, and

Charles H. Page (New York: Van Nostrand, 1954), pp. 62–63. It is difficult, however, to disaggregate the effects of similar social status and formal position from those of occupational demands.

33. See Chapter 6.

34. James D. Thompson, *Organizations in Action: Social Science Bases of Administrative Theory* (New York: McGraw-Hill, 1967), pp. 20–24.

35. See Philip B. Heymann, "The Problem of Coordination: Bargaining and Rules," *Harvard Law Review* 86(1973): 797–877.

36. David K. Lewis, *Convention* (Cambridge, Mass.: Harvard University Press, 1969), p. 14, as quoted by Russell Hardin, *Collective Action* (Baltimore: Johns Hopkins University Press, 1982), p. 158. My assessment of informal norms in this study was based on observation of behavior, responses to questions in personal interviews, and minutes of meetings.

37. Herbert A. Simon, Donald W. Smithburg, and Victor A. Thompson, *Public Administration* (New York: Alfred A. Knopf, 1964), p. 91.

38. Donald Chisholm, "A California Ocean: Tales of the Coastal Zone Conservation Commission" (Master's thesis, University of California, Berkeley, 1976), p. 26.

39. Robert A. Kagan, *Regulatory Justice: Implementing a Wage-Price Freeze* (New York: Russell Sage, 1978).

40. See Chapter 7 for a detailed discussion of the role of the RTA in Bay Area transit coordination.

41. Regional Transit Association of the Bay Area, "Minutes of Meetings of the Board of Control and Staff-Level Committees, 1979–1980" (typescript).

42. Chisholm Washington Interview #2.

43. The pioneering work of Richard Fenno on Congressional committees made clear the importance of socialization to informal norms for the effective operation of the Congress. See his *Congressmen in Committees* (Boston: Little, Brown, and Co., 1973), esp. chap. 4. See also John Manley, *The Politics of Finance: The House Committee on Ways and Means* (Boston: Little, Brown, and Co., 1970), esp. chap. 3; Nelson W. Polsby, "The Institutionalization of the U.S. House of Representatives," *American Political Science Review* 62(1968): 144–68; and Herbert B. Asher, "The Learning of Legislative Norms," *American Political Science Review* 67(1973): 499–513.

44. Charles E. Lindblom, *The Intelligence of Democracy* (New York: The Free Press, 1965), pp. 66–84.

45. *Washington Star,* 17 March 1981.

46. *Washington Star,* 17 March 1981.

47. An analysis of the problems involved in allocating Metrobus operating revenues and costs is found in Harvey A. Levine, "Formulae for Metrobus Operating Revenues and Costs," a progress report to WMATA presented at Airlie X Workshop, 1974 (typescript).

48. *Washington Star,* 21 March 1981.

49. Lindblom, *Democracy,* p. 92.

50. Cordi Bay Area Interview #14.

51. Peter M. Blau, *Exchange and Power in Social Life* (New York: John Wiley and Sons, 1964), p. 60.

52. Chisholm Bay Area Interview #7.

53. Landau, Chisholm, and Webber, *Redundancy,* p. 36.

54. Herbert A. Simon, *Administrative Behavior,* 2nd ed. (New York: The Free Press, 1957), chap. 3. Value premises, at least, are comparable with conventions and norms as I have used the terms in this study.

55. Thompson, *Organizations,* p. 65.
56. Lindblom, *Democracy,* p. 122.

Chapter Five: The Fruits of Informal Coordination

1. Chisholm Bay Area Interview #19.
2. Chisholm Bay Area Interviews #19, #23.
3. Chisholm Bay Area Interview #23.
4. Chisholm Bay Area Interview #19.
5. Chisholm Bay Area Interview #7.
6. Chisholm Bay Area Interview #19.
7. Chisholm Bay Area Interview #43.
8. Chisholm Bay Area Interview #43.
9. Chisholm Bay Area Interview #47.
10. Chisholm Washington Interview #22.
11. The following account is based primarily on personal interviews conducted by the author with BART and AC personnel, with additional information supplied by articles in the *San Francisco Chronicle.* I am also indebted to Jonathan Bendor for material made available to me in a research memorandum written by him.
12. Chisholm Bay Area Interview #42.
13. Chisholm Bay Area Interview #42.
14. Chisholm Bay Area Interview #36.
15. Chisholm Bay Area Interview #43.
16. Chisholm Bay Area Interview #40.
17. Chisholm Bay Area Interviews #40, #42.
18. Chisholm Bay Area Interview #41.
19. Chisholm Bay Area Interview #20.
20. Chisholm Bay Area Interview #50.
21. Chisholm Bay Area Interview #4.
22. Chisholm Bay Area Interview #16.
23. Chisholm Bay Area Interview #13.
24. Chisholm Bay Area Interview #49.
25. Chisholm Bay Area Interviews #5, #11, #12, #14.
26. Chisholm Bay Area Interview #16.
27. Chisholm Bay Area Interview #17.
28. Chisholm Bay Area Interview #25.
29. Chisholm Bay Area Interviews #3, #11.
30. Chisholm Bay Area Interview #25.
31. Chisholm Bay Area Interviews #46, #47.
32. Chisholm Bay Area Interview #47.

Chapter Six: Factors Facilitating Informal Organization

1. Because of the qualitative character of the data collected on interdependence and on informal channels in this study, attempting to control for level of interdependence to ascertain the effects of other factors on the development of informal channels would require stretching the data. Therefore, this chapter is an exploratory effort intended to generate propositions to be tested in later research.
2. For recent studies on the emergence of norms, see, for example, Robert Axel-

rod, *The Evolution of Cooperation* (New York: Basic Books, 1984), esp. parts 2 and 5. See also Russell Hardin, *Collective Action* (Baltimore: Johns Hopkins University Press, 1982), chaps. 10–14; and Edna Ullmann-Margalit, *The Emergence of Norms* (Oxford: Oxford University Press, 1977).

3. I use the term "norm" interchangeably with the term "convention." For a precise definition of "convention," see Chapter 4.

4. Alvin Gouldner, "The Norm of Reciprocity: A Preliminary Statement," *American Sociological Review* 25(1960): 174.

5. Ibid., p. 171.

6. Ibid.

7. In a discussion of friendship ties in organizations, Lincoln and Miller distinguish between "instrumental" and "primary" ties between individuals, but fail to develop an argument about the relationship between the two. See James R. Lincoln and Jon Miller, "Work and Friendship Ties in Organizations: A Comparative Analysis of Relational Networks," *Administrative Science Quarterly* 24(1979): 181–99.

8. Peter M. Blau, *Exchange and Power in Social Life* (New York: John Wiley and Sons, 1964), pp. 15–16.

9. Victor A. Thompson, *Bureaucracy and the Modern World* (Morristown, N.J.: General Learning Press, 1976), p. 17. See also Chapter 2 of this study.

10. Ross K. Baker, in his *Friend and Foe in the U.S. Senate* (New York: The Free Press, 1980), p. 6, notes that "friendships among U.S. Senators are at one and the same time political and personal; what varies is which of the two qualities is dominant and defines the nature of the friendship." Cited by Gregory A. Caldeira and Samuel C. Patterson, "Political Friendship in the Legislature," *Journal of Politics* 49 (1987): 955.

11. Blau, *Exchange and Power,* pp. 91–97.

12. For a discussion of different relational types, see David Knoke and James H. Kuklinski, *Network Analysis* (London: Sage Publications, 1982), pp. 15–16.

13. However, insofar as the relationship of the parties involved is characterized by some minimal level of interdependence, the parties retain the capacity to hurt each other in some future interaction. See my discussion later in this chapter.

14. Gouldner, "Reciprocity," p. 171.

15. Blau, *Exchange and Power,* p. 98.

16. Cordi Bay Area Interview #2.

17. Blau, *Exchange and Power,* p. 108.

18. Robert Axelrod, *The Evolution of Cooperation* (New York: Basic Books, 1984).

19. Ibid., p. 10.

20. Ibid., p. 3.

21. Gouldner and Axelrod reinforce each other's conclusions quite strongly; however, Axelrod does not appear to be aware of Gouldner's work.

22. Axelrod (*Cooperation,* p. 182) takes a somewhat different view: "The foundation of cooperation is not really trust, but the durability of the relationship. . . . Whether the players trust each other or not is less important in the long run than whether the conditions are ripe for them to build a stable pattern of cooperation with each other."

23. Blau, *Exchange and Power,* p. 98.

24. Ibid., p. 94.

25. Ibid., p. 98.

26. Gouldner, "Reciprocity," p. 175.

27. Ibid.

28. Ample evidence exists for the importance of the norm of reciprocity within legislative bodies characterized by fairly stable memberships.

29. Chisholm Bay Area Interview #8.

30. Blau, *Exchange and Power*, p. 114.

31. Cordi Bay Area Interview #13.

32. Chisholm Bay Area Interview #12.

33. See Chapter 8 for a discussion of the substantive coordination achieved by RTA.

34. Chisholm Bay Area Interview #12.

35. Chisholm Bay Area Interview #12.

36. Chisholm Bay Area Interview #11.

37. Chisholm Bay Area Interview #8.

38. Chisholm Bay Area Interview #12.

39. Chisholm Bay Area Interview #21.

40. Chisholm Washington Interview #3 and various Airlie Conference documents (typewritten).

41. For a summary of such studies, see Anders Edstrom and Jay R. Galbraith, "Transfer of Managers as a Coordination and Control Strategy in Multinational Organizations," *Administrative Science Quarterly* 22(1977): 248–63. See also G. B. Baty, W. A. Evan, and T. W. Rothermel, "Personnel Movement as Interorganizational Relations," *Administrative Science Quarterly* 16(1971): 430–43; and Jeffrey Pfeffer and Huseyn Leblebici, "Executive Recruitment and the Development of Interim Organizations," *Administrative Science Quarterly* 18(1973): 449–61.

42. Chisholm Bay Area Interview #6.

43. The coordinative value of similar decision premises is discussed in Chapter 4.

44. Chisholm Bay Area Interview #49.

45. Chisholm Bay Area Interview #8.

46. Chisholm Bay Area Interviews #7, #23, #26.

47. Edstrom and Galbraith, "Managers," p. 249.

48. Ibid., p. 261.

49. See the discussion on "latent coordination" in Chapter 4.

50. Pfeffer and Leblebici, "Executive Recruitment," p. 449.

51. Chisholm Bay Area Interview #12.

52. Chisholm Bay Area Interviews #4, #30.

53. Chisholm Bay Area Interview #5.

54. Chisholm Bay Area Interview #29.

55. Chisholm Bay Area Interview #29.

56. Chisholm Bay Area Interview #34.

57. Wilbert E. Moore, *Industrial Relations and the Social Order* (New York: Macmillan, 1951), p. 293.

58. Chisholm Bay Area Interview #27.

59. Chisholm Bay Area Interview #28.

60. Chisholm Bay Area Interview #29.

61. Chisholm Bay Area Interview #28.

62. Chisholm Bay Area Interview #49.

63. As quoted in Alvin Gouldner, *Patterns of Industrial Bureaucracy* (New York: The Free Press, 1954), p. 180.

64. Cordi Bay Area Interviews #2, #5.

65. Cordi Bay Area Interview #5.

66. Cordi Bay Area Interview #2.

67. Cordi Bay Area Interview #13.

68. Chisholm Bay Area Interview #35.

69. Chisholm Bay Area Interview #29.

70. See James D. Thompson, *Organizations in Action: Social Science Bases of Administrative Theory* (New York: McGraw-Hill, 1967), and Chapter 4 of this study.

71. Chisholm Bay Area Interview #34.

72. Chisholm Bay Area Interview #13.

73. Robert K. Merton, *Social Theory and Social Structure* (New York: The Free Press, 1968), p. 199.

74. Chisholm Bay Area Interview #8.

75. Personality traits affecting the development of informal channels should be the same as those affecting the ability of individuals to establish and maintain friendships: "self-confidence, self-esteem, openness, tolerance for the views of others, and fairmindedness." Caldeira and Patterson, "Political Friendship," p. 961.

76. Chisholm Bay Area Interview #8.

77. Chisholm Bay Area Interviews #12, #29.

78. Chisholm Bay Area Interview #10.

79. Chisholm Bay Area Interview #7.

80. In fact, Caldeira and Patterson ("Political Friendship," p. 969) have developed a "propinquity model" as an explanation for the development of friendship ties in legislative bodies. They found that indeed "spatial proximity facilitates the development of political friendships in a big way. Where a legislator sits or lives partly determines who will nominate him; across the board, propinquity increases the likelihood that a friendship will come to fruition." See also R. Robert Huckfeldt, "Social Contexts, Social Networks, and Urban Neighborhoods: Environmental Constraints on Friendship Choice," *American Journal of Sociology* 89(1983): 651–59; and R. Athanasion and G. Yoshioka, "The Spatial Character of Friendship Formation," *Environment and Behavior* 5(1973): 43–65.

81. Chisholm Bay Area Interview #15.

82. Chisholm Bay Area Interview #5.

83. Chisholm Bay Area Interview #21.

84. Chisholm Bay Area Interview #11.

Chapter Seven: Informal Weaknesses and Formal Compensations

1. Max Weber, *The Theory of Social and Economic Organization,* ed. and introd. Talcott Parsons (Glencoe, Ill.: The Free Press, 1964).

2. Some governments, such as that of Hong Kong, have officially banned such informal contacts between agency personnel.

3. See Chester I. Barnard, *The Functions of the Executive* (Cambridge, Mass.: Harvard University Press, 1971).

4. Martin Landau, "Linkage, Coding, and Intermediacy," *Journal of Comparative Politics* 2(1971): 416.

5. Ibid., pp. 416–18.

6. See F. J. Roethlisberger and William J. Dickson, *Management and the Worker* (Cambridge, Mass.: Harvard University Press, 1947).

7. See, for example, Wilbert E. Moore, *Industrial Relations and the Social Order* (New York: Macmillan, 1951); and Victor A. Thompson, *Bureaucracy and the Modern World* (Morristown, N.J.: General Learning Press, 1976).

8. Chisholm Bay Area Interview #35.

9. See Chapter 6.

10. See James G. March, "The Business Firm as Political Coalition," *Journal of Politics* 24(1962): 662–78; James D. Thompson, *Organizations in Action: Social Science Bases of Administrative Theory* (New York: McGraw-Hill, 1967); and Donald Chisholm, *Organizational Adaptation to Environmental Change,* IGS Studies in Public Organization, Working Paper no. 86-1 (Berkeley: University of California, 1986).

11. Chisholm Bay Area Interview #11.

12. Herbert A. Simon, Donald W. Smithburg, and Victor A. Thompson, *Public Administration* (New York: Alfred A. Knopf, 1964), p. 88.

13. See Chapter 6.

14. See Chapter 6.

15. Jonathan B. Bendor, *Redundancy in Public Transit, Part IV: Structure, Competition and Reliability in Planning and Operations* (Berkeley: University of California, Institute of Urban and Regional Development, 1980), p. 80.

16. See Chapter 4.

17. See Chapter 6.

18. However, emergency social systems composed of rearranged pieces of existing social structures show the capacity to arise almost immediately following disasters. They are synthesized into a new whole in remarkably little time. Development time is probably, at least partially, a function of importance and urgency. See James D. Thompson and Robert Hawkes, "Disaster, Community Organization, and Administrative Process," in *Man and Society in Disaster,* ed. George W. Baker and Dwight W. Chapman, with a foreword by Carlyle F. Jacobsen (New York: Basic Books, 1962), pp. 268–304.

19. See Chapter 6.

20. See Charles E. Lindblom, *The Intelligence of Democracy* (New York: The Free Press, 1965).

21. Thomas C. Schelling, "An Essay on Bargaining," *American Economic Review* 48(1956): 281–306.

22. Fritz W. Scharpf, "Interorganizational Policy Studies: Issues, Concepts, and Perspectives," in *Interorganizational Policy Making: Limits to Coordination and Central Control,* ed. Kenneth Hanf and Fritz W. Scharpf (London: Sage Publications, 1978), pp. 345–70.

23. This key point is clearly and persuasively argued by Robert Axelrod, *The Evolution of Cooperation* (New York: Basic Books, 1984); see esp. chap. 3.

24. Cordi Bay Area Interview #3.

25. Roland Warren, "Comprehensive Planning and Coordination: Some Functional Properties," *Social Problems* 20(1973): 359.

26. Chisholm Bay Area Interview #49.

27. Elizabeth Dorosin and David W. Jones, Jr., *Case Study #3: MTC and "The Big Five" Transit Operators: Groping Toward Coordination* (Berkeley: University of California, Institute of Transportation Studies, no date), p. 2.

28. Ibid.

29. Martin Landau, Donald Chisholm, and Melvin Webber, *Redundancy in Public Transit, Volume I: On the Idea of an Integrated Transit System* (Berkeley: University of California, Institute of Urban and Regional Development, 1980), p. 41.

30. Ibid.

31. See Chapter 5.

32. Cordi Bay Area Interview #14.

33. Landau, Chisholm, and Webber, *Redundancy,* pp. 41–42. Recent changes in UMTA funding resulting from Reagan administration policies have effectively reduced funds available for disbursement by MTC. This should have the dual effects of

reducing the danger of MTC becoming too powerful and reducing the ability of MTC to alter distributions of costs and benefits of alternative coordination solutions.

34. Ibid., p. 43.

Chapter Eight: Coordination and Tradeoffs with Other Values

1. Herbert A. Simon, "On the Concept of Organizational Goal," *Administrative Science Quarterly* 9(1964): 7.

2. William Niskanen, *Bureaucracy and Representative Government* (New York: Aldine-Atherton, 1971), p. 201. Niskanen's approach is consistent with Simon's distinction between procedural and substantive forms of rationality.

3. None of these goals has any intrinsic value; they are important only for their instrumentality in achieving other goals.

4. W. Ross Ashby, "Principles of the Self-Organizing System," in *Principles of Self-Organization,* ed. Heinz von Foerster and George W. Zopf, Jr. (New York: Pergamon Press, 1962), p. 266.

5. Christopher Alexander, *Notes on the Synthesis of Form* (Cambridge, Mass.: Harvard University Press, 1979).

6. Charles E. Lindblom, "The Science of Muddling Through," *Public Administration Review* 19(1959): 79–88.

7. Jackson Turner Main, *The Anti-Federalists: Critics of the Constitution, 1781–1788* (New York: Norton, 1974), p. 129; emphasis added.

8. Since the time the research reported here was conducted, Santa Clara has built and commenced operating a light-rail transit system along its most heavily traveled corridor.

9. However, as this was being written, AC's budget woes had prompted it to commission a study of its routing structure. The tentative conclusions of that study were that AC should use a "hub and spoke" arrangement in part of its system, in combination with a grid arrangement for the other part. *San Francisco Chronicle,* 4 May 1987, p. A-7.

10. The descriptions of the specific problems facing each major transit operator in the Bay Area that follow are accurate for the 1978–80 period.

11. Elizabeth Dorosin and David W. Jones, Jr., *Case Study #3: MTC and "The Big Five" Transit Operators: Groping Toward Coordination* (Berkeley: University of California, Institute of Transportation Studies, no date), p. 15.

12. Since the research was conducted for this study, Golden Gate has replaced its gas-turbine propulsion units with more reliable and less expensive diesel engines.

13. Charles E. Lindblom, *The Intelligence of Democracy* (New York: The Free Press, 1965), p. 198.

14. Ibid.

15. Robert K. Merton, *Social Theory and Social Structure* (New York: The Free Press, 1968), p. 198.

16. Ibid., p. 200.

17. Philip Selznick, *Leadership in Administration: A Sociological Interpretation* (New York: Harper and Row, 1957), pp. 17–18, 20–21.

18. Chisholm Bay Area Interviews #20, #23.

19. James D. Thompson, *Organizations in Action: Social Science Bases of Administrative Theory* (New York: McGraw-Hill, 1967), p. 128.

20. Ibid.

21. Edward L. Katzenbach, Jr., "The Horse Cavalry in the Twentieth Century," in *The Use of Force*, ed. Robert J. Art and Kenneth N. Waltz (Boston: Little, Brown, and Co., 1971), pp. 277-97. See also Donald Chisholm, *Organizational Adaptation to Environmental Change*, IGS Studies in Public Organization, Working Paper no. 86-1 (Berkeley: University of California, Institute of Governmental Studies, 1986).

22. Cordi Bay Area Interview #11.

23. Steven Zwerling, *Mass Transit and the Politics of Technology* (New York: Praeger, 1974), p. 6.

24. David B. Truman, *The Governmental Process: Political Interests and Public Opinion* (New York: Alfred A. Knopf, 1964), pp. 264-70.

25. Ibid., p. 264.

26. Herbert J. Storing, *What the Anti-Federalists Were For: The Political Thought of the Opponents of the Constitution* (Chicago: University of Chicago Press, 1981), p. 17.

27. Ibid.

28. As quoted by Storing, ibid., p. 17.

29. Lindblom, *Democracy*, p. 229.

30. Lindblom, *Democracy*, p. 151.

31. Lindblom, *Democracy*, p. 151.

32. See Chapter 7.

33. On this point, see Harold Seidman, *Politics, Position, and Power*, 3rd ed. (New York: Oxford University Press, 1980).

34. *Oakland Tribune*, 10 September 1982, p. B-6.

35. See Chapter 7.

36. Robert Bish, "Intergovernmental Relations in the United States: Some Concepts and Implications From a Public Choice Perspective," in *Interorganizational Policy Making: Limits to Coordination and Central Control*, ed. Kenneth Hanf and Fritz W. Scharpf (London: Sage Publications, 1978), p. 30.

37. Chisholm Bay Area Interview #50.

38. Chisholm Bay Area Interview #29.

39. Seymour Adler, *Redundancy in Public Transit, Part III: The Political Economy of Transit in the San Francisco Bay Area, 1945-1963* (Berkeley: University of California, Institute of Urban and Regional Development, 1980), p. 156.

40. Ibid., p. 196.

41. Ibid.

42. Ibid.

43. Ibid., p. 197.

44. Ibid., p. 237.

45. Ibid., p. 239.

46. Ibid., p. 206.

47. Ibid., p. 240.

48. Conversation with Wolfgang S. Homburger, 16 July 1982.

49. Jonathan B. Bendor, *Redundancy in Public Transit, Part IV: Structure, Competition, and Reliability in Planning and Operations* (Berkeley: University of California, Institute of Urban and Regional Development, 1980), p. 288.

50. Ibid.

51. Herbert A. Simon, *Administrative Behavior*, 2nd ed. (New York: The Free Press, 1957), pp. 26-28.

52. Cordi Bay Area Interview #7.

53. Vincent Ostrom, Charles Tiebout, and Roland Warren, "The Organization of

Government in Metropolitan Regions," *American Political Science Review* 55(1961): 837.

54. Bendor, *Redundancy*, p. 254.

55. Herbert A. Simon, Donald W. Smithburg, and Victor A. Thompson, *Public Administration* (New York: Alfred Knopf, 1964), p. 493.

56. On this point, see Aaron Wildavsky, "The Political Economy of Efficiency," in his *Speaking Truth to Power* (Boston: Little, Brown, and Co., 1979).

57. See Brett W. Hawkins and Thomas R. Dye, "Metropolitan 'Fragmentation': A Research Note," *Midwest Review of Public Administration* 4(1970): 17–24, for an assessment of the influence of organizational fragmentation on public spending in metropolitan areas. They conclude that the effect of fragmentation on spending is very weak when compared with environmental factors such as the sociopolitical values involved.

58. Martin Landau, "Redundancy, Rationality, and the Problem of Duplication and Overlap," *Public Administration Review* 29(1969): 346–58.

59. See Jonathan B. Bendor, *Parallel Systems: Redundancy in Government* (Berkeley: University of California Press, 1985), for an extensive consideration of the role of reliability and redundancy in public transit operations and planning as well as generalizations to other public services.

60. Landau, "Redundancy," p. 349.

61. Ibid., p. 350.

62. See Chapter 5.

63. Bendor, *Redundancy*, p. 252.

64. Ibid., pp. 289–90.

65. Ibid., p. 291.

66. Simon, "Concept of Organizational Goal," p. 3.

Chapter Nine: Conclusion

1. Herbert A. Simon, "The Structure of Ill Structured Problems," *Artificial Intelligence* 4(1973): 181–201.

2. Harold Seidman, *Politics, Position, and Power*, 3rd ed. (New York: Oxford University Press, 1980).

3. Martin Landau and Russell Stout, "To Manage Is Not to Control or the Folly of Type II Errors," *Public Administration Review* 39(1979): 148–56.

4. *San Francisco Chronicle*, 19 May 1987, p. A-6.

5. Kenneth Arrow, *The Limits of Organization* (New York: W. W. Norton, 1974), p. 33.

6. Philip B. Heymann, "The Problem of Coordination: Bargaining and Rules," *Harvard Law Review* 86(1973): 802.

7. Arrow, *Organization*, p. 38.

8. Charles E. Lindblom, *The Intelligence of Democracy* (New York: The Free Press, 1965), p. 190.

9. Ibid.

10. As quoted by Vincent Ostrom, "Nonhierarchical Approaches to the Organization of Public Activity," *Annals of the American Academy of Political and Social Science* 466(1983): 137.

11. Heymann, "Coordination," pp. 827–43.

12. Herbert A. Simon, *Reason in Human Affairs* (Stanford, Calif.: Stanford University Press, 1983), p. 3.

13. A. F. von Hayek, *Studies in Philosophy, Politics, and Economics* (London: Routledge and Pane, 1967), 13.

14. Ibid.

15. Warren Weaver, "Science and Complexity," *American Scientist* 36(1948): 537.

16. Ibid., p. 538.

17. Ibid., p. 539.

18. Ibid., p. 540.

19. Simon, "Ill Structured Problems," p. 187.

20. Ibid., p. 190.

21. Ibid., p. 191.

22. James D. Thompson and Arthur Tuden, "Strategies, Structures, and Processes of Organizational Decision," in *Comparative Studies in Administration,* ed. James D. Thompson (Pittsburgh: University of Pittsburgh Press, 1959), pp. 195–216.

23. See John Dewey, *The Public and Its Problems* (New York: Henry Holt and Co., 1927).

24. Ostrom, "Public Activity," p. 147.

25. Ibid.

26. Ibid.

27. Heymann, "Coordination," p. 870.

28. Herbert A. Simon, "Style in Design," in *Proceedings of the Second Annual Design Research Association Conference, October 1970,* ed. J. Archea and C. Eastman (Pittsburgh: Carnegie-Mellon University, 1975), p. 2.

29. Ibid.

Chapter Ten: An Afterword

1. The discussion that follows is based largely on documents published by the MTC and the RTA. For a more detailed analysis, see the *Transit Coordination Evaluation,* published annually by MTC between 1981 and 1986. I also reinterviewed several key actors at the transit operators, especially in reference to informal agreements between them.

2. *San Francisco Chronicle,* 17 December 1987, p. A-22.

3. *San Francisco Chronicle,* 18 December 1987, p. A-3.

4. *Oakland Tribune,* 12 December 1987, p. A-9.

5. BART, for example, increased its fares by 30 percent in January 1986. BART surveys of its riders indicate that many have formed carpools.

6. *San Francisco Chronicle,* 17 December 1987, p. A-22.

7. This section relies on information supplied in two newspaper articles, one in the *San Francisco Chronicle,* 14 April 1987, pp. A-1, A-18, written by Harry W. Demoro, a long-time transit reporter in the Bay Area, and one from the *San Francisco Chronicle,* 17 December 1987, pp. A-1, A-22, by Ramon G. McLeod, and on information from various MTC reports.

8. Metropolitan Transportation Commission, *Transit Coordination Evaluation, Report for FY 1986* (Oakland, Calif.: Metropolitan Transportation Commission, 1986), p. C1.

9. Ibid., p. C3.

10. This is only a short summary of some of the more important arrangements. For complete details of all interoperator coordinative arrangements in the Bay Area public transit system, see the *Transit Coordination Evaluation* reports produced annually by MTC.

11. Metropolitan Transportation Commission, *Transit Coordination Evaluation,* p. 24.

12. *San Francisco Chronicle,* 19 May 1987, p. A-6.

13. Metropolitan Transportation Commission, *Transit Coordination Evaluation,* p. 1.

14. Ibid.

15. Ibid., p. 4.

16. Ibid., p. 14.

17. *San Francisco Chronicle,* 19 May 1987, p. A-6. I find this particularly ironic in the face of concern by the individual operators that MTC represented a significant threat to their independence and in fact was perceived, initially at least, to favor consolidation.

18. *San Francisco Chronicle,* 19 May 1987, p. A-6. I cannot help but regard these as rather flimsy grounds for any major reorganization of Bay Area public transit.

19. As it is, AC, BART, Santa Clara, and Golden Gate spend an estimated combined $800,000 annually on lobbyists in Sacramento and Washington (*San Francisco Chronicle,* 19 May 1987, p. A-6).

Bibliography

Adler, Seymour. *Redundancy in Public Transit, Part III: The Political Economy of Transit in the San Francisco Bay Area, 1945–1963*. Berkeley: University of California, Institute of Urban and Regional Development, 1980.

Aiken, Michael, and Robert Alford. "Community Structure and Innovation: The Case of Urban Renewal." *American Sociological Review* 35(1970): 650–65.

Aiken, Michael, and Jerald Hage. "Organizational Interdependence and Intra-organizational Structure." *American Sociological Review* 23 (1968): 912–30.

Aldrich, Howard. "Organizational Boundaries and Interorganizational Conflict." *Human Relations* 24(1971): 279–93.

———. "Resource Dependence and Interorganizational Relations." *Administration and Society* 7(1976): 419–55.

Alexander, Christopher. *Notes on the Synthesis of Form*. Cambridge, Mass.: Harvard University Press, 1979.

Allen, Michael. "The Structure of Interorganizational Elite Cooptation: Interlocking Corporate Directorates." *American Sociological Review* 39(1974): 393–406.

Allen, Thomas J., and Stephen I. Cohen. "Information Flow in Research and Development Laboratories." *Administrative Science Quarterly* 14 (1969): 12–19.

Alt, R. M. "The Internal Organization of the Firm and Price Formation: An Illustrative Case." *Quarterly Journal of Economics* 63(1949): 92–110.

Altshuler, Alan. "The Politics of Urban Transportation Innovation." *Technology Review* (May 1977): 51–58.

Amir, Shaul. "Group Issue Analysis of a Planning Controversy." *Traffic Quarterly* 28(1974): 185–96.

Argyris, Chris. *The Applicability of Organizational Sociology.* Cambridge: Cambridge University Press, 1972.

Arrow, Kenneth. *The Limits of Organization.* New York: W. W. Norton, 1974.

Ashby, W. Ross. "Principles of the Self-Organizing System." In *Principles of Self-Organization,* pp. 255–78. Edited by Heinz von Foerster and George W. Zopf, Jr. New York: Pergamon Press, 1962.

Asher, Herbert B. "The Learning of Legislative Norms." *American Political Science Review* 67(1973): 499–513.

Assael, Henry. "Constructive Role of Interorganizational Conflict." *Administrative Science Quarterly* 14(1969): 573–82.

Athanasion, R., and G. Yoshioka. "The Spatial Character of Friendship Formation." *Environment and Behavior* 5(1973): 43–65.

Axelrod, Robert. *The Evolution of Cooperation.* New York: Basic Books, 1984.

Baker, Ross K. *Friend and Foe in the U.S. Senate.* New York: The Free Press, 1980.

Banfield, Edwin C. *Political Influence.* New York: Free Press, 1961.

Barber, Bernard. "Structural Functional Analysis: Some Problems and Mis-Understandings." *American Sociological Review* 21 (1956): 129–35.

Barnard, Chester I. *The Functions of the Executive.* Cambridge, Mass.: Harvard University Press, 1971.

Barton, Allen. "The Emergency Social System." In *Man and Society in Disaster,* pp. 222–67. Edited by George W. Baker and Dwight W. Chapman. Foreword by Carlyle F. Jacobsen. New York: Basic Books, 1962.

Baty, G. B., W. A. Evan, and T. W. Rothermel. "Personnel Movement as Interorganizational Relations." *Administrative Science Quarterly* 16 (1971): 430–43.

Bauer, Kurt W. "Regional Planning in Southeastern Wisconsin." *Traffic Quarterly* 28(1974): 551–72.

Baum, Bernard H. *Decentralization of Authority in a Bureaucracy.* Englewood Cliffs, N.J.: Prentice-Hall, 1961.

Beckman, Norman. "Impact of the Transportation Planning Process." *Traffic Quarterly* 20(1966): 159–73.

Bendor, Jonathan B. *Redundancy in Public Transit, Part IV: Structure, Competition and Reliability in Planning and Operations.* Berkeley: University of California, Institute of Urban and Regional Development, 1980.

———. *Parallel Systems: Redundancy in Government.* Berkeley: University of California Press, 1985.

Benson, J. A. "The Interorganizational Network as a Political Economy." *Administrative Science Quarterly* 20(1975): 229–49.

Berelson, Bernard R., Paul F. Lazarsfeld, and William N. McPhee. *Voting: A Study of Opinion Formation in a Presidential Campaign.* Chicago: University of Chicago Press, 1954.

Berliner, Joseph. "The Informal Organization of the Soviet Firm." *Quarterly Journal of Economics* 66(1952): 353–65.

———. *Factory and Manager in the USSR.* Cambridge, Mass.: Harvard University Press, 1957.

Bertalanffy, Ludwig von. *General System Theory: Foundations, Development, Applications.* New York: George Braziller, 1968.

Beveridge, W. I. B. *The Art of Scientific Investigation.* New York: Vintage Books, 1957.

Bish, Robert. "Intergovernmental Relations in the United States: Some Concepts and Implications from a Public Choice Perspective." In *Interorganizational Policy Making: Limits to Coordination and Central Control,* pp. 19–36. Edited by Kenneth Hanf and Fritz W. Scharpf. London: Sage Publications, 1978.

Bish, Robert, and Roland Warren. "Scale and Monopoly Problems in Urban Government Services." *Urban Affairs Quarterly* 8(1972): 97–122.

Black, Bertram, and Harold Kase. "Interagency Cooperation in Rehabilitation and Mental Health." *Social Service Review* 37(1963): 26–32.

Blau, Peter M. *The Dynamics of Bureaucracy.* Chicago: University of Chicago Press, 1955.

———. "Patterns of Choice in Interpersonal Relations." *American Sociological Review* 27(1962): 41–55.

———. *Exchange and Power in Social Life.* New York: John Wiley and Sons, 1964.

———. "The Hierarchy of Authority in Organizations." *American Journal of Sociology* 73(1968): 453–67.

———. *The Organization of Academic Work.* New York: Wiley, 1973.

Blau, Peter M., and W. Richard Scott. *Formal Organizations.* San Francisco: Chandler, 1962.

Blau, Peter M., Wolf Heydebrand, and Robert Stauffer. "The Structure of Small Bureaucracies." *American Sociological Review* 31(1966): 179–91.

Blumberg, Arthur, and William Wiener. "One from Two: Facilitating an Organizational Merger." *Journal of Applied Behavioral Science* 7(1971): 87–102.

Bott, Elizabeth. *Family and Social Network: Roles, Norms, and External Relationships in Ordinary Urban Families.* London: Tavistock Press, 1957.

Bracken, Paul. *The Command and Control of Nuclear Forces.* New Haven: Yale University Press, 1983.

Braybrooke, David, and Charles E. Lindblom. *A Strategy of Decision: Policy Evaluation as a Social Process*. New York: Free Press, 1970.

Bredemeier, Harry C. "The Methodology of Functionalism." *American Sociological Review* 20(1955): 173–80.

Brieger, Roland. "Career Attributes and Network Structure." *American Sociological Review* 41(1976): 117–35.

Brown, Bonnie E. "Rational Planning and Responsiveness: The Case of the HSA's." *Public Administration Review* 41(1981): 437–44.

Browne, William P. "Organizational Maintenance: The Internal Operation of Interest Groups." *Public Administration Review* 38(1978): 48–57.

Buckley, W., T. R. Burns, and L. D. Meeker. "Structural Resolutions of Collective Action Problems." *Behavioral Science* 19(1974): 277–97.

Buell, Thomas B. *Master of Sea Power: A Biography of Fleet Admiral Ernest J. King*. Boston: Little, Brown, and Co., 1980.

Burcham, John B., Jr. "The Politics of Transportation in the National Capital Region." Washington, D.C.: Washington Metropolitan Area Transit Authority, [no date]. Typescript.

Burns, T., and G. M. Stalker. *The Management of Innovation*. London: Tavistock Publications, 1961.

Caldeira, Gregory A., and Samuel C. Patterson. "Political Friendship in the Legislature." *Journal of Politics* 49(1987): 953–75.

Caro, Robert A. *The Power Broker: Robert Moses and the Fall of New York*. New York: Vintage Books, 1975.

Chisholm, Donald. "A California Ocean: Tales of the Coastal Zone Conservation Commission." Master's thesis, University of California, Berkeley, 1976.

————. *Problems of Systems Analysis: Informal Organization and Bay Area Transit*. Berkeley: University of California, Institute of Transportation Studies, 1980.

————. *Organizational Adaptation to Environmental Change*. IGS Studies in Public Organization, Working Paper no. 86-1. Berkeley: University of California, Institute of Governmental Studies, 1986.

————. "Ill Structured Problems, Informal Mechanisms, and the Design of Public Organizations." In *Bureaucracy and Public Choice*, pp. 77–94. Edited by Jan-Erik Lane. London: Sage, 1987.

Clark, Burton. "Interorganizational Patterns in Education." *Administrative Science Quarterly* 10(1965): 224–37.

Coker, Francis W. "Dogmas of Administrative Reform." *American Political Science Review* 16(1922): 399–411.

Cordi, Thomas. "The Bay Area Transit Community as an Ecology of Games." Berkeley: University of California, [1979]. Typescript.

Corwin, Ronald G. "Patterns of Organizational Conflict." *Administrative Science Quarterly* 14(1969): 507–20.

Crane, Diana. "Social Structure in a Group of Scientists: A Test of the 'Invisible College' Hypothesis." *American Sociological Review* 34(1969): 335–52.

Crawford, Susan. "Informal Communication Among Scientists in Sleep and Dream Research." Ph.D. diss., University of Chicago, 1970.

Crozier, Michel. *The Bureaucratic Phenomenon.* Chicago: University of Chicago Press, 1964.

Cyert, Richard M., and James G. March. *A Behavioral Theory of the Firm.* Englewood Cliffs, N.J.: Prentice-Hall, 1963.

Darwin, F. *Life and Letters of Charles Darwin.* London: John Murray, 1888.

Devons, Ely. *Planning in Practice: Essays in Aircraft Planning in Wartime.* Cambridge: Cambridge University Press, 1950.

———. *Papers on Planning and Economic Management.* Edited by Sir Alec Cairncross. Manchester: Manchester University Press, 1970.

Dewey, John. *The Public and Its Problems.* New York: Henry Holt and Co., 1927.

Dill, William R. "Environmental Influence on Managerial Autonomy." *American Sociological Quarterly* 2(1958): 409–43.

Dillon, Robert J., and Robert E. Quinn. "Interorganizational Systems: A Computerized Approach to Improved Coordination and Productivity." *Public Productivity Review* 4(1980): 63–83.

Doig, Jameson W. *Metropolitan Transportation Politics and the New York Region.* New York: Columbia University Press, 1966.

Dorosin, Elizabeth, and David W. Jones, Jr. *Case Study #3: MTC and "The Big Five" Transit Operators: Groping Toward Coordination.* Berkeley: University of California, Institute of Transportation Studies, [no date].

Durkheim, Emile. *The Rules of Sociological Method.* Glencoe, Ill.: The Free Press of Glencoe, 1938.

Edstrom, Anders, and Jay R. Galbraith. "Transfer of Managers as a Coordination and Control Strategy in Multinational Organizations." *Administrative Science Quarterly* 22(1977): 248–63.

Engelen, Rodney E., and Darwin G. Stuart. "Changing Roles in Regional Planning." *Traffic Quarterly* 28(1974): 537–50.

Eschewege, Henry, and John Vialet. "Stimulating Transportation Innovation—The Federal Role." *Traffic Quarterly* 34(1980): 305–12.

Evan, William M. "The Organization Set." In *Approaches to Organizational Design,* pp. 173–91. Edited by James D. Thompson. Pittsburgh: University of Pittsburgh Press, 1966.

———. "Toward a Theory of Interorganizational Relations." *Management Science* 11(1965): 217–30.

Everett, Martin, and Juhani Nieminen. "Partitions and Homomorphisms in Directed and Undirected Graphs." *Journal of Mathematical Sociology* 7(1980): 91–111.

Fenno, Richard. *Congressmen in Committees*. Boston: Little, Brown, and Co., 1973.

————. "Observation, Context, and Sequence in the Study of Politics." *American Political Science Review* 80(1986): 3–15.

Fiksel, Joseph. "Dynamic Evolution in Societal Networks." *Journal of Mathematical Sociology* 7(1980): 27–46.

Fox, Kenneth. *Better City Government: Innovations in American Urban Politics, 1850–1937*. Philadelphia: Temple University Press, 1977.

Franklin, William D. "Benefit-Cost Analysis in Transportation: The Economic Rationale of Resource Allocation." *Traffic Quarterly* 22(1968): 69–76.

Friedell, Morris F. "Organizations as Semi-lattices." *American Sociological Review* 32(1967): 46–53.

Friedkin, Noah E. "University of Social Structure and Social Networks Among Scientists." *American Journal of Sociology* 83(1978): 1444–65.

George, Alexander. "The Case for Multiple Advocacy in Making Foreign Policy." *American Political Science Review* 6(1972): 751–85.

Goodsell, Charles T. *The Case for Bureaucracy: A Public Administration Polemic*, 2nd ed. Chatham, N.J.: Chatham House, 1985.

Gouldner, Alvin. *Patterns of Industrial Bureaucracy*. New York: The Free Press, 1954.

————. "Reciprocity and Autonomy in Functional Theory." In *Symposium on Sociological Theory*, pp. 241–70. Edited by Llewellyn Gross. New York: Harper and Row, 1959.

————. "Organizational Analysis." In *Sociology Today: Problems and Prospects*, pp. 400–28. Edited by R. K. Merton, L. Broom, and L. S. Cotrell, Jr. New York: Basic Books, 1959.

————. "The Norm of Reciprocity: A Preliminary Statement." *American Sociological Review* 25(1960): 161–78.

Granovetter, Mark. "The Strength of Weak Ties." *American Journal of Sociology* 78(1973): 1360–80.

————. *Getting a Job: A Study of Contacts and Careers*. Cambridge, Mass.: Harvard University Press, 1974.

————. "Network Sampling: Some First Steps." *American Journal of Sociology* 81(1976): 1287–303.

Gregor, A. James. "Political Science and the Uses of Functional Analysis." *American Political Science Review* 62(1968): 425–39.

Gross, Bertram M. "Planning in an Era of Social Revolution." *Public Administration Review* 31(1971): 259–97.

————. "An Organized Society." *Public Administration Review* 33(1973): 323–27.

Hage, Jerald, and Michael Aiken. "Program Change and Organizational

Properties: A Comparative Analysis." *American Journal of Sociology* 72(1967): 503–19.

Hammer, Muriel. "Predictability of Social Connections Over Time." *Social Networks* 2(1979–80): 165–80.

Hanf, Kenneth, and Fritz W. Scharpf, ed. *Interorganizational Policy Making: Limits to Coordination and Central Control.* London: Sage Publications, 1978.

Hardin, Russell. *Collective Action.* Baltimore: Johns Hopkins University Press, 1982.

Hassell, John S., Jr. "How Effective Has Urban Transportation Planning Been?" *Traffic Quarterly* 34(1980): 5–20.

Hawkins, Brett W., and Thomas R. Dye. "Metropolitan 'Fragmentation': A Research Note." *Midwest Review of Public Administration* 4(1970): 17–24.

Hayek, A. F. von. *Studies In Philosophy, Politics, and Economics.* London: Routledge and Pane, 1967.

Hebert, Budd. "Urban Morphology and Transportation." *Traffic Quarterly* 30(1976): 633–50.

Hempel, Carl G. "The Logic of Functional Analysis." In *Symposium on Sociological Theory,* pp. 271–307. Edited by Llewellyn Gross. New York: Harper and Row, 1959.

Heymann, Philip B. "The Problem of Coordination: Bargaining and Rules." *Harvard Law Review* 86(1973): 797–877.

Hickson, D. J., C. R. Hinings, C. A. Lee, R. E. Schenck, and J. M. Pennings. "A Strategic Contingencies Theory of Intraorganizational Power. *Administrative Science Quarterly* 16(1971): 216–29.

Hirschman, Albert O., and Charles E. Lindblom. "Economic Efficiency, Research and Development, Policy Making: Some Converging Views." *Behavioral Science* 7(1962): 211–22.

Hirten, John E. "The Bias in Transit Planning." *Modern Railroads,* May 1975, 70–73.

Holland, Paul, and Samuel Leinhardt. "A Dynamic Model for Social Networks." *Journal of Mathematical Sociology* 5(1977): 5–20.

Homans, George C. "The Western Electric Researches." In *Human Factors in Management,* pp. 210–41. Edited by S. D. Hoslett. New York: Harper and Brothers, 1951.

Homburger, Wolfgang S., and James A. Desveaux. *Joint Transit Fares in a Multi-operator Region: A Conceptual Plan for the San Francisco Bay Area.* Berkeley: University of California, Institute of Transportation Studies, 1980.

Homburger, Wolfgang S., and Vukan R. Vuchic. "Federation of Transit

Agencies As a Solution for Service Integration." *Traffic Quarterly* 24 (1970): 373–91.

Huckfeldt, R. Robert. "Social Contexts, Social Networks, and Urban Neighborhoods: Environmental Constraints on Friendship Choice." *American Journal of Sociology* 89(1983): 651–69.

Hyneman, Charles S. "Administrative Reorganization." *Journal of Politics* 1(1939): 62–75.

Imerstein, Allen W., Larry Polivka, Sharon Gordon-Girvin, Richard Chakerian, and Patricia Martin. "Service Networks in Florida: Administrative Decentralization and Its Effects on Service Delivery." *Public Administration Review* 46(1986): 161–78.

International Encyclopedia of the Social Sciences. S.v. "General Systems Theory," by Anatol Rapaport. New York: Macmillan, 1968.

———. S.v. "Social Systems," by Talcott Parsons.

———. S.v. "Cooperation," by Robert Nisbet.

Janowitz, Morris. "Changing Patterns of Organizational Authority: The Military Establishment." *American Sociological Quarterly* 3(1959): 473–93.

Jervis, Robert. *Perception and Misperception in International Politics.* Princeton, N.J.: Princeton University Press, 1976.

Jones, Bryan D., and Clifford Kaufman. "The Distribution of Urban Public Services: A Preliminary Model." *Administration and Society* 6(1974): 337–60.

Jones, David W., Jr. *The Politics of Metropolitan Transportation Planning and Programming.* Berkeley: University of California, Institute of Transportation Studies, 1976.

———. "Conventional Transit: Financing and Budget Constraints." Paper presented at the Conference on Urban Transport Service Innovations. September 1977.

———. *Case Study #2: MTC, Its Citizen Constituency and Local Government: "Bottoms Up" Planning; "Top Down" Funding.* Berkeley: University of California, Institute of Transportation Studies, [no date].

———. "Transportation in the Bay Area: A Challenge to Institutional Reform." *Public Affairs Report* 19(1978): 1–9.

Kagan, Robert A. *Regulatory Justice: Implementing a Wage-Price Freeze.* New York: Russell Sage, 1978.

Kahn, Alfred J. *Planning Community Services for Children in Trouble.* New York: Columbia University Press, 1963.

Kaplan, Abraham. *The Conduct of Inquiry: Methodology for Behavioral Science.* San Francisco: Chandler Publishing Company, 1964.

Katzenbach, Edward L., Jr. "The Horse Cavalry in the Twentieth Century."

In *The Use of Force*, pp. 277–97. Edited by Robert J. Art and Kenneth N. Waltz. Boston: Little, Brown, and Co., 1971.

Kaufman, Herbert. *The Forest Ranger: A Study in Administrative Behavior.* Baltimore: Johns Hopkins University Press, 1963.

———. "Administrative Decentralization and Political Power." *Public Administration Review* 39(1969): 3–15.

———. "The Direction of Organizational Evolution." *Public Administration Review* 33(1973): 300–7.

———. "The Natural History of Organizations." *Administration and Society* 7(1975): 131–49.

———. "Reflections on Administrative Reorganization." In *Setting National Priorities: The 1978 Budget*, pp. 391–418. Edited by Joseph A. Pechman. Washington, D.C.: The Brookings Institution, 1978.

Kesselman, Mark. "Overinstitutionalization and Political Constraint." *Comparative Politics* 3(1970): 21–44.

Killworth, Peter D., and H. Russell Bernard. "Informant Accuracy in Social Network Data III: A Comparison of Triadic Structure in Behavioral and Cognitive Data." *Social Networks* 2 (1979): 19–46.

Kindermann, Ross P., and J. Laurie Snell. "On the Relation Between Markov Random Fields and Social Networks." *Journal of Mathematical Sociology* 7(1980):1–13.

King, Alan L. "Identifying Community Transportation Concerns." *Traffic Quarterly* 29(1975): 317–32.

Klein, Burton. "A Radical Proposal for R and D." *Fortune,* May 1958, 112–13, 218, 222, 224, 226.

Knoke, David, and James H. Kuklinski. *Network Analysis.* London: Sage Publications, 1982.

Kochen, Manfred, and Karl W. Deutsch. "Toward a Rational Theory of Decentralization: Some Implications of a Mathematical Approach." *American Political Science Review* 63(1969): 734–49.

Kropotkin, P'ter. *Mutual Aid: A Factor of Evolution.* Foreword by Ashley Montagu. Boston: Extending Horizons Books, 1955.

Landau, Martin. "Redundancy, Rationality, and the Problem of Duplication and Overlap." *Public Administration Review* 29(1969): 346–58.

———. "Linkage, Coding, and Intermediacy." *Journal of Comparative Politics* 2(1971): 401–29.

———. "Federalism, Redundancy and System Reliability." *Publius* 3 (1973): 173–96.

———. "On the Concept of a Self-correcting Organization." *Public Administration Review* 33(1973): 533–42.

———. *Political Theory and Political Science.* Atlantic Highlands, New Jersey: Humanities Press, 1979.

Landau, Martin, Donald Chisholm, and Melvin Webber. *Redundancy in Public Transit, Volume I: On the Idea of an Integrated Transit System.* Berkeley: University of California, Institute of Urban and Regional Development, 1980.

Landau, Martin, and Russell Stout. "To Manage Is Not to Control or the Folly of Type II Errors." *Public Administration Review* 39(1979): 148–56.

Laszlo, Ervin. *Introduction to Systems Philosophy: Toward a New Paradigm of Contemporary Thought.* New York: Gordon and Breach, 1972.

———. *The Systems View of the World.* New York: George Braziller, 1972.

Lazarsfeld, Paul F., and Robert K. Merton. "Friendship as a Social Process: A Substantive and Methodological Analysis." In *Freedom and Controversy in Modern Society,* pp. 18–66. Edited by Morroe Berger, Theodore Abel, and Charles H. Page. New York: Van Nostrand, 1954.

Lee, Douglas B., Jr. "Consequences of Service Reduction in Municipal Transit: San Francisco's Muni." *Transportation* 2(1973): 195–218.

Leinhardt, Samuel. "Social Network Research: Editor's Introduction." *Journal of Mathematical Sociology* 5(1977): 1–4.

Lemann, Nicholas. "Survival Networks: Staying in Washington." *The Washington Monthly,* June 1978, 23–32.

Levine, Harvey A. "Formulae for Metrobus Operating Revenues and Costs." A progress report to WMATA presented at Arlie X Workshop. Typescript.

Levine, Sol, and Paul E. White. "Exchange as a Conceptual Framework for the Study of Interorganizational Relationships." *Administrative Science Quarterly* 5(1964): 583–601.

Levine, Sol, Paul E. White, and Benjamin D. Paul. "Community Interorganizational Problems in Providing Medical Care and Social Services." *American Journal of Public Health* 53(1963): 1183–95.

Lewis, David K. *Convention.* Cambridge, Mass.: Harvard University Press, 1969.

Lima, Peter M., Theodore H. Positer, and Bradley T. Hargroves. "Transportation and Substate Regionalism." *Traffic Quarterly* 32(1978): 67–86.

Lincoln, James R., and Jon Miller. "Work and Friendship Ties in Organizations: A Comparative Analysis of Relational Networks." *Administrative Science Quarterly* 24(1979): 181–99.

Lindblom, Charles E. "The Science of Muddling Through." *Public Administration Review* 19(1959): 79–88.

———. *The Intelligence of Democracy.* New York: The Free Press, 1965.

———. "Still Muddling, Not Yet Through." *Public Administration Review* 39(1979): 517–26.

Lipson, Leon. "Statement Before the U.S. House of Representatives Select

Committee on Intelligence, Subcommittee on Program and Budget Allocation," Washington, D.C., 24 January 1980.

Litwak, Eugene, and Lydia Hylton. "Interorganization Analysis: A Hypothesis on Coordinating Agencies." *Administrative Science Quarterly* 6(1962): 395–426.

Litwak, Eugene, and Henry J. Meyer. "Theory of Coordination Between Bureaucratic Organizations and Community Primary Groups." *American Sociological Quarterly* 11(1966): 31–58.

Lockwood, Stephen C. "Transportation Planning in a Changing Environment." *Traffic Quarterly* 28(1974): 521–36.

London, Jack. *The Road.* London: Arco Publications, 1967.

Long, Norton. "The City as a Political Economy." *Administration and Society* 12(1980): 5–35.

Lorrain, François, and Harrison C. White. "Structural Equivalence of Individuals in Social Networks." *Journal of Mathematical Sociology* 1(1971): 49–80.

Lowi, Theodore S. "Toward Functionalism in Political Science: The Case of Innovation in Party Systems." *American Political Science Review* 57 (1963): 570–83.

Lowrie, S. Gale. "Centralization vs. Decentralization." *American Political Science Review* 16(1922): 379–86.

Macaulay, S. "Non-contractual Relations in Business: A Preliminary Study." *American Sociological Review* 28(1963): 55–67.

McCord, Edward. "Structural-Functionalism and the Network Idea: Towards an Integrated Methodology." *Social Networks* 2(1979–80): 371–83.

McGregor, Eugene, Jr. "Politics and the Career Mobility of Bureaucrats." *American Political Science Review* 68(1974): 18–26.

Main, Jackson Turner. *The Anti-Federalists: Critics of the Constitution, 1781–1788.* New York: Norton, 1974.

Manley, John. *The Politics of Finance: The House Committee on Ways and Means.* Boston: Little, Brown, and Co., 1970.

Marando, Vincent L. "The Politics of Metropolitan Reform." *Administration and Society* 6(1974): 229–62.

March, James G. "The Business Firm as a Political Coalition." *Journal of Politics* 24(1962): 662–78.

March, James G., and Herbert A. Simon. *Organizations.* New York: John Wiley and Sons, 1958.

March, James G., and Johan P. Olson. "Organizing Political Life: What Administrative Reorganization Tells Us About Government." *American Political Science Review* 77(1983): 282–96.

Marrett, Cora Bagley. "On the Specification of Interorganizational Dimensions." *Sociology and Sociological Research* 56(1971): 83–99.

Matthews, John M. "State Administrative Reorganization." *American Political Science Review* 16(1922): 387–98.

Mayworm, Patrick, Armando M. Lago, and J. Matthew McEnroe. *Patronage Impacts of Changes in Fares and Services.* Washington, D.C.: U.S. Government, Department of Transportation, Urban Mass Transportation Administration, 1980.

Mencher, S. "Principles of Social Work Organization." *Social Casework* 44(1963): 262–66.

Merkle, Judith. *Management and Ideology: The Legacy of the International Scientific Management Movement.* Berkeley: University of California Press, 1980.

Mertins, Herman, Jr. "The New Federalism and Federal Transportation Policy." *Public Administration Review* 33(1973): 243–52.

Merton, Robert K. *On the Shoulders of Giants: A Shandean Postscript.* New York: The Free Press, 1965.

―――. *Social Theory and Social Structure.* New York: The Free Press, 1968.

Metcalfe, Lee. "Organizational Strategies and Interorganizational Networks." *Human Relations* 29(1976): 327–43.

Meyer, Marshall. "Two Authority Structures of Bureaucratic Organizations." *Administrative Science Quarterly* 13(1968): 211–28.

Miller, David R. "New Challenges, New Institutions." *Public Administration Review* 33(1973): 236–42.

Miller, Walter. "Interinstitutional Conflict as a Major Impediment to Delinquency Prevention." *Human Organization* 17(1958): 20–23.

Milward, H. Brinton. "Interorganizational Policy Structures and Research on Public Organizations." *Administration and Society* 13(1982): 457–78.

Mindlin, Sergio E., and Howard Aldrich. "Interorganizational Dependence: A Review of the Concept and a Reexamination of the Findings of the Aston Group." *Administrative Science Quarterly* 20(1975): 382–92.

Mitchell, Wesley C. "Facts and Values in Economics." *Journal of Philosophy* 41(1944): 212–19.

Mock, Ron. "Intergovernmental Power and Dependence." *Public Administration Review* 39(1979): 556–61.

Moore, Wilbert E. *Industrial Relations and the Social Order.* New York: Macmillan, 1951.

Mullins, Nicholas C. "The Distribution of Social and Cultural Properties in Informal Communication Networks among Biological Scientists." *American Sociological Review* 33(1968): 786–97.

Naftalin, Arthur. "Mass Transit in Hamburg." *Transportation Engineering* (December 1977): 36–43.

Nakamoto, Takuya. *Interorganizational Contacts and Service Coordination: Case Study of the San Francisco Municipal Railway.* Berkeley: University of California, Institute of Urban and Regional Development, [1979].

Niskanen, William. *Bureaucracy and Representative Government.* New York: Aldine-Atherton, 1971.

————. "Competition Among Government Bureaus." In *Making Bureaucracies Work,* pp. 167–74. Edited by Carol H. Weiss and Allen H. Barton. London: Sage Publications, 1980.

Nuehring, Elane M. "The Character of Interorganizational Task Environments: Community Mental Health Centers and Their Linkages." *Administration and Society* 9(1978): 425–46.

Olcott, Edward S. "Innovative Approaches to Urban Transportation Planning." *Public Administration Review* 33(1973): 215–24.

Onibokun, Adponju G., and Martha Curry. "The Ideology of Citizen Participation: The Metropolitan Seattle Transit Case Study." *Public Administration Review* 36(1976): 269–77.

Ostrom, E., Roger B. Parks, and Gordon P. Whitaker. "Defining and Measuring Structural Variations in Interorganizational Arrangements." *Publius* 4(1974): 87–108.

————. "Do We Really Want to Consolidate Urban Police Forces? A Reappraisal of Some Old Assertions." *Public Administration Review* 33 (1973): 423–32.

Ostrom, Vincent. "Nonhierarchical Approaches to the Organization of Public Activity." *Annals of the American Academy of Political and Social Science* 466(1983): 135–47.

Ostrom, Vincent, and E. Ostrom. "A Behavioral Approach to the Study of Intergovernmental Relations." *Annals of the American Academy of Political and Social Science* 359(1965): 137–46.

Ostrom, Vincent, Charles Tiebout, and Roland Warren. "The Organization of Government in Metropolitan Regions." *American Political Science Review* 55(1961): 831–42.

O'Toole, Laurence J., Jr., and Robert S. Montjoy. "Interorganizational Policy Implementation: A Theoretical Perspective." *Public Administration Review* 44(1984): 491–503.

Paige, John H. "Comprehensive Planning for Highways: A Political Perspective." *Traffic Quarterly* 28(1974): 307–19.

Parsons, Talcott. *Structure and Process in Modern Societies.* Glencoe, Ill.: The Free Press, 1960.

Perrow, Charles. *Complex Organizations: A Critical Essay.* Glenview, Ill.: Scott, Foresman and Co., 1972.

Pfeffer, Jeffrey, and Huseyn Leblebici. "Executive Recruitment and the Development of Interim Organizations." *Administrative Science Quarterly* 18(1973): 449–61.

Pfiffner, James P. "Management and Central Controls Reconsidered." *The Bureaucrat* 10(1981–82): 13–16.

Pitkin, Hanna. "Obligation and Consent—II." *American Political Science Review* 60(1966): 39–52.

Plunkitt, George Washington. *Plunkitt of Tammany Hall*. Recorded by William L. Riordan. Introduction by Arthur Mann. New York: E. P. Dutton, 1963.

Polsby, Nelson W. "The Institutionalization of the U.S. House of Representatives." *American Political Science Review* 62(1968): 144–68.

Pondy, Louis R. "Varieties of Organizational Conflict." *Administrative Science Quarterly* 14(1969): 499–505.

Price, Don K. *Government and Science*. New York: Oxford University Press, 1962.

Pugh, D. S., D. J. Hickson, C. R. Hinings, and C. Turner. "Dimensions of Organizational Structure." *Administrative Science Quarterly* 13(1968): 65–105.

Quenstadt, Warren. "Statement Before the U.S. Senate Committee on the District of Columbia," Washington, D.C., 3 March 1976.

Ranson, Stewart, Bob Hinings, and Royston Greenwood. "The Structuring of Organizational Structures." *Administrative Science Quarterly* 25 (1980): 1–17.

Regional Transit Association of the Bay Area. Minutes of Meetings of the Board of Control and Staff-Level Committees, 1978–1980. Typescript.

Reid, William. "Interagency Coordination in Delinquency Prevention and Control." *Social Service Review* 38(1964): 418–28.

Rider, Robert. "Decentralizing Land Use Decisions." *Public Administration Review* 40(1980): 594–602.

Riggs, Fred W. "Organizational Structures and Contexts." *Administration and Society* 7(1975): 150–90.

Riley, Matilda White, and Richard Cohn. "Control Networks in Informal Groups." *Sociometry* 21(1958): 30–49.

Roethlisberger, F. J., and William J. Dickson. *Management and the Worker*. Cambridge, Mass.: Harvard University Press, 1947.

Rogers, Everett M., and Rekha Agarwala-Rogers. *Communication in Organizations*. New York: The Free Press, 1976.

Rose, Arnold M. " 'Official' vs. 'Administrative' Criteria for Classification of Combat Breakdown Cases." *American Sociological Quarterly* 2(1958): 185–94.

Rowbottom, R. W. "Organizing Social Services: Hierarchy or . . . ?" *Public Administration* 51(1973): 291–305.

Sapolsky, Harvey M. *The Polaris System Development: Bureaucratic and Programmatic Success in Government.* Cambridge, Mass.: Harvard University Press, 1972.

Savas, E. E. "An Empirical Study of Competition in Municipal Service Delivery." *Public Administration Review* 37(1977): 717–24.

————. "Intra-city Competition Between Public and Private Service Delivery." *Public Administration Review* 41(1981): 46–51.

Scharpf, Fritz W. "Interorganizational Policy Studies: Issues, Concepts, and Perspectives." In *Interorganizational Policy Making: Limits to Coordination and Central Control,* pp. 345–70. Edited by Kenneth Hanf and Fritz W. Scharpf. London: Sage Publications, 1978.

Schelling, Thomas C. "An Essay on Bargaining." *American Economic Review* 48(1956): 281–306.

Schermer, Julie Hetrick. "Interest Group Impact Assessment in Transportation Planning." *Traffic Quarterly* 29(1975): 29–51.

Schick, Allen. "The Coordination Option." In *Federal Reorganization: What Have We Learned?,* pp. 85–113. Edited by Peter Szanton. Chatham, N.J.: Chatham House, 1981.

Schiesl, Martin J. *The Politics of Efficiency: Municipal Administration and Reform in America, 1800–1920.* Berkeley: University of California Press, 1977.

Schiller, F. C. S. "Scientific Discovery and Logical Proof." In *Studies in the History and Method of Science,* pp. 235–89. Edited by Charles Singer. Oxford: Clarendon Press, 1917.

Schmidt, S. M., and T. A. Kochan. "Interorganizational Relationships: Patterns and Motivations." *Administrative Science Quarterly* 22(1977): 220–34.

Schulz, David F., Joseph L. Schofer, and Neil J. Pedersen. "An Evolving Image of Long-Range Transportation Planning." *Traffic Quarterly* 33 (1979): 443–58.

Scott, James C. "Corruption, Machine Politics and Political Change." *American Political Science Review* 63(1969): 1142–58.

Scott, W. Richard. "Developments in Organization Theory, 1960–1980." *American Behavioral Scientist* 24(1981): 407–22.

————. *Organizations: Rational, Natural, and Open Systems.* Englewood Cliffs, N.J.: Prentice-Hall, 1981.

Seidman, Harold. *Politics, Position, and Power.* 3rd edition. New York: Oxford University Press, 1980.

Selznick, Philip. "An Approach to a Theory of Bureaucracy." *American Sociological Review* 8(1943): 47–54.

————. *TVA and the Grassroots: A Study in the Sociology of Formal Organization.* Berkeley: University of California Press, 1949.

————. *Leadership in Administration: A Sociological Interpretation.* New York: Harper and Row, 1957.

Shaw, Peter L., and Renee B. Simon. "Changing Institutional Relationships—The Los Angeles County Transportation Commission Experience." *Traffic Quarterly* 35(1981): 569–88.

Simmel, Georg. *The Sociology of Georg Simmel.* Translated and edited by Kurt H. Wolff. New York: The Free Press, 1950. Originally published in 1908.

Simon, Herbert A. "Rational Choice and the Structure of the Environment." *Psychological Review* 63(1956): 129–38.

————. *Administrative Behavior.* 2nd edition. New York: The Free Press, 1957.

————. "The Architecture of Complexity." *Proceedings of the American Philosophical Society* 106(1962): 467–82.

————. "On the Concept of Organizational Goal." *Administrative Science Quarterly* 9(1964): 1–22.

————. *The Sciences of the Artificial.* Cambridge, Mass.: M.I.T. Press, 1969.

————. "The Structure of Ill Structured Problems." *Artificial Intelligence* 4(1973): 181–201.

————. "Applying Information Technology to Organization Design." *Public Administration Review* 33(1973): 268–78.

————. "Style in Design." In *Proceedings of the Second Annual Design Research Association Conference, October 1970,* pp. 1–10. Edited by J. Archea and C. Eastman. Pittsburgh: Carnegie-Mellon University, 1975.

————. *Reason in Human Affairs.* Stanford, Calif.: Stanford University Press, 1982.

————. "Human Nature and Politics: The Dialogue of Psychology with Political Science." *American Political Science Review* 79(1985): 293–304.

Simon, Herbert A., Donald W. Smithburg, and Victor A. Thompson. *Public Administration.* New York: Alfred A. Knopf, 1964.

Simpson, Richard L. "Vertical and Horizontal Communication in Formal Organizations." *Administrative Science Quarterly* 4(1959): 186–96.

Singer, Charles, ed. *Studies in the History and Method of Science.* Oxford: Clarendon Press, 1917.

Spencer, Herbert. *The Principles of Sociology,* Volume 1. New York: Appleton-Century-Crofts, 1897.

Sperry, R. W. "Orderly Function With Disordered Structure." In *Principles of Self-Organization,* pp. 279–90. Edited by Heinz von Foerster and George W. Zopf, Jr. New York: Pergamon Press, 1962.

Springer, Fred, and Richard Gable. "The Impact of Informal Relations on Organizational Rewards." *Comparative Politics* 12(1980): 191–210.

Stein, Robert M. "Functional Integration at the Sub-State Level: A Policy Approach." *Urban Affairs Quarterly* 16(1980): 211–33.

Stern, Robert N. "The Development of An Interorganizational Control Network: The Case of Intercollegiate Athletics." *Administrative Science Quarterly* 24(1979): 242–66.

Stinchcombe, Arthur L. *Constructing Social Theories.* New York: Harcourt, Brace, and World, 1968.

Stokes, B. R. "Bay Area Rapid Transit: A Transportation Planning Breakthrough." *Public Administration Review* 33(1973): 206–14.

Storing, Herbert J. *What the Anti-Federalists Were For: The Political Thought of the Opponents of the Constitution.* Chicago: University of Chicago Press, 1981.

Stymne, Bengt. "Interdepartmental Communications and Organizational Strain." *Acta Sociologica* 11(1968): 82–100.

Taggart, Robert, and David W. Jones, Jr. *Case Study #1: MTC's Incremental Plan-making: Planning As Persuasion.* Berkeley: University of California, Institute of Transportation Studies, [no date].

Thoenig, Jean-Claude. "State Bureaucracies and Local Government in France." In *Interorganizational Policy Making: Limits to Coordination and Central Control,* pp. 167–97. Edited by Kenneth Hanf and Fritz Scharpf. London: Sage Publications, 1978.

Thomas, Kerry, ed. *Attitudes and Behavior.* London: Penguin Books, 1971.

Thompson, James D. "Organizational Management of Conflict." *American Sociological Quarterly* 4(1960): 389–409.

———. "Organizations and Output Transactions." *American Journal of Sociology* 68(1962): 309–24.

———. *Organizations in Action: Social Science Bases of Administrative Theory.* New York: McGraw-Hill, 1967.

———. "Society's Frontiers for Organizing Activities." *Public Administration Review* 33(1973): 327–45.

———. "Social Interdependence, the Polity, and Public Administration." *Administration and Society* 6(1974): 3–20.

Thompson, James D., and Robert Hawkes. "Disaster, Community Organization, and Administrative Process." In *Man and Society in Disaster,* pp. 268–304. Edited by George W. Baker and Dwight W. Chapman. Foreword by Carlyle F. Jacobson. New York: Basic Books, 1962.

Thompson, James D., and William McEven. "Organizational Goals and Environment: Goal-Setting as an Interaction Process." *American Sociological Review* 23(1958): 23–31.

Thompson, James D., and Arthur Tuden. "Strategies, Structures, and Processes of Organizational Decision." In *Comparative Studies in Administration*, pp. 195–216. Edited by James D. Thompson. Pittsburgh: University of Pittsburgh Press, 1959.

Thompson, Victor A. *The Regulatory Process in OPA Rationing*. New York: King's Crown Press, 1950.

———. *Bureaucracy and the Modern World*. Morristown, N.J.: General Learning Press, 1976.

Thurman, Blake. "In the Office: Networks and Coalitions." *Social Networks* 2(1979–80): 47–63.

Truman, David B. *The Governmental Process: Political Interests and Public Opinion*. New York: Alfred A. Knopf, 1964.

Turk, Herman. "Interorganizational Networks in Urban Society: Initial Perspectives and Comparative Research." *American Sociological Review* 35 (1970): 1–19.

———. *Interorganizational Activation in Urban Communities*. Washington, D.C.: American Sociological Association, 1973.

Ullmann-Margalit, Edna. *The Emergence of Norms*. Oxford: Oxford University Press, 1977.

Wachs, Martin. "Fostering Technological Innovation in Urban Transportation Systems." *Traffic Quarterly* 25(1971): 39–54.

Wachs, Martin, Barclay M. Hudson, and Joseph L. Schofer. "Integrating Localized and Systemwide Objectives in Transportation Planning." *Traffic Quarterly* 28(1974): 159–84.

Walton, Richard, John Dutton, and Thomas Cafferty. "Organizational Context and Interdepartmental Conflict." *Administrative Science Quarterly* 14(1969): 522–42.

Warren, Roland. "A Municipal Services Market Model of Metropolitan Organization." *Journal of American Institute of Planners* 30(1964): 193–204.

———. *Government in Metropolitan Regions: A Reappraisal of Fractionated Political Organization*. Davis, Calif.: Institute of Governmental Affairs, 1966.

———. "The Interorganizational Field as a Focus for Investigation." *Administrative Science Quarterly* 12(1967): 396–419.

———. "Comprehensive Planning and Coordination: Some Functional Aspects." *Social Problems* 20(1973): 355–64.

Washington Metropolitan Area Transit Authority. "Short History of the Financing of the Transportation System for the National Capital Region." April 1975. Typescript.

———. "Airlie XVII Conference Background Papers, December 1980. Typescript.

———. "Chronology," [no date]. Typescript.

Weaver, Warren. "Science and Complexity." *American Scientist* 36(1948): 536–44.

Webber, Melvin M. *The BART Experience—What Have We Learned?* Berkeley: University of California, Institute of Urban and Regional Development and Institute of Transportation Studies, 1976.

Weber, Max. *The Theory of Social and Economic Organization.* Edited with an introduction by Talcott Parsons. Glencoe, Ill.: The Free Press, 1964.

Weick, Karl E. *The Social Psychology of Organizing.* Reading, Mass.: Addison-Wesley, 1969.

Wellman, Barry. "Public Participation in Transportation Planning." *Traffic Quarterly* 31(1977): 639–56.

White, Harrison C., Scott A. Boorman, and Ronald L. Brieger. "Social Structure From Multiple Networks. I. Blockmodels of Roles and Positions." *American Journal of Sociology* 81(1976): 730–80.

White, Paul E. "Intra- and Inter-Organizational Studies: Do They Require Separate Conceptualizations?" *Administration and Society* 6(1974): 107–52.

Whitten, Norman E., Jr., and Alvin W. Wolfe. "Network Analysis." In *Handbook of Social and Cultural Anthropology,* pp. 717–46. Edited by John J. Honigmann. Chicago: Rand McNally, 1973.

Whyte, William Foote. "Social Organization in the Slums." *American Sociological Review* 8(1943): 34–39.

Wildavsky, Aaron. "The Self-Evaluating Organization." *Public Administration Review* 32(1972): 509–20.

———. *Speaking Truth to Power.* Boston: Little, Brown, and Co., 1979.

Williams, A. "The Optimal Provision of Public Goods in a System of Local Government." *Journal of Political Economy* 74(1966): 18–33.

Woolfe, Patricia. "The Second Messenger: Informal Communication in Cyclic AMP Research." *Minerva* 13(1975): 349–73.

Wright, Deil. *Understanding Intergovernmental Relations.* North Scituate, Mass.: Duxbury Press, 1978.

Yates, Douglas. *The Ungovernable City: The Politics of Urban Problems and Policy-Making.* Cambridge, Mass.: M.I.T. Press, 1977.

Yin, Robert K. "Life Histories of Innovations: How New Practices Become Routinized." *Public Administration Review* 41(1981): 21–28.

Zwerling, Steven. *Mass Transit and the Politics of Technology.* New York: Praeger, 1974.

Index

Accountability, 142, 145, 200
AC Transit. *See* Alameda Contra Costa County Transit District
Administrative orthodoxy, 17
Alameda, county of, 46, 179
Alameda Contra Costa County Transit District
  busbridge agreement with BART, 81, 94, 96–98
  changes in since initial study, 204
  and conflict with BART, 55–56, 181
  constituencies of, 178–79
  express bus service for BART, 81, 109
  formation of, 178–79
  and informal channels with other operators, 66–68, 72–74, 76, 77, 127–29
  and interdependence with other operators
    with BART, 169, 184
    bilateral and multilateral, 53
    with Muni, 165
    natural, artificial, and voluntary, 60–62
    operations, 45–47
    planning, 50–52
    service-related, 40, 45, 47–50
  localizing interdependence, 199
  major problems faced by, 168, 205–6
  merger with other operators, 2
  Northern California Demonstration Project, 120
  operating environment of, 164

operating subsidies for, 158
and personnel movement to and from other operators, 123–25, 129
regional transit information centers, 208
relations with MTC, 158
and rental of buses to Golden Gate, 111
RTA meetings, 121
and subsets of informal networks, 80–83
Transbay Terminal, 105
transbay tube fire, role in, 99–104
and transfer arrangements with other operators
  arrangements with other operators, 107
  changes in, since initial study, 209–10
  and connections with BART, 105, 107–8, 154
  daily transfers, numbers of, 48, 53–56
  and interdependence, 40–41, 53–56, 60–61
  and role of MTC in facilitating, 154–56
American Public Transit Association, 135
Antifederalists, the, 163, 164
Antioch, city of, 205
Arrow, Kenneth, 23, 112, 194
Ashby, Ross, 9
Assembly Transportation Committee, California state, 3

Compositor: G&S Typesetters
      Text: Times Roman 10/12
   Display: Goudy Bold
   Printer: Princeton Univ. Press/Printing
    Binder: Princeton Univ. Press/Printing